RESTFUL
REFLECTIONS

*Nighttime Inspiration
to Calm the Soul,
Based on Jewish Wisdom*

**Rabbi Kerry M. Olitzky
Rabbi Lori Forman**

JEWISH LIGHTS PUBLISHING

WOODSTOCK, VERMONT

Restful Reflections:
Nighttime Inspiration to Calm the Soul, Based on Jewish Wisdom
© 2001 by Kerry M. Olitzky and Lori Forman

Library of Congress Cataloging-in-Publication Data
Restful reflections : nighttime inspiration to calm the soul, based on Jewish wisdom / [edited by] Kerry M. Olitzky & Lori Forman.
p.   cm.
Sequel to: Sacred intentions
Includes bibliographical reference and index.
ISBN 1-58023-091-1 (pbk.)
1. Jewish devotional calendars. 2. Jewish meditations.
3. Spiritual life—Judaism. I. Olitzky, Kerry M. II. Forman, Lori.
III. Sacred Intentions.
BM724.R46   2000
296.7'2—dc21
00-011957

10 9 8 7 6 5 4 3 2 1

Manufactured in the United States of America

Cover design: Big Eyedea
Text design: Susan Ramundo

Published by Jewish Lights Publishing
A Division of LongHill Partners, Inc.
Sunset Farm Offices, Route 4, P.O. Box 237
Woodstock, VT 05091
Tel: (802) 457-4000 • Fax: (802) 457-4004
www.jewishlights.com

For Terry Elkes,
and for the vision that he inspires
KO

For Maya, my daughter,
to inspire, guide, and comfort her in the years ahead
LF

Featuring contributions to rekindle the spirit writte

Yosef I. Abramowitz
Bradley Shavit Artson
Leila Gal Berner
Jonathan Jaffe Bernhard
Tsvi Blanchard
Barry H. Block
Terry A. Bookman
Herbert Bronstein
Ayelet Cohen
Jerome K. Davidson
Avram Davis
Lavey Derby
Malka Drucker
Amy Eilberg
Edward Feinstein
Yehudah Fine
Mordecai Finley
James A. Gibson
Melvin J. Glazer
James Scott Glazier
Edwin C. Goldberg
Elyse Goldstein
James Stone Goodman
Irving Greenberg
Daniel Gropper
Judith HaLevy
Brad Hirschfield
Elana Kanter
Stuart Kelman

Francine Klagsbrun
Peter S. Knobel
Jeffrey Korbman
Jonathan Kraus
Irwin Kula
Neil Kurshan
Mark H. Levin
Levi Meier
Steven Heneson Moskow
David Nelson
Vanessa L. Ochs
Nessa Rapoport
Jack Riemer
Jeffrey Salkin
Nigel Savage
Ismar Schorsch
Harold M. Schulweis
Rami Shapiro
Rick Sherwin
Jeffrey Sirkman
Marcia Cohn Spiegel
Liza Stern
Michael Strassfeld
Michael White
Arnold Jacob Wolf
Joel H. Zaiman
Josh Zweiback
Raymond A. Zwerin

CONTENTS

ACKNOWLEDGMENTS

This book is a sequel. It is part of an ongoing project of reaching into the rich reservoir of Jewish thought in order to draw from it wisdom and inspiration for everyday—and every night—living. Therefore, we must begin by thanking all those people who read and were inspired by each daily entry in our first book, *Sacred Intentions,* and encouraged us to prepare a second volume. We also thank all of our colleagues who enriched our own writing by contributing many thoughtful pieces, some of which we were unable to use owing to the sheer volume of contributions.

We express our profound appreciation to staff members at Jewish Lights Publishing who carefully shepherded this volume page by page. In particular, we thank Martha McKinney, who constantly kept us on track and looked out for each administrative and creative detail. Our profound gratitude goes to Sandra Korinchak, who took this project on herself among her editorial responsibilities at Jewish Lights Publishing. The words are ours, but their final form is due in significant measure to the editorial care she took in helping to shape each entry.

Words are inadequate to express the abiding gratitude that I feel toward both Stuart, publisher of Jewish Lights, and Antoinette Matlins. They have stood by me, from the early days of only dreaming about their sacred intention of creating an inclusive Jewish community through the expression of sacred words. It has been a privilege to be part of this unfolding enterprise. Everyone who participates in it with them is truly blessed. I want to acknowledge with abiding appreciation my colleagues and coworkers at the Jewish Outreach Institute, particularly Dr. Egon Mayer and Nastaran Afari, and Terry Elkes, president of our organization. In a short time, they have welcomed me into an environment in which people from all walks of Jewish life feel at home—particularly those who previously felt as if they were on the periphery. In the environment that we are working to create, we are helping to bring to reality a more inclusive Jewish community.

As many words as there are in this book and in the others that I have been blessed to write, they are insufficient to articulate the depth of support, encouragement and love I receive from my family. Each word stands on the firm foundation that they have created for me. Whether we plumb the valley or ascend to the peaks, we do it together. In the midst of the richness of their lives, sometimes simple words are best to express the deepness of our feelings. To my wife, Sheryl, and to our sons, Avi and Jesse: I thank you with every ounce of my being. Whatever I am and whatever I am yet to be is all because of you. RABBI KERRY (SHIA) M. OLITZKY

It has been a true journey writing both *Sacred Intentions* and this sequel with Kerry. I thank him for his wisdom and guidance as we compiled these two volumes of inspiration. I continue to be grateful to UJA Federation of New York for supporting me in my work as I search for creative ways to teach and connect our Jewish values with our organization's mission. I am also greatly appreciative of the assistance Stephanie McFadden gives me as my secretary, which allows me to take on interesting projects. One of my many projects has been to write "The Jewish Thought of the Day," which is the backbone of my entries herein. I thank all my readers for their continued interest and support. I am forever in awe of the warm responses I receive for these daily messages.

I worked on this book while I was home on maternity leave with my daughter, Maya. As Maya is my first child, little did I realize what it would mean to experience motherhood for the first time and to write simultaneously. Though being disciplined was challenging, Maya's birth filled me with such joy and love that hopefully this perspective on life comes through in my writing. I hope that these words of inspiration guide her as she grows and matures. To my husband, Simcha, who is my true partner in our lives together, my love and thanks for supporting and nurturing me as I continue to grow and explore new territory as mother, wife, rabbi, and teacher.   RABBI LORI FORMAN

HOW TO USE THIS BOOK

This book follows the daily Gregorian calendar and is designed to be used as a companion to daily life. It may be used in conjunction with the book *Sacred Intentions: Daily Inspiration to Strengthen the Spirit* (which is focused on the beginning of each day) or on its own. Most of its entries are tied to the themes that emerge from the calendar. Sometimes dates that have become part of the fabric of North American society are noted. At other times, attention is given to the general season. Since Jewish calendar dates are generally not tied to the secular calendar, they are noted with some measure of flexibility.

Place the volume by your bed and as you get ready to sleep, read the entry for the day that is coming to a close. Let it provide a framework for you to review the day at its end. Some people will want to reflect on an entry late in the day (perhaps reading it at the end of the work day, or even with family members around the dinner table) and then once again before retiring for the night. You may also want to read an entry once again in the morning.

Don't feel compelled to follow the book's daily format. If there are things that weigh on your mind, use the index to choose a selection that might better reflect what you feel. Flip through the pages. Read entries that catch your attention as they speak to you.

This is not a book that you read quickly and then put aside. Rather, take time to read each entry slowly. Drink in the words of text that begin each selection, before working your way through the entry itself. In the case of texts that have been selected from sacred literature, think about what the text meant to the generation in which it emerged. For contemporary selections, react to it directly. Then read through the entry in order to see how we have mined the text's wisdom for the everyday.

Whatever approach you take to this book, set your critical and analytic mind aside for a few moments. Let the words speak to your heart and soul so that you may feel inspired and enriched.

INTRODUCTION

As the sun sets, darkness begins to cover the earth. Our instinct is to dispel the darkness with light. We turn on lamps. We light candles. The seasons change, and fall fades into winter. As many of us leave our homes for work while it is still dark or come home after the sun has already set, we even set automatic timers so that lights are on in our homes before we come home at night. Some even illuminate as we approach them. When we were children, many of us slept with little night-lights glowing in the dark, or we left our doors open slightly in order to catch the light from the hallway. And now, particularly as we find ourselves awakening in the middle of the night, some of us still use night-lights so that we don't stumble in the blackness.

This kind of darkness is easy to drive away, but what do we do about the darkness that inhabits the soul, particularly when it rears its head at night? We turn to our tradition for inspiration, insight, guidance, and courage.

Continuing in the format of the book *Sacred Intentions,* which was designed to help the reader start the day with wisdom and encouragement, this volume of readings is designed to help you reflect on the day that has just ended and ease you into sleep. This is particularly appropriate, since, according to the Hebrew calendar, we begin counting days starting with the evening before. Thus, these readings help you prepare for the day ahead—before you go to sleep at night.

Saadya Gaon reminds us that there is something special about praying at night. And Maimonides similarly suggests that there is something special about studying at night. Although both are forms of dialogue with different emphases, it might be said that with prayer we talk to God and with study we listen to God or listen for God's voice in the world.

The title of this volume comes from an approach that we have adopted in our own lives. At the end of the day, we reflect on what has taken place during the previous eighteen hours or so. Often we view our reflection through the lens of a particular text, something that has been taught from Jewish tradition, something that we have read or heard from one of our many spiritual teachers. While the approach of *Sacred Intentions* is to help you *prepare* for the day ahead, *Restful Reflections* helps you *reflect* on daily life in order to bring the lessons you've learned and the insights you've gained into the upcoming days. And at the end of each daily reflection, you'll rest better because of it.

JANUARY

Setting Goals and Their Limits

1 JANUARY

The meaning of our life is the road, not the goal. For each answer is elusive, each fulfillment melts away between our fingers and the goal is no longer the goal once it is achieved.

ARTHUR SCHNITZLER[1]

At the beginning of the year, many of us write out a list of goals for ourselves. Each year the list seems to get longer. We may plan to lose weight, take up a hobby, go back to school. Some of us may be more inclined to set new goals in our professional lives, asking ourselves questions such as, "What do I hope to accomplish this year?" "Will I get promoted?" Goals are useful tools in helping us to move forward in our life's journey. They can give us focus and provide us with concrete ways to mark our progress. And when we reach them, we feel a certain sense of accomplishment. But as we pursue them and as we continue to grow, the original goals we set early in the year may slowly fade into memory as new aspirations emerge to take their place. Some things won't seem quite as important or as urgent as they once did. Our lives take various twists and turns that impact directly on our goals. We get surprised along the way. As we embark on our journey this year, there will be times that we will be able to walk upright, sometimes even run. At other times, we may trip and stumble. But however life's path unfolds, let us not mistake the goals we set out along the way for the journey itself. Goals come and go, but the path continues. As we begin this new year, let us be open to the fullness of life so we can savor the many experiences we encounter along the way. As Rabbi Nachman of Breslov said, "Believe that none of the effort you put into coming closer to God is ever wasted—even if in the end you don't achieve what you are striving for."   LF

Asking the Right Questions

2 JANUARY

Learn the difference between today and tomorrow.
TALMUD[2]

There is something about the days after the secular New Year that makes it special even to those of us who do not really go out of our way to celebrate it. We don't jump right into the new year. We kind of ease our way into it. While I try to stay off the roads and away from the many places that are crazy on the eve of January 1, I really avoid them for a few days thereafter as well. After all the parties and the big sales, I want to finally get down to the real business of living. No matter how we try to avoid it, the entire month of December is consumed by holiday parties (a polite euphemism) and intensive shopping excursions (thank God for the Internet!), especially for those whose Hanukkah observance has been caught by the frenzy of gift-giving. But in January things settle down for what I like to call the long haul of winter. Often the weather reminds us of the road that lies ahead of us before we can even think about spring. Even if you live in warm climes, the seasons change—and our attitudes change according to the calendar. So we return to the challenges that, weeks ago, we had temporarily set aside.

There are lots of questions that remain unresolved, and more have crept into our minds in the meantime. What can we do to ensure that our relationships with the ones we love continue? How do we plot out our job change? What kind of additional training will be necessary to ensure our career advancement? How can we help our children—or our parents—meet the challenges that they are facing?

How do we begin to find answers to these questions? The Talmud, as quoted above, offers us some insight. To help discern the answers, that is, to tell "the difference between today and tomorrow," we must first discover the questions that need to be asked, setting aside the clutter that has accumulated over these past few weeks. Now it's time to look for the answers: inward to ourselves, outward to others, and upward to God.   KO

Above the Stars
3 JANUARY
Look now toward heaven, and count the stars . . .
GENESIS 15:5

Before you go into your bedroom and place your head upon your pillow, take a moment to peer through a window at the night sky outside. As you gaze up at the stars, you may be overcome by a sense of wonder and awe, as you experience the grandeur and scope of the universe. You will be sharing the experience of our patriarch Abraham, who was told to gaze at the stars and think of all the future generations who would descend from him. That vision gave him a sense of mission, continuity, and confidence. The stars symbolized the Divine promise that a multitude of his descendants would carry on his teachings in perpetuity and transmit them to the world.

There is another, precious lesson to be learned from this episode. The great biblical commentator Rashi teaches us that the way to really look at the stars is to imagine yourself high *above* them in the heavens, gazing *down* at them. God has put you *above* the stars, not under the power of any heavenly body or constellation. Some people believe that they were born under a certain sign that controls their fate. However, the Torah teaches us that our fate is not predetermined by circumstances of nature or nurture. You can always create your destiny no matter when you were born, no matter what things may have happened during your day to disrupt your equilibrium and equanimity.

During the day and at night, the choice is always yours. If you see yourself as existing *under* the stars, you might feel that you have to accept your predetermined fate. However, if you look *down* at the stars, you will find yourself empowered, as you create your own destiny.   RABBI LEVI MEIER

Turning Dreams into Reality
4 JANUARY
The Jewish state is essential to the world;
therefore it will be created.
THEODOR HERZL[3]

Who would have ever thought that such a crazy idea could become a reality? Yet, Herzl was spurred to action to put an end to the insidious anti-Semitism he saw in Western Europe. He uses his fervor, passion, and dedication to change his dream—a dream shared by the Jewish people throughout its two-thousand-year exile—into a reality.

Today many of us visit Israel with ease. Some of us may come and go many times during the course of a year; others may save for years in order to make one special pilgrimage in their lifetime to our land of promise. As we walk the same streets the prophets walked, as we touch the ground that our ancestors consecrated, we must remember that one lone man, Theodor Herzl, rallied an entire population and the leaders of several European nations to support the return of the Jewish people to their homeland. Turning your own dreams—whether they are the dreams you would like to achieve tomorrow or larger dreams you plan for the longer-term future—into accomplishments may not be quite as complex a task as Herzl's. But may we each have his courage to take action and challenge anyone or anything to realize our own dreams!   LF

Bringing in the Light
5 January

God called the light "day," and the darkness,
God called "night." There was evening
and there was morning, one day.
GENESIS 1:5

Evening and then morning. A familiar text. One day at a time. A familiar approach. And at the end of each day, like an artist standing back from a canvas and admiring her work, God stood back—so to speak—from the canvas of creation and admired each aspect of the newly created world. Why does creation—and therefore the Hebrew calendar—begin with darkness (sunset) and not with the light of a new day, or even with midnight? Perhaps it is because the world began in darkness, before divine light was brought into the world. That light forces out the darkness.

No matter how many times we do it, or how many winters we experience it, it still feels strange for our day to start before sunrise. Similarly, when we arrive home after sunset, we feel as if the day were already over. Perhaps when we are inside all day—and in the winter, we may even avoid a lunchtime outing—we don't get the sense of the cycle of day and night or of the slow movement of one season into another.

But it does get dark later each evening, as the sun and moon continue their cycles of rotation with the earth. While there is a scientific explanation for this, there is a spiritual message here as well. God created humans as partners in creation. It is our responsibility to complete what God began. Thus, while God's light forced out the darkness at creation, it is our obligation to use God's light to force out the darkness of each ensuing day. We know that the darkness returns with the night. However, it is the divine light we carry into the world that illumines each new day and brightens even the bleakest winter night.   KO

Lighten Up

6 JANUARY

Whenever a person eats and drinks and gets pleasure from his or her labor it is a gift from God.

ECCLESIASTES 3:12B

Critics of American culture claim that we are too materialistic. They are wrong. Materialists have fun. Materialists enjoy the things they have. We don't.

We work long hours so we can take a nice vacation and then spend the time worrying about all the work that awaits us when we return. We scrimp and save to afford a nice house and then never stay home long enough to enjoy it. We buy a good car, computer, or stereo and keep drooling over the next model. We shop for just the right outfit and then refuse to wear it a second time, because everyone has seen it.

The Talmud says that we will be penalized for every legitimate pleasure we fail to experience in this life. What do we in America do with those legitimate pleasures? We tax them, and we call that tax a sin tax! That says it all. Pleasure is sinful. We are not to have any pleasure, and when we do, we have to poison it with guilt. This may be good American ideology, but it is bad Judaism. And in this case, I opt for the Talmud.

So as good Jews, here is what we should pledge this year: enjoy ourselves a little more. Lighten up. How?

First, stop worrying about having too much. Yes, there are many people who have too little; help them have enough so they can begin worrying about having too much. Feeling guilty over our success without helping others succeed as well is egotistical foolishness. Guilt is easy and cheap. If you are really bothered by the inequality between the haves and the have-nots, do something tangible to make things more just. But stop feeling guilty about your success and good fortune. Most people work hard to earn what they want and there is no shame in that.

Second, stop worrying about having enough. Yes, there are many people with more, but so what? If there is something you want, go about getting it honestly. And then enjoy it once it is yours. The problem with resenting what others have is that you must denigrate what you have. You rob yourself of legitimate pleasure.

Happiness is not a steady experience measured in things. Happiness is a feeling that pops in and out of our experience. To base the quality of life on whether or not you are happy is to base it on something so unstable that you will only make yourself miserable.

So stop worrying about being happy and stop wishing each other a happy new year. Some days will be happy and some will be horrible. Just like last year. Just like next year. Instead, wish each other and yourself a more playful new year. While we may not be able to make ourselves happy, we can make ourselves play a little more. And, who knows, maybe if we are more playful, we might bump into happiness a little more often as well.

Rabbi Rami Shapiro

Honoring the Elderly
7 January
You shall rise before the elders and allow the beauty, glory and majesty of their faces to emerge.
Leviticus 19:32[4]

Each of us is created in the image of God, so Jewish tradition tells us. But as we age, we become quickly aware of the many changes and challenges that we face: our hair grays, our eyesight dims, our memory fades. Even beforehand, we see it in our parents. It may not have always been that way—at least, that is what one midrash has to say. It suggests that the appearance of old age did not exist before Abraham. He complained to God that no one could tell him apart from his son, Isaac. Abraham said to God, "There needs to be a way to distinguish father and son, youth from elder." Upon waking the following morning, Abraham found himself blessed with a head of gray hair.

It is not the color of our hair that counts, though we may put dyes into it. Our faces may wrinkle and our girth widen. We rush to retain what we remember as the appearance of our youth. No matter how we age, whether with grace or difficulty, our divine nature remains intact. What remains for eternity is the divine spark within us, that part of God that lies deep within and is never extinguished. If we can find our spiritual center through a program of religious discipline, it will carry us through the many challenges that life has to offer. May we embrace the fullness of life as we continue to grow tonight, tomorrow, and through the years.   LF

The Making of the Self

8 January

More of us than we care to admit live in self-made dungeons behind bars erected by our own resentment.

RABBI CHARLES SHERMAN

The perspective that shaped our basic attitude to the world has probably become buried—over time—beneath the inner recesses of our souls.

As the years progressed, some of our dreams got somehow dashed. We certainly don't remember when it happened. We can't pinpoint the time. We may not even remember the details any longer, what we were going to do, and with whom we were going to do it. Somehow life just crept in and we were forced to "ride its wave." Relationships. Jobs. Relocation. Marriage and children, perhaps. Responsibilities. Along the way, our sense of self may have become clouded over along with our original dream. As a result, resentments may have slowly surfaced and colored our relationships with others. But now we are prepared to change this attitude toward ourselves.

We can rediscover our early dreams. It is not too late to reclaim them or ourselves as we once were. If we begin to understand that it is we, and not others, who erected the dungeons that we live in—though we many times blame their construction on others—perhaps we will be better prepared to do what needs to be done and not fault others for what we feel we have become. It's always easier to place the blame on others. It removes the responsibility for change from us. But change is the only way we can move forward, make progress, and return—both to God and to ourselves. So let's make the change now, before the sun rises on another day.   KO

The Forgiveness of Sin

9 JANUARY

God, who is merciful, forgives sin,
and does not destroy.
God restrains the Divine wrath,
And does not release all Divine anger.

LITURGY[5]

The first prayer in the morning service is *Modeh Ani,* a prayer of thankfulness and gratitude for having been given a new day of life. The first prayer of the afternoon service is *Ashrei,* a prayer that thanks God for the privilege of being able to pray and dwell in God's house. But the evening service begins with the verses above, which speak of sin and wrath and anger.

Perhaps the end of the day makes us conscious of the time we have wasted and the follies we have committed in this day that is now gone. We started the day with sacred intentions, and now we look back and we see how much time we have frittered away and how little we really accomplished.

Rabbi Abraham Joshua Heschel explains it differently. He said that just as if you were to say to a culturally literate American "four score and seven years ago" or "we hold these truths to be self-evident," she could continue the text, so if you quoted a fragment of a psalm to a literate Jew, he could finish the text as well. The passage that introduces the evening service comes from Psalm 78, which reminds us of the sin of praying without meaning what we say. It is the sin of flattering God with our mouths and praising God with our lips but inwardly not meaning the words that we utter.

Prayer is not a contest of speed. Prayer is not a marathon. What counts in prayer is not how many words we say or how fast we can pray or even how precisely we pronounce the words. What counts in prayer is the intention of the heart.

RABBI JACK RIEMER

Forward-Looking Visions

10 JANUARY

Is it not enough that you brought us from *a land flowing with milk and honey to have us die in the wilderness, that you would lord it over us?*

NUMBERS 16:13

On first read, these do not sound like uplifting words of Torah. They were spoken by two relatively unknown characters in the Bible, Datan and Amiran, who joined with their leader, Korach, in a rebellion against Moses. They accuse Moses of being distant from the people. They decry what they claim to be his autocratic approach to leadership. We may even be tempted to be sympathetic to their cause, especially because democratic principles are basic to the country that many of us have called home our entire lifetime. But read the words of these rebels carefully. They claim that Moses has led them *from* a land flowing with milk and honey. But the Israelites came from Egypt, a land of slavery, not a land of milk and honey. As can happen, in the midst of their journey through the wilderness, they got lost along the way. Returning to Egypt, with all its "knowns," became more appealing than the promise—and the *unknown*—that awaited them in the land of Israel.

It's natural to cling to the familiar, especially when new directions in our lives—changes in personal situation or family, even our location—seem too challenging. However,

Korach and his followers remind us that vision must take us forward, not backward. The journey from the "known" to the new is difficult. But the answer is not to turn back. The only solution is to push ahead. Face the unknown tomorrow with God. That is the key to *know*ledge.   LF

Opening Up
11 JANUARY

*Holy One, may You open my mouth so that
my lips may sing Your praises.*
LITURGY[6]

I like to say this phrase very slowly so that I can focus on each word and direct it to God from the depths of my soul. While it has a specific function in the midst of my regular prayers, it represents a posture that I strive to maintain throughout my day, especially as I interact with people and the world around me. This short prayerful phrase helps us to posture ourselves for our regular communication with God, as it introduces the core set of prayers in every worship service. It is a *kavannah,* a sacred mantra, that helps direct all our thoughts and feelings as we begin to pray. Through its incantation, we shut out all the errant thoughts that surface while we are trying to focus on prayer. We try to put aside our worries about the trivial and the everyday so that our communication with the Holy One of Blessing is pure. And each time I repeat it in prayer (once or twice never seems enough), I can feel the world pushing back from me so that I can be clear and focused.

Not only do I repeat this line over and over as I prepare for the *Amidah,* I also reflect on it throughout the day, whenever I want to return to that place of prayer even when my routine of prayer does not require it. It is even helpful to say it to myself as I prepare for sleep, thinking about what I said to people during the day and how I will continue that conversation and relationship tomorrow.

With these few words, we ask God to help us express ourselves so that in that expression, all that we do may be in praise of the Divine. This is part of the spiritual logic implicit in the liturgy that is made manifest when we pray. The words of the liturgy spill over into the rest of what we do. And what are those "praises" that we are preparing to sing to God? A list of adjectives seems inadequate and unnecessary. Maybe we should start with just one. Perhaps thanking God for the day just past is a way of praising God, as is asking for God's guidance in anticipation of the day yet to come.   KO

The Power of Song

12 JANUARY

God is my strength and my song.

EXODUS 15:2A

So much of the Jewish spiritual journey happens through song. And while listening to music can be transporting and can move the soul from one place to a higher place, being part of the music, as a singer or musician, can alter one's Jewish spiritual consciousness even more radically. The experience can be so powerful that, to use the vernacular, "it blows you away," that is, it leaves you startled, unhinged even, and open to sacred connection.

I know from my own experience that chanting *niggunim,* sacred melodies, is always unspeakably deep for me. I am put into a state that merges intense *kavannah* (spiritual attentiveness), catharsis, and waves of pain and joy. In the chanting, I lose myself in the sear of voices, the barriers between self and other being dissolved.

Of course, I am well socialized to have such an experience. I have heard and sung *niggunim* since early childhood. I understand some things about how a wordless tune connects one soul to another soul, and many souls to God. Before you sleep tonight, *hava nashira shira halleluyah*. I invite you to sing your song to God.   VANESSA L. OCHS[7]

Spiritual Ladders
13 JANUARY

A woman once asked Rabbi Jose ben Halfta, "If creation took place during the first six days of the world, what has God been doing since?" The rabbi answered, "God spends the time building ladders: for some to ascend and others to descend."

MIDRASH[8]

God as a contractor. Interesting idea. Hiring painters, electricians, and plumbers. But the ladders of which the midrash speaks are "spiritual ladders." Too often the routines of life get us down. At times we all need a little lift to reach higher. At these moments, God provides a ladder for us to "ascend." And we are reminded that life is full of awe and wonder. But there are other times when our arrogance and self-confidence take control. Sometimes it is simply about living in the abstract without regard to the real needs of daily living. At these times we might need to come down the ladder somewhat, to reestablish our footing in the world. God helps us there, too. The spiritual path is not only about seeking spiritual heights or peak experiences. Rather, it is about finding the right height in the midst of our everyday responsibilities. We should climb the ladders toward Heaven but recognize that the bottom of the ladder must be secured on the ground.

Life is full of "spiritual ladders." Our challenge is to recognize them and then place our foot on that next rung. And if you slip, God will be there to catch you as you fall. If you climb too high, God will be there as well. Count on it!   LF

Enough
14 January

Sometimes just to live is blessing enough.
Sometimes just to see is miracle enough.
Sometimes just to think is wonder enough.
Sometimes just to love is all there is.
Rabbi Steven Carr Reuben[9]

This insight helps us to transcend those feelings of inadequacy caused by our often insatiable appetites for pleasure and for the acquisition of the many goods that are available to us in the marketplace. Just when we think that acquiring a particular object will make us feel better, we come to understand that the accumulation of more things—no matter how luxurious—may make us feel worse. No matter what we acquire, we will never have *enough* "stuff." Consider the options that are now in front of us all the time. Our mailboxes overflow with catalogs, each one promising more than the next. And when we order one thing, that seems to be a signal to mail-order companies—and the number of catalogs we receive increases exponentially. Ironically, the important mail (who even remembers getting letters?) becomes overwhelmed by the junk.

We can never "get" enough to help us understand Rabbi Reuben's teaching, for his lesson transcends the material world. Although there is nothing wrong with acquiring possessions that make our lives more comfortable, while we are seeking to acquire, we run the risk of losing sight of the loving relationship that is required to make any of our acquisitions worthwhile. We see. We think. We breathe. We acknowledge that we are alive. But what makes this, and more, possible? Nurturing and supportive love—human and divine.

Sometimes repeating these phrases as part of our daily routine reminds us of the import of their message. To the person with whom we share our lives: I love you. To God: *I thank you for your love and the love that you share through those who love me.* Sometimes that alone is enough.   KO

Looking for God in All the Wrong Places
15 JANUARY
Let God be your companion.
MIDRASH[10]

It is not the lack of belief in God that causes people spiritual pain. Atheists do not have angst over being atheists. It is, rather, the growing up and growing out of childhood notions about God, and having nothing mature or sophisticated to replace them with, that is the real root of the "search for spirituality" we find so common today. People often tell me proudly that they don't believe in God. "Really?" I ask. "Which God is it that you don't believe in?" Most often they will describe the old man with a beard on a throne in heaven. "Well, guess what? I don't believe in Him, either." Oh, now we can talk.

Imagine if I told you that you had to retain all your adolescent beliefs about sex: Everything you knew and felt about sexuality at the age of thirteen was what you would experience now. Or imagine that your beliefs about love never changed from when you were six. That's how grown adults deal with God. Whatever we believed around the time of bar or bat mitzvah is generally where we stay, unless we have a crisis of faith, as many of us have, and then we start again.

I believe so many of us go looking for God in all the wrong places. We rest on the old stereotypes of God as some grand magician when we teach the stories of Egypt. We conjure up God as a heavenly puppeteer, pulling the strings up there, when we talk about birth and death. We reopen and reinvent the old man with a beard on a throne through the images of traditional liturgy.

God is a strict Judge and Loving Compassionate Father/Mother and Birthing Womb and Nurturing Breast and Fierce Warrior and Spirit of the Universe all at the same time. And as each child is a multifaceted conglomerate of his parents' nature and nurture, then becomes an adult when she attends to her own needs and discovered truths, so God becomes more real to us when we are ready to let go of our parents' dreams and listen attentively to our own soul's stirrings. And then we will be able to discover God for ourselves.

RABBI ELYSE GOLDSTEIN

How We Use Ourselves
16 JANUARY

There are six parts of the body that serve a person. Three are under your control and three are not. The eyes, the ears and the nose are not under your control. You see (what you want to see or) what you don't want to see, hear (what you want to hear or) what you don't want to hear, and smell (what you want to smell or) what you don't want to smell. The mouth, the hand, and the foot are under your control. If you want, you can use your mouth to study Torah or to gossip. You can use your hand to give charity or to steal or kill. You can use your feet to walk to synagogue or houses of study, or to brothels.

MIDRASH[11]

This midrash might be an answer to the question: How do we use the gifts that God has given us? Certainly there are things that come our way that are nearly impossible to avoid. What we see, hear, and smell may not always be ours to control. We may try to avert our gaze, walk away from gossip, or hold our noses, but such approaches can only take us so far. A risqué billboard is as hard to block out as is, on the positive side, the wafting smell of fresh-baked challah. When we find ourselves in situations where we would rather not be, it is up to us to find a way to extricate ourselves gracefully if possible. The senses of sight, hearing, and smell may be involuntary, but there are many ways we use ourselves in our work and in our interpersonal relationships that are in our control. How we use those parts of ourselves over which we have control—in this example from the Midrash, how we speak, to what degree we give, and when and where we show up—say a lot about us as individuals. Are you cautious about how you speak about others? Do you give with a generous spirit? Do you show up when called upon? For tomorrow, think about ways you can better use the faculties God has given you with wisdom and discernment.   LF

Parental Wisdom
17 January
My child, heed your father's musar *and your mother's Torah.*
PROVERBS 1:8

This text from Proverbs, the book that Jewish tradition attributes to King Solomon, seems like guidance only for young children, the kind of lesson one is taught in elementary school. Most of us don't consider ourselves children any longer. And we seem to listen less to our parents as we grow older, even if we recognize the wisdom of their experience. Somehow what they live through and want to teach us does not seem quite relevant. "It's the gap!" as my kids like to say, referring to the gap that separates my generation from theirs. I certainly feel it in the same way between my parents and me.

But the *musar* (ethical guidance and advice) of our father and the torah (insight) of our mother have the potential to carry us into and through adulthood, if we are prepared to listen to it, something we generally eschew as rebellious adolescents. To listen, we have to open our ears and our hearts. After so many years we may have forgotten many of the things that our parents taught us. Then something we learned from them resurfaces many years later, perhaps even after they are gone. (That's one of the ways we know that their memory and influence are indeed still alive.) How many times have we heard ourselves saying something that our parents used to say, even when we are not conscious of its source or when we rejected it when we first heard it from their lips? It is never too late to thank our parents, never. Teach what you learned to someone else. Both the learning and their memory stay alive.

As you go to sleep this evening, think about what your parents may have taught you, the bit of wisdom that they offered when you needed it most. Call it to mind now. You'll rest a lot easier. KO

What Faith Can Do
18 JANUARY
The righteous live by their faith.
HABAKKUK 2:4

Abraham was the first man of faith, and because God chose him, we might have expected a saga of success, joy, family harmony, and enjoyment of life. That is not the way it ever was in the Bible, and that is certainly not the way it is here and now. Look at our biblical heroes: Isaac was almost murdered by his father, and later becomes blind and is lied to by his son Jacob. This Jacob, in turn, has plenty of problems with his own family: his daughter Dinah is raped; his sons hate their youngest brother, Joseph, and sell him into slavery while lying to their father about his whereabouts. Joseph becomes famous as an interpreter of dreams in Egypt and then is thrown into jail because he won't sleep with the boss's wife. No one has it easy, no one's life is without struggle and challenge, and no one's life is without disappointment.

Faith to me means that *no matter what happens in my life,* God will be there for me. *No matter what.* I believe that God gives us all the strength we need to handle whatever we are given. The life script we live out today is *never* the life script we thought we were getting when we were younger. Things happen, times change, other people change, *we change.* Life is so much more interesting and challenging than we could ever have imagined. And sometimes we get hurt, even those of us who believe in the goodness of God. But throughout it all, God is there, waiting patiently for us to remember that we are not alone.

Faith does not mean magic, faith does not make the pain of our lives go away. But faith does heal our wounds. Faith does challenge us to get on with our lives, knowing that we *can.* Knowing that God wants us to live, to love, and to be happy. God wants us not to be defeated by defeat but to be strengthened by our own strength. That is what faith is, that is what faith can do.   RABBI MELVIN J. GLAZER

The Limits of Worry

19 JANUARY

*It is forbidden to worry about these two things: What is
possible to fix and what is impossible to fix. Fix what is
possible and don't worry. How will worrying
about what you can't fix help?*

ADAPTED FROM RABBI YECHIEL MIKHAL OF ZLOTCHOV[12]

Some of us may be born "worriers." We fill our hours worrying about things both big and small, many of which may be out of our control. "Will I have enough money for my retirement? "Did I say the right thing last night at the board meeting?" "Will I live to an old age?" All these thoughts, or others like them, are certain to have crossed your mind at one time or another. At night, some of us may experience an intensified period of worrying. Somehow, the night stillness causes our fears to surface. Maybe it is because the interruptions of the day are no longer at hand.

Many times our worrying is a means to attempt to control situations that are often beyond our control. If we worry about them, then we (incorrectly, of course!) feel we are "doing something." However, one of life's struggles is for us to learn how to live despite our lack of control. Rabbi Yechiel Mikhal suggests a wise approach: Fix what we can and let go of what is beyond us. The activity of worrying drains us of a lot of mental and emotional activity. As you end this day and prepare for sleep, redirect this energy toward constructive and life-enriching actions.   LF

Worldly Wisdom

20 JANUARY

If they tell you that there is wisdom
among the nations, believe them.

MIDRASH[13]

At times we might tend to think that Judaism has a monopoly on wisdom. But it just isn't so. During the month of January, we are particularly mindful of the wisdom of the Reverend Martin Luther King, Jr. Many of his words have stayed with me and goaded me on, such as: "The ultimate measure of a man is not where he stands in moments of comfort, but where he stands at times of challenge and controversy." His wisdom and spiritual strength inspired our teachers, like Rabbi Abraham Joshua Heschel, who marched together with him. They taught one another from their different traditions, and our world is better for it.

For a long time, Judaism ostensibly prohibited studying the wisdom of other traditions. My grandfather, my *zeyde,* went so far as to cross to the other side of the street when we walked past a church. It was a behavior that he brought with him from Europe, one of the few that he taught me that I have chosen to let go. But it was his way of demonstrating to me that Christianity and what it represented was off-limits and had nothing to say to us, as Jews. Obviously, I was prohibited as a young child from entering even the outermost precincts of a church—or any other religious institution that was not Jewish. As an adult, I have learned from the people and activities of a variety of other religions and gained from the wisdom there.

The Talmud is filled with parables and discussions about those who were tempted to pursue the wisdom outside Judaism. For most of us today, everyday contact with other religious traditions is taken for granted. It is part of who we are and what we have become. Rabbi Rami Shapiro sees it this way: "The true person of faith seeks to learn from every tradition while being at home in her own."[14] In my own search, I have learned one thing: Though there is indeed "wisdom among the nations," Judaism's insightful interpretation of the challenges we face in daily life—and its big questions—is ours alone to share with the world.   KO

Commanded
21 JANUARY

*God called Moses to the top of the mountain
and Moses went up.*

EXODUS 19:20B

Scholars will argue over the exact text of the Ten Commandments. Is it the version in Exodus or the one in Deuteronomy? Or was it replaced altogether by the commandments given to Moses when he returned for what was supposed to be the videotape replay in Exodus 33? How many commandments were given to Moses? Ten? Six hundred thirteen? Or are these merely convenient numbers by which to remember them?

I think there is a more important question to be asked. Do we still believe that we are commanded at all? Is there an authority greater than ourselves that can demand our allegiance and our behavior? Or is life merely listening to myself and doing what is best for me (and for my family)? Have we traded God for self?

I do not mean the lip service almost everyone pays to belief. We say, "I believe in God." The words roll easily off our tongues. But what does that belief entail? What does it mean for the way in which I live my life? Is there anything that we do (or refrain from doing) because God wants us to? Is there anything that would force me to say, "I would love to . . . but God has commanded me not to do so . . . so I won't"? Anything?

We have made "individual conscience" our highest authority. We have declared that it is more moral to do or not to do something because we have internalized the value or ideal. But is it really? Is it more moral to give some spare change to a person on the street because I feel like it, or because God wants me to do it? And which is more likely to get you to do it next time and the time following? Though made in the image of God, we humans are limited, capable of rationalizing away even the most despicable of behaviors. We get lazy, look aside. Having the external authority of God pushing us to our highest selves seems to me the straightest path to righteousness.

The Ten Commandments challenge us, then as now, to find the place of God in our lives, to place God squarely in the center. "Is this what God wants?" That needs to be our first and foremost question. If it is, and we honestly struggle to answer it, we need not worry over the particulars and the differences in the way we carry out the Divine will. That will grow and change with us and with the times, just as it always has. God would not have created us unique if we were all to conform to the same behavior, all look and dress alike, all do the exact same things. There are many paths to the one God. We need only ask ourselves, "Am I on the path?"

RABBI TERRY A. BOOKMAN

Seeking Advice

22 January

Plans are foiled for want of counsel, but they succeed through many advisors.

PROVERBS 15:22

Sometimes we think we may be beyond any learning curve. Perhaps we spend much of our time lecturing, mentoring, or teaching others the skills we have acquired. We may wonder if there is anything more for us to learn. We may even be in substantial positions of decision-making and responsibilities—in our work or in our families—where others turn to us to make significant, hard choices. If you find yourself in this situation, you may be in danger of thinking you no longer need advice. When we reach "the top," so to speak, it may be hard to find a mentor for ourselves. To whom do we turn when we are struggling or when we need a reality check? Wisdom matures when we are open to receiving input, feedback, and advice from others no matter the extent of our own accomplishments. Often these words of wisdom may not come from a peer but rather from a student or someone who answers to us. Sometimes this may mean we have to contract our egos in order to hear what others have to say. As Proverbs reminds us, no one who thinks he or she has all the answers can succeed in this life. Let us remain open to the others around us so that we can deepen our wisdom and maintain our willingness to grow and adapt to life's ever-changing situations. Tomorrow let us look for the opportunity to ask for advice.   LF

The Acquisition of Knowledge

23 JANUARY

If you lack knowledge, what have you acquired?
If you acquire knowledge, what do you lack?

MIDRASH[15]

What is the primary goal of this life? That seems to be the bottom line question. It's a tough one, too. It is the question that increasingly dogs most of our adult years, particularly when we realize that material success can only get us so far. Generally we wait to ask it until we have achieved some measure of success and recognition. Then we have to sit back and determine what really gives life meaning. Often we ask these questions at night, at the end of a day that was rushed and busy and exhausting.

When the Rabbis write about the acquisition of knowledge, they are generally writing about Torah-based knowledge: laws, customs, ceremonies, scholarship. They also hint at knowledge of God, for even though God may be unknowable, any hint of knowledge of God is acquired through an intimate relationship. And intimacy evolves through (here comes the company line) prayer, study, and the practice of meaningful ritual.

But knowledge alone, even knowledge of God, is never enough. What do we do with this knowledge? To use a contemporary idiom: Are we prepared to walk the walk or merely talk the talk?

Knowledge must lead to action in the world. Otherwise the prayer and study and ritual are limited and limiting. And action implies an overflowing passion. For that "passionate overflow" is what makes living real.   KO

Be There

24 January

God said to Moses, "Come up to the mountain and be there."
EXODUS 24:12A

In the midst of the listing of various ethical and ritual laws in the Torah, God tells Moses to ascend the mountain and receive the law. As one Hasidic commentator points out, there is no apparent reason why God should say, "Come up to me on the mountain" and then "be there." After all, where else would Moses be? And yet, as the Hasidic sage relates, it is possible to be even on the top of a mountain and in the presence of God and yet not to truly be there. For "being there" is not merely a geographical description, it is also a spiritual statement.

If spiritually "being there" was a challenge for Moses, then we can conclude that it's also difficult for us. To "be there" in the everyday happenings in life is no small task. So often we are mired in the past, in consideration of what we did or didn't do. Or we are anxious about the future. So often we are physically with someone but mentally off in another world, and an opportunity for true communication is squandered.

Why is it so hard to "be there" in the moment? Perhaps it's because we need training in such practices. This is the rationale behind many types of meditation, in which we are told, "Don't just do something, sit there!" Such a command is not easy to obey. As most beginning meditation students know, nothing can be harder than trying to think about nothing. If meditation experts are correct, however, then we can learn from them that to focus on the present is a great spiritual challenge. To "be there" with a friend, family member, or even by ourselves is not easy. But what could be a better way to show our gratitude to God for our lives than to enjoy them as they come, in the moments in which we live them?

May we all become better at "being there," and in so doing know that, like Moses, we stand in the presence of God.

RABBI EDWIN C. GOLDBERG

Acting with Pure Motives

25 JANUARY

If you wish to find out whether your motive is pure, test yourself in two ways: whether you expect recompense from God or anyone else, and whether you would perform the act in the same way if you were alone, unbeknown to others.

BACHYA IBN PAKUDA

Our actions are often conditioned by the reward we hope for or even expect. We may wonder whether we will be praised, receive a bonus, or be noticed by others. When we are honest with ourselves, we know that there are plenty of times that we extend ourselves in order to receive recompense, be it financial or emotional.

As we develop spiritually, we can reflect on whether we are taking on responsibilities from an inner place free of expectations or whether we are harboring hopes that greater recognition will come our way. When we can discern our motives, we can at least gain clarity and proceed in awareness. It is not that we must always do things selflessly; certainly there are situations, in our jobs or community work, for example, that require us to undertake projects, and we do so to show our loyalty and to advance ourselves. Yet we can also ask ourselves, "What things do we do for which we do not expect any reward or payback?" I suspect we can each find a few. For we do extend ourselves in many ways, both big and small, to those we love and care most about. Think of the areas in your life where you do this with little effort. Can you expand these actions tomorrow in some small yet significant way?　　LF

Silent Wisdom

26 JANUARY

Rabbi Akiva said, "Silence is a fence for wisdom."
MISHNAH[16]

Does a fence keep things out or keep things in? In prisons and maximum security compounds, there are often two fences. One fence is there to prevent the outsider (or the insider) from getting to the second fence. It depends on in which direction you are heading. Like most things in life, it all depends on your perspective. So is the Mishnah telling us that silence enhances wisdom or limits its acquisition? When we are overwhelmed by noise, we cannot gain wisdom. Perhaps silence itself is a form of wisdom, beyond knowing when to speak and when not to speak. And silence is what we yearn for at the end of the day, as we are preparing to sleep. We want to shut out the noise of the world, the noise that is outside our homes, and the noise that intrudes on our thoughts no matter how hard we try to shake ourselves free of it.

It's true that sometimes we thrive on the noise, especially in the midst of a sports spectacular, such as Super Bowl Sunday, which always occurs this time of year. It's okay to welcome the noise as long as we know that it is for a short period of time, for a specific event. Then we can embrace the silence once again.

It may seem odd that a rabbi—whose wisdom is generally known by words—would make such a statement about silence. Like music that is made by the spaces between the notes, the Rabbis have taught us that the silent spaces between the words of Torah speak to us as well. If we keep silent, perhaps we will be able to hear what they want to teach us.   KO

The Wonderment of Being Led

27 JANUARY

Who is like You, Adonai . . . awesome in splendor,
working wonders!

EXODUS 15:11

Like our own lives, most of the Torah is occupied with one story: the experience in the wilderness. It is here we receive the Torah. It is here that a group of slaves is transformed into a people. Our forty years of wandering, filled with occasional moments of joy, but also difficulties and challenges, serve a critical purpose. Still, a curiosity remains. Even in the most demanding of circumstances, and even with a group of six hundred thousand souls, the trek from Egypt to Canaan should take no more than one month. How is it that we became so lost? The Torah tells us: "God led the people roundabout by way of the wilderness."

God intentionally transforms a one-month journey into a forty-year experience. Writing in his *Star of Redemption,* Franz Rosenzweig suggests that God purposefully misleads. Only if God's intentions are hidden from us can we freely respond, for then our response is not swayed by knowing God's motivations. So God must conceal and at times mislead. We could accept this if all our years in the wilderness—and all our years of life—were filled with good and not tragedy. But the mystery of life, and of those forty years, is that we cannot (and perhaps should not) understand God's intent. We cannot fathom the "whys." Often we become frustrated.

We would do better to praise God and, like the Israelites, break out in song, "Who is like You, Adonai . . . awesome in splendor, working wonders!" But it is difficult to praise God—especially in the midst of tragedy. Thanking God becomes easier only when we look back through the years, when we stand

on the other side of the sea and behold our journey as a pilgrimage. Then we can begin to sing God's praises.

Unexpected, unplanned, unforeseen turns can, and often
do, become blessings. We do not lead, but are led "roundabout"—by God.   RABBI STEVEN HENESON MOSKOWITZ[17]

The Discipline of Prayer

28 JANUARY

*A musician must practice by prearranged schedule, regardless
of his inclination at the moment. So with the devout soul . . .
it must work. The person who folds his hands, waiting for
the spirit to move him to think of God—who postpones
worship for the right mood and the perfect setting, a forest or
mountain peak—will do little meditating or praying.*

RABBI MILTON STEINBERG[18]

Our lives are so overscheduled that, most of us wonder,
"How can I also find a free time slot for prayer?"
Traditionally, Jews pray three times a day. The underlying
idea is that in the course of the busy day we should stop,
reconnect with others, and thank God for all we have. Today
many of us do not even stop for lunch. We ask ourselves,
"How could I possibly slow down for a prayerful ten minutes?" Yet, can you think about taking some short period of
time—either at the day's start or now at the day's end—to
reflect and offer a prayer to God?

When we make time in our schedules on a regular basis,
we build a foundation, a reservoir within ourselves that connects us with the Holy One. We realize that some nights our
words will flow and other days we may feel tongue-tied. Yet
there will be those special moments when we are transported
to an entirely different realm. No two days will be exactly
alike. We come to understand that without an ongoing

prayerful dialogue, it is hard, if not impossible, to access a meaningful relationship with God—a relationship that we often need most when we are in crises. Think of prayer as an ongoing habit and make it a daily, or nightly, practice.   LF

Tomorrow's Hope
29 JANUARY

*If we are not better tomorrow than we are today,
why have a tomorrow?*

RABBI NACHMAN OF BRESLOV[19]

The purpose of today is to prepare us for tomorrow. So we have to make use of today as preparation. If we don't, then perhaps we are not deserving of tomorrow. And today is filled with time. If we waste it, if we kill it, if we abuse it, we don't get it back. Only if we make the most out of that time do we have the possibility of its coming back to us through what we have learned during it.

Some take Rabbi Nachman's comment as messianic, that is, as a theological reference to another world. Thus, this life becomes preparation for the next life. That is an important understanding of his teaching, but I think that in this case Rabbi Nachman was writing regarding this world. He wanted to encourage us to appreciate our daily blessings and use them to improve our own lives and benefit the lives of others.

Other rabbis offered his teaching a little differently. Those who recorded their teachings in *Pirke Avot* wrote, "Repent the day before your death." Of course, no one really knows which will be the last day he or she spends on this earth. But we all know how to repent and steer our lives back to the right course. The question is not how but when. Rabbi Nachman says the time is now. And I would add, now before you sleep—until tomorrow or forever!   KO

The Bottom

30 JANUAR

God is hiding from the world. (
divine emerge from

RABBI ABRAHAM JOSH

There were two young brothers, eig...
who were exceedingly mischievous. Whatever went wrong
the neighborhood, it turned out that they had a hand in it.
Their parents were at their wits' end trying to control them.
Hearing about a rabbi nearby who worked with delinquent
boys, the mother suggested to her husband that she would
ask the rabbi to talk with the boys, and he agreed. The mother went to the rabbi and made her request. He agreed but
said he wanted to see the younger boy first and alone. So the
mother sent the younger boy to the rabbi. The rabbi sat the
boy down across his huge, impressive desk. For about five
minutes they just sat and stared at each other. Finally, the
rabbi pointed his forefinger at the boy and asked, "Young
man, where is God?"

The boy looked under the desk, in the corners of the room,
all around, then said nothing. Again, louder, the rabbi pointed at the boy and asked, "Where is God?" Again, the boy
looked all around but said nothing. A third time, in a louder,
firmer voice, the rabbi leaned far across the desk and put his
forefinger almost to the boy's nose and asked, "Young man, I
ask you, where is God?"

The boy panicked and ran all the way home. Finding his
older brother, he dragged him upstairs to their room and into
the closet, where they usually plotted their mischief. He finally said, "We're in bi-i-i-ig trouble." The older boy asked,
"What do you mean 'big trouble'?" His brother replied, "I'm
telling ya,' we're in big trouble. God is missing and they
think we did it!"

...missing from the world, then we did do it. As ...ham Joshua Heschel said, "God is hiding from the ...ur task is to let the divine emerge from our deeds." ...can bring God back into the world. God is waiting for ...nvitation.   RABBI JEFFREY SALKIN

Shabbat as Repair

31 JANUARY

Shabbat restores a modicum of balance for us between the value of the individual and the value of community. This-worldly salvation, which is what Judaism seeks above all, can be found in bonding with each other to repair collectively what we have damaged or destroyed individually.

RABBI ISMAR SCHORSCH[20]

Shabbat is our weekly day of renewal. Though often called a day of rest, it has many aspects, including that of connection, of rebonding with the others in our life. We step back from the pressures of work and we step into the realm of family and community. During the week, our responsibilities can keep us so frantic that our connections with friends and family are hurried and brief through e-mail, cell phones, and pagers. We may not even speak to our loved ones at any length until the weekend arrives. Reconnecting in person around the warmth of a Shabbat meal, here we face one another and can speak to one another in an unhurried way. We can be fully present for those whom we love. To experience time differently, we can even refrain from wearing a watch on Shabbat so as not to be tied to the clock. Let us use Shabbat as a day to repair our relationships and restore the bonds that keep us connected one to another, to community, and also to God.   LF

FEBRUARY

Sunny Days
1 FEBRUARY

*The sun will no more be your light by day ... but Adonai
will be to you an everlasting light.*
ISAIAH 60:19

Although February—even in a leap year—is the shortest
month of the year, it always seems to me to be the longest.
(That might be one of the reasons why the Hebrew calendar
boasts of an entire extra month in its leap year.) It is in the
heart of winter and even though the days are actually getting
longer, spring seems a long way away. I often feel as if I were
living primarily in darkness. It seems that we are constantly
forced to confront our days through artificial light in the
winter. Winter weather in the Northeast especially accentu-
ates the cold and darkness of what seems to be an unwelcom-
ing world.

So, like most people, I anxiously look forward to the sun's
rising as I make my way through the traffic and the crowds
on the way to work in the early morning. But in the winter,
even when the sun finally makes an appearance, the skies
often remain dark and dismal. The weather report puts it at
"partly cloudy." Here the text from Isaiah is particularly useful for getting me through the day. The sun's powerful light is

limited. Its ability to warm the world seems limited in the winter. Only divine light can pierce the darkness. The light of the sun may be able to warm the body, but only God's light can warm the soul. Tomorrow let's bring that warmth to someone else who feels cold like we once did. KO

Creating a Jewish Home
2 FEBRUARY

A container is defined by its contents. A pitcher of water is water. A crate of apples is apples. A house, too, is defined by what it contains. Fill your house with books of Torah and your house becomes Torah. Affix tzedakah *boxes to its walls and your house becomes a wellspring of charity. Bring those who need a warm home to your table, and your house becomes a lamp in the darkness.*
RABBI MENACHEM MENDL SCHNEERSON

We are always concerned about our future, whether we are speaking about the weather (and the groundhog's prediction!) or other more important issues.

When we move into a new home we often spend a great deal of time and energy—not to mention money—buying and arranging furniture and possessions. Our homes are a reflection of our tastes and who we are. When we walk into others' homes, we learn a lot about them: Perhaps our hosts are collectors of special artwork, or we learn that they are slobs. Some homes just seem to exude a feeling of learning, *tzedakah,* hospitality, and warmth. We look around and see Jewish books lining the bookshelves, *tzedakah* boxes out in the open. We smell freshly baked or warmed challah and hear the sounds of laughter and life. Of course, the things we place in the rooms of our homes only say so much. Much of who we are is expressed nonverbally and cannot be captured in the things we own. In fact, we can walk into a home that is sparsely furnished and yet feel great warmth and love. As we strive to create rich Jewish lives, let us remember that adding special objects to our homes can help create an atmosphere that reminds us of the role that Judaism plays in our lives each day. Using these ritual objects helps to pave our way to God and the *ultimate* future beyond tomorrow.   LF

A Mission Statement for Life

3 FEBRUARY

And be a blessing.

GENESIS 12:2

As we prepare to retire for the night, we think back over our day. What did we do and why did we do it? Why did we choose one course of action over another? Did we act out of conscience and conviction or out of some ulterior motive? What brought us joy, and what caused us pain? Whom did we help and whom did we hurt?

Feelings of anger, regret, or remorse may keep us from the peaceful slumber that we so crave. One prescription that I would suggest for a good night's sleep is the adoption of a special life mission statement for yourself and your family. In this way, you will be able to see the events of the day within a holy perspective. The Divine words that were spoken to Abraham—"And be a blessing"—can become the guiding force in your life, just as they were for him.

Throughout your day—and your life—you will feel pulled in more than one direction by competing forces. It may be difficult to decide what to do. But remembering to "be a blessing" will guide you to act in a loving fashion—in thought, words, and action.

The Hebrew word for "blessing" *(berakhah)* is very similar to the word for "pool of water" *(berekhah)*. Just as a pool is made up entirely of water, the blessings that you give and receive should be completely genuine and wholehearted. Being a blessing will transform you into a dynamic spring of water, a vitalizing, purifying source of thoughts, words, and actions, allowing the flow of Divine energies to inspire you in everything you do. RABBI LEVI MEIER

Worldly Wisdom
4 FEBRUARY
Who is wise? Someone who can see what is coming.
TALMUD[21]

Usually we think of wisdom as something sublime and limited to the profound challenges of life rather than anything concerning the routine of everyday living. I also imagined that those who possessed wisdom somehow came to it in rather remarkable ways, often through a transformational experience that emerged out of a revelation or life-threatening trauma. Perhaps those whom we call wise retired to a study or office—filled with shelves of books, a desk brimming with ancient parchments and tattered correspondence—each evening after dinner just to think. Or perhaps they were constantly sought after for advice or even just their presence. People would, I imagine, come to them for guidance because of a particular role they held in the community or a reputation that developed over time. Maybe they were physicians or judges or rabbis. Their training, their experience, and their professional role made them well suited for this "job." In my secret moments of younger fantasy, I might even have allowed myself to fantasize that role for myself.

But there are other kinds of wisdom that are often overlooked in our pursuit of a more venerated form of wisdom. And these forms are more real and certainly more important. Among them is the wisdom that comes from survival and self-preservation, the kind that our people learned through its history of interaction with peoples and nations that were not so supportive or nurturing. This kind of wisdom comes from the school of "hard knocks," the kind that can distinguish an enemy from a friend and then turn that enemy into a friend, the kind that we learn through the simple events and encounters that make up each day, the kind that teaches us how to survive each day and each night that precedes it.   KO

Shabbat—the Pinnacle of Creation

5 FEBRUARY

"Remember," in Hebrew, "zakhor" *begins with the letter* "zayin," *which stands for the number seven. Let every day of the week be directed toward the seventh, the crown of creation, the day on which God completed all work and rested.*

BIBLICAL COMMENTARY[22]

A common expression, "Thank God it's Friday," conveys our yearning for a respite from the workweek. In the Jewish perspective of time, the end of the week is much more than a mere day off. The seventh day, Shabbat, is called the pinnacle of creation because God created rest on it. Thus, just as God rested, so do we. Resting doesn't mean lounging around, watching TV, or doing errands. No. In Judaism, the quality of resting that is associated with Shabbat has to do with restoring our *neshamot*, our souls. On Shabbat we can spend quality time with our family and friends that the pace of our week precludes. On Shabbat we praise God for creating the world. We can only feel this sense of gratitude if we step back from our daily routine. Otherwise, it is difficult to see the world and its beauty with awe and wonder if we are perpetually in motion. The rabbis teach that we acquire a *nefesh yiterah,* an additional soul on Shabbat. The only way to feel this gift is if we dedicate time to renewing our soul on a deep level by withdrawing from our daily responsibilities and worries and refocusing our energies. Shabbat comes each and every week. So the next time Friday rolls around, instead of saying, "Thank God it's Friday," say to yourself and to others, "Thank God Shabbat is coming!"   LF

Forgiving Those Who Hurt Us

6 FEBRUARY

I hereby forgive whoever hurt me this day.

RABBI ISAAC LURIA[23]

One of the giants of spiritual history, Rabbi Isaac Luria, or the Ari (the Lion), as he was called, had his own prayer book. The Ari felt that he simply could not recite the words of the evening service, praising God for being merciful and forgiving, unless he was willing to be the same. And so he added his own prelude to the one that is printed in most prayer books. Only after he had put anger and irritation out of his own heart did he feel that he had the right to ask God to do the same for him.

We ought to take the custom of the Ari and make it our own. What if once a day, before we go to sleep, we say his prayer? What if once a day we let go of the grudges and the resentments and the irritations that have accumulated in our souls during the day? We would sleep better and travel through life much lighter.   RABBI JACK RIEMER

The Time for Mercy

7 FEBRUARY

*The gates of mercy are open all the time and anyone who
wants to enter through them may do so.*

TALMUD[24]

If you have gotten in tune with the rhythm of the Jewish calendar, you may be used to thinking about God's mercy
around the time of the fall holidays: Rosh Hashanah and
Yom Kippur. That's the theme of those holidays and it colors
the entire period of time. It's also the time of year that most
Jews find their way into the synagogue even if they have been
absent from the pews all year long—and even if they do not
stay the entire time. We consider our deeds, sit through long
services and sermons, maybe even brave a brief dialogue with
the Almighty. We pray that if there is some sort of Book of
Life, our names—and the names of those we love—are
recorded in it. It seems that, for most of us, the idea of divine
mercy is restricted to this one time of year, while other religious ideas shape the remainder of the seasons.

So if the fall holidays are reserved for repentance and spiritual renewal, then why are we talking about it at the beginning of February? The only Jewish holiday that comes to mind
during this time of year is Tu Bishevat, that rather inflated
minor holiday that celebrates the trees. Sure, Shabbat takes
place at the end of each week and we continue our cyclical
reading of the Torah. Some of us slip away on vacation
around Presidents' Day weekend, later in the month. But it's
the middle of winter and not much is going on in the calendar.

But spiritual logic is often counterintuitive. The rabbis of
the Talmud want to teach us through this text that God's
mercy is always available—no matter what time of day, no
matter what time of year. All we have to do is ask for it. If
that's the case, what are we waiting for?   KO

Seeking Truth

8 FEBRUARY

The letters that form the word emet, *"truth" in Hebrew, are spaced far apart in the Hebrew alphabet. Conversely, the letters that form the word* sheker, *"deceit" in Hebrew, follow one after another. This suggests that it is difficult to act in trust, while deception is as close as one's ear.*

COMMENTARY ON THE TALMUD[25]

The Rabbis love to draw insights from the meaning of words. Here the midrashist finds an important lesson based on the distance between the letters of two words—*emet* and *sheker*—as they appear in the Hebrew alphabet! This text leads us to consider an important question: "What is the difference between telling the truth or a lie?" In other words, why does lying seem to come more easily than telling the truth? Even when we know that the truth is the correct, and even higher, path to pursue, we each get caught up in telling lies from time to time so as not to embarrass ourselves or to cover up an error. Truth is also not always apparent. Like a treasure, it may take some seeking. Lies, on the other hand, are always known to those who speak them. We may say we are not lying, but in our hearts we know we are. Our lies may deceive others for a short time, and yes, they can even lull us into believing they are only harmless "white lies." Yet, in the end, lies have a way of catching up with us. Lies beget more lies, while truth telling begets the practice of seeking the path of truth. Let us remember that truth is the path we seek no matter how distant it may take us from where we are. Whether we are at the beginning, middle, or end of our journey, we can change course and step onto the path of truth. It is never too late. LF

Keep It Burning

9 FEBRUARY

*You yourself command the people of Israel to bring
you pure oil of pounded olives for lighting to
cause the lamp to burn continually.*

EXODUS 27:20

The *ner tamid,* a lamp that burned perpetually in the ancient Tabernacle, was one lamp among many that were used to bring light into that sacred space. Unlike the menorah, which was used for illumination, the light of this lamp was largely symbolic. God does not need our light. It is we who need its light. And it is we who must keep the lamp burning.

Each of us is a light that both does and does not go out. Our lives are a finite flame. In the normative course of things we are born, we grow, we make our mark on the world, age, and then die. None of us, no matter how powerful, no matter how rich or famous, none of us can escape that reality. And yet there is a part of us, we call it the soul, which will never die, a flame that will never go out.

God is a light that never goes out. There is nothing finite about God. And so, through soul, we share in God's eternality. The *ner tamid,* the eternal light that is housed in each and every synagogue, is our attempt to remind us of this reality. The attempt must be a communal one. Each of us forgets sometimes. That is part of what it means to be human. But as a people, as a community, we can do it. In that way, our human unity, fragile as it is at times, can remind us of God's unity, which can never be shattered. All that from a single flame.

What are you doing to keep the flame from going out?

RABBI TERRY A. BOOKMAN

Plain Wisdom

10 FEBRUARY

If you've got it, hold it. If you are capable, do!
YIDDISH PROVERB

My grandparents were simple people. As young children, they came from Russia to America, traveling in steerage on a large ship. No English. No money. And this mind-set remained throughout their lives. Even after living in the United States for sixty-five years, they were immigrants. Somehow they survived, eked out a living, and brought their basic values to bear on the shaping of the family they raised—even if their level of Jewish observance was slowly worn away through the years. It was for me and the generation of my children to recapture and renew what they had left behind for us. We could afford to do it, because of what they bequeathed to us and because of how the American Jewish community evolved. They may have let go of many things, but of these basic values, as expressed in their Yiddish and broken English, they never let go.

The Yiddish expression above, translated into English, was something my grandparents taught me, something with which they goaded me in childhood and, through my memory of them, into adulthood as well. Make sure that you hold on to things that are dear to you. Let the other things slip away, because they are not worth keeping. And if you are capable of doing something, especially to lead, then do it. And do it now. God would expect no less and neither would they.   KO

The Gift of Expression
11 FEBRUARY
The ability to express what is hidden in the heart is a rare gift.
RABBI ABRAHAM JOSHUA HESCHEL

We feel many things over the course of a day, much more over the course of a year or a lifetime. Sometimes our many emotions are not only hard to reach, they may also be hard to express; we may be able to express only very few of the deep and the more subtle everyday emotions that lie below our surface. Some of us may access our more interior realms through writing, dancing, music, or other artistic expressions. Others of us may use prayer and contemplation as ways to quiet our minds and reach our inner world. Dreams at night provide another doorway. There is no need to be an artist to yearn for access to that which lies in our hearts and to desire to give it full expression. Too often we have learned to protect our hearts, and thus we do not feel safe to express what lies therein. Let us not allow our heart's truths to be eclipsed by either the harried lives we lead or past hurts. Rather, let us nurture our gifts so that we can find the means to express ourselves fully. Let your evolving relationship with God guide the expression of your soul.   LF

Finding What We Lost
12 FEBRUARY
O God, Your ways are holiness.
PSALM 77:14a

We may be in danger of losing the sense that some times are holier than others—that Shabbat is not like Wednesday (or even like Saturday); that many of us can skip or go late to work on the first day of Sukkot or Pesach. Even this day of

President Abraham Lincoln's birthday—which was acknowledged quite patriotically when many of us were children—has become lost in Presidents' Day later in the month, part of our quest for convenience in all of our holidays. We are in danger of losing the sense that *yahrzeit* is a command appearance in the synagogue, and not a date that we can skip or move. We are in danger of losing the sanctity of our life cycle moments, because we have become blind to the choreography and deaf to the poetry that is within them. We are in danger of losing the holiness of the synagogue, seeing it as yet another institution in our lives.

And how did we lose that sense of the sacred?

The sixties helped us lose holiness; our generation's credo was "Let it all hang out, and whatever you do, don't be judgmental." The universities helped us lose holiness; no one talked about the holy at college.

American consumerism helped us lose holiness. And last but not least: Our own fears, our own reticence, our own bashfulness, helped us lose holiness. We were afraid to talk about it. We were afraid that if we spoke of the holy we would become "holier than thou," and that if we talked about sanctity then we might become sanctimonious.

So, that is where we lost holiness. But I sense that we can find it again as a spiritually seeking community. All of our words for our Jewish hopes and dreams provide us with the path to holiness: "recover," "find," "rediscover," not "invent." And they all take us back to one road. That is the meaning of *teshuvah*—to return to those things that we thought we had lost. Won't you come along?

RABBI JEFFREY SALKIN

The Limits of Self-Prese

13 FEBRUARY

Hillel taught, "If I don't stand up for my
But if I am only self-centered, what g

MISHNAH[26]

In this unusual, rather poetic translation by Rabbi Eugene Borowitz (a leading liberal Jewish theologian in North America) of a well-known text from *Pirke Avot,* the Rabbis offer us advice out of their own experience, a perspective that often informs their teaching. In his translation, Rabbi Borowitz places his own spin on it as well. He views a classic text through the lens of postmodernity, as he would call it, and then derives an important spiritual lesson for us. The lesson is in the challenge that stands between self-preservation and self-aggrandizement. The challenge is where the self and the other join forces rather than standing at odds with one another.

As we think about the day that is now drawing to a close, we look at the way we acted. We consider ourselves and others. Did we do right? Should we have stood up to someone else on our own behalf? Should we have stood up on someone else's behalf? How do we know how to establish that balance? How do we know how to find the "golden mean," as the philosophers like to call that midpoint?

Sometimes we just know what to do. It is a rare insight, but we know as soon as we act that we have done the right thing. And often we don't think about it at all. It just comes from the center of the self and it feels good. But most times, we find that place in the middle of self and other as a result of navigating our way through the world, guided and nurtured by the Divine. It comes from trial and error, from the guidance of others. It comes through prayer and insight. And slowly, as the years accumulate, so does our wisdom.   KO

The Power of Prophecy

14 FEBRUARY

Would that all of God's people were prophets!

NUMBERS 11:29

As we can all imagine, the task of leading the People of Israel through their desert trek was a heavy burden for Moses. Even great leaders get tired. Tired from leading an often disgruntled, complaining people, Moses cried out to God at one point that the load was too heavy for him to carry alone. As a result, the leadership responsibilities were redistributed, now to be shared by a council of seventy elders. A pair of Israelites named Eldad and Medad are inspired at this time and prophesy throughout the camp. The people, though, feel their prophecy and behavior is somehow "over the top." Maybe they were too passionate, maybe too direct. Moses' response, though, is not one of concern or alarm. Rather, he boldly proclaims, "Would that all of God's people were prophets!"

Each of us has the ability to be a prophet, in that we can speak out and motivate our friends, family, and community with a vision for the future. We can each become leaders drawing on our abilities to motivate through inspiration and vision. While some people may be alarmed like Joshua, Moses' prodigy who pleaded with Moses to restrain Eldad and Medad, others will have the wisdom of Moses to embrace their voices of wisdom and not be afraid. Not all of us can be a Moses, but we can each become a prophet. Let us not leave this task for others.   LF

From Terror to Love

15 February

Jacob [said to the angel], "I will not let you go unless you bless me."
GENESIS 32:27B

Before Jacob met his angel, he was terrified of what his brother, Esau, might do. But when his body had been marked and morning had broken, his blessing won, his name changed, then Jacob-Israel could come near his brother without fear. And his brother could run to him, and embrace him, and fall upon him, and kiss him. And together they could weep.

Terror is the prelude to love. Solitude and struggle, darkness and injury. But day breaks. The sun dispels the night. The adversary does not prevail. The wound becomes the sign of aristocracy. And I, in the middle of my years, read as if for the first time past the story of the lonely night, past the confrontation in the dark, to the story of *chesed,* of grace and lovingkindness, in which Jacob, the accumulator, the hoarder, can meet his brother face-to-face and say: Take my gifts. Take my blessing. *Ki yesh li kol.* I have enough. I have all.

For the giving and receiving of love is everything.

NESSA RAPOPORT

Divine Delay

16 February

God may delay, but God does not forget.
LADINO PROVERB

This comment, from a part of Jewish folk culture that is often not celebrated, may emerge from a deeply held religious conviction. Like most folk wisdom, it comes from the accumulated experience of individuals, and its truth is confirmed by its passing from one person to the next, from one generation to the one that comes after it. It may also reflect an attempt by people, regular everyday people like you and me, to explain why those who do evil seem to be rewarded, while bad things often happen to those who do good. The comment reminds us of a profound lesson that emerges from our own experience. God's action cannot be measured in the same units of time as we measure our own deeds. What appears as divine silence should not be interpreted as divine approval or disapproval. Rather, silence on behalf of God may merely be a delay. As the rabbis have taught, we may have free will, and we may freely exercise it, but all is known by the Almighty.

I believe that there is a motivation on God's part in this delay. God wants to give us an opportunity to change our behavior, to repair what we may have broken, and to return to a path that leads back toward a relationship with God. The delay may not be one that we deserve. Thus, it is a form of divine mercy and compassion.

About six months have passed since the fall holidays. A half year since God sealed us in the Book of Life—or not—according to Jewish tradition. We are alive to read these words and contemplate the day just passed and the weeks and months that preceded. God does not forget, says the proverb. What is it that we have done today that we want God to remember? Hurry. Don't delay. Perhaps neither will God.   KO

Renewing Faith

17 FEBRUARY

It is hard to trust when we have been hurt. It is hard to hope again when we have known tragedy. It is hard to stop flinching, to stop responding to past pains. Help me, God. Restore me. Revive in me all the optimism that I once had. Remind me of the person I used to be. Help me to return to life, to openness, and to You, my God.

RABBI NAOMI LEVY[27]

Each of us has gone through times of pain and suffering. Many of us have lost people we loved dearly. Some of us may remember physical illness that caused us great pain, while others of us may recall psychological distress that led to suffering. No one is immune from some amount of pain as we make our way through life. How do we get through these difficult times and renew our sense of hope and faith? Hopefully, we reach out to our community to sustain and nurture us, and we turn to God. At times though, optimism seems impossible. When we have been betrayed and our trust has been broken, we can choose cynicism and harden our hearts, we can pray, or we can incline our hearts and minds for a complete healing of our spirit. This requires that we seek an openness that, right now, might be closed off or scarred over. So let us begin by turning to God and asking to have our spirit and trust restored in fullness and strength.   LF

Seek Alternate Route

18 FEBRUARY

When you go forth on a journey,
seek the counsel of your Maker.

TALMUD[28]

For those of you who take advantage of holiday weekends, you might find yourself snarled in traffic on Presidents' Day. While I was stuck in traffic, I found myself staring at a construction sign. The yellow letters were flashing advice to drivers; I think they flashed at me at least a dozen times before the message penetrated: *Expect Delays/Seek Alternate Route.* I wondered if our ancestors, the ancient Israelites, would have appreciated that kind of sign as they wandered along their circuitous route toward the Promised Land. Certainly, the journey, which took them forty years, could have been accomplished in a matter of months with a better map! And I wonder if I could have appreciated that message, if it had been posted in some conspicuous spot as I embarked upon my life's journey. Would it have reassured me? Depressed me? Given me patience or perspective?

Without a doubt, most of us who have built careers or raised families or nurtured relationships or established reputations—you name it—have come to learn to expect delays. And those of us who have risen to the challenge of rebuilding any of these—career, family, relationship, or reputation— have had to learn to be flexible. Seeking alternative routes may be the key to eventual good fortune and the successful completion of our journey.   RABBI LIZA STERN

Mastery of Learning

19 FEBRUARY

God desires the purity of spirit that all can bring and not the learned mastery with which only some are gifted.

TALMUD[29]

There are many calendars that govern our lives. In addition to my electronic daily planner, I have a drawer full of calendars that I have to consult before I make any plans: a Hebrew calendar that is filled with holidays and Torah readings and lots of other items that shape my religious life, the program calendar for the organization in which I work, my wife's work and travel schedule, my older son's college calendar, and my younger son's day school calendar. And we receive plenty of calendars in the mail offering lectures and courses in the community that have to be added as well. We may want to take advantage of these courses (if our other calendars permit), because they promise to teach us mastery in a variety of subjects. So we dutifully register for whatever we can. We think that such mastery allows us greater control of our environment and our lives—as well as better access to the holy. Often we think that knowledge will allow us to resolve the challenges of daily living. We may also think that knowledge, particularly the "how-to" of Jewish life, will lead us directly to God. Ironically, the rabbis of the Talmud, whom we would expect to encourage such mastery, surprise us by suggesting that God prefers purity of spirit over subject mastery. They might even go so far as to say that you cannot gain *mastery* of such subjects without a purity of spirit.

So before you sign up for more courses or add any more books to your library, consider the spirit with which you approach any new learning. Attempt not to be its master. Rather, let wisdom lead you.   KO

Acting with Zeal

20 FEBRUARY

You can talk all you want, but it gets nothing done.
A meowing cat catches no mice.
Laughing is easy, doing is tough.
Nobody is born a virtuoso.
Nothing comes easily.

YIDDISH PROVERBS

Throughout Jewish ethical literature, the Rabbis talk about an inner quality they call *zerrizut,* which means zeal. At one time or another we have each experienced bouts of procrastination. We put off doing an action that we know needs to be done. When it comes to fulfilling the tasks in front of us, whether these are family responsibilities, work assignments, or communal commitments, it is incumbent on us to call upon the zeal inside us to do them in a timely manner. The rabbis go so far as to say that we have a religious obligation to be constructively busy. Laziness is never esteemed. These Yiddish proverbs remind us that all success comes with hard work and an inner discipline. We can talk all we want, but if we don't exert effort, all our words and aspirations will be for naught. So tomorrow morning, if you are feeling lazy or have the urge to put aside an important project or task, remember the wisdom of our ancestors and their proverbs, that with *zerrizut* you can transform the world.   LF

Knowing the Self in the Other

21 FEBRUARY

*The greater the person, the more
one must seek to discover oneself.*

RABBI ABRAHAM ISAAC KOOK[30]

My teacher, Rabbi Harold M. Schulweis, taught this to me; in turn, I want to share it with you: An old rabbi living in a faraway village [it seems that many classic stories start out this way] was visited by Jews from all over Europe because he possessed the remarkable ability to counsel the most difficult men, women, and children. Thieves, drug addicts, prostitutes and drunkards were his visitors. One day the rabbi's bravest disciple asked him, "How is it that you who are so immersed in prayers and books, who rarely go out to mix with people in the marketplace, are able to relate to these troubled people who come to you from another world?"

The rabbi thought and answered, "I listen deeply to their words and look into their eyes. I hear and see echoes and reflections of my own self. Not that I have done everything that they have done, but I do recognize in them my *yetzer,* my lusts and drives and ambitions, my imaginations of the heart." The disciple asked him whether he had ever failed to recognize the sins of others. The rabbi thought a long while and then confessed. "Yes, once I heard this man confessing a sin that I could find no hint of in myself. It was at that moment that I realized I was hiding something of myself and I searched deeper to find it out."

Our imagination allows us to know each other, and the more I find myself in you, the better I understand myself. As we take time to reflect, gain introspection, and even judge ourselves at the end of the day, may we be emboldened to act with generosity, kindness, and compassion toward ourselves and others. RABBI MALKA DRUCKER

True Faith

22 FEBRUARY

If we dare to be true persons of faith, we can unite in our unknowing: Doing justly, loving mercy, and walking humbly with God and each other.

RABBI RAMI SHAPIRO[31]

How do we unite in something that we do not know? That is why we call it faith. We believe and yet we do not, cannot, fully know. Some might even say that God is unknowable. While we might grow closer in relationship to God—and that should be our goal—we can never really know the Divine. This is hard for some people to accept, especially those of us who have been brought up to believe that knowledge is power, that knowledge is the key to understanding, that knowledge can lead us to fixing things that are broken.

Borrowing a phrase from the prophet Micah (where he responds to the reflective question: What does God require of you?), Rabbi Shapiro suggests that our faith in God demands that we join together to do justice, love mercy, and walk humbly with one another. But it is our recognition, and acceptance, of our unknowing that motivates us to act. This unknowing is what we share in common with others. Such an acknowledgment leads us to one another and to God.

This approach is particularly instructive for those of us who generally consider ourselves as masters in our own universe, which can keep us from being fully sensitive to the needs of others. Such an approach will lead us to a different kind of knowledge than we thought was necessary to navigate our way in the world. This kind of knowledge brings us to personal repair and repair of a broken world. To recognize that we have that ability, when we choose to act, is indeed a humbling experience. KO

Torah Study for Its Own Sake

23 FEBRUARY

Rabbi Eliezer ben Zadok said: Do good deeds because of your regard for God and study words of Torah for their own sake. Do not use them as a crown to magnify yourself with, or as a spade with which to hoe.

TALMUD[32]

So many of the activities we pursue in our lives we do for reward, status, recognition, or some other motive. What, though, do we do for its own sake? Studying Torah for its own sake in Hebrew is called *Torah lishmah*. When it comes to Torah study, we are taught that we are to do it without any expectations, hope for reward, or even a time schedule. It doesn't matter how long it takes us to finish reading the Bible or study a volume of Talmud. Unlike other areas of our lives, here the watchword is: The slower the better. We undertake Torah study with the intention to gain knowledge, but we continue our study whether we arrive at insights with ease or with difficulty.

Torah study is also about character development in its broadest sense. We learn about ourselves, our relationships with others, and our relationship with God by delving into the ancient words of Torah. At times they become like a Rorschach test. For example, how we respond to Abraham's near-sacrifice of Isaac tells us much about ourselves, our relationship to our father, and our ambivalence about God's authority. The questions we ask when we read about the Exodus from Egypt speak to our own yearning for freedom from all experiences of slavery.

Whenever you study Torah, do not do so in a rote manner. Rather, allow the holy words of Torah to flow through you, touch your soul, and inform your life.   LF

Leaving, Then Going To

24 FEBRUARY

And Jacob came upon a certain place and stopped there for the night, for the sun had set.

GENESIS 28:11A

Our sages teach us that there is no chronology in the Torah. Events may appear in any order. Distances do not matter. Time sequences do not exist. Therefore, everything occurs in God's world simultaneously. Only in our world, an aberration of God's perspective, do dimensions exist.

The events of our material lives are chronological. We plan for them. We anticipate them. We believe they constitute the fabric, the warp and woof of our lives. Day begins. Waking, we think about the events upcoming. Dressing the children. Meals. The demands we must meet throughout the day. Schedules. The business of everyday living. This appears to be our reality. But behind that reality exists a greater, larger, more demanding but quieter reality: God's presence. "Jacob awoke from his sleep and said, 'Surely God is present in this place and I did not know it. . . . How awesome is this place! This is none other than the abode of God and that is the gateway to heaven.'"

What do we learn from Jacob's experience? Our material lives, our daily schedules, are linear, chronological, sensible. We have joys and sorrows, our obligations and our responsibilities. We meet them and move on.

But there exists another level, a level in which there is no before and no after, only the eternal present. In that moment ultimate significance intersects with the material and the transient now. In that moment, the gateway to eternity opens to human view. We experience just a glimpse of divinity, the eternal Presence enters the material. Now. And we are able to experience an indelible moment. God was in this place and I did not know it!   RABBI MARK H. LEVIN

Going Beyond

25 FEBRUARY

*To begin to understand God, we must learn to go beyond
our own mind, our own ego, our own tools of perception.
Only then will God emerge.*

RABBI MENACHEM MENDEL SCHNEERSON[33]

This statement by the late leader of the Chabad-Lubavitch
Hasidim is extremely thought-provoking, especially for those
who have been brought up in a society that focuses on personal autonomy and the self. We are talking here about the
same tools of perception that help us to navigate this world.
It is that sensory data that has helped us to function since we
were infants. And now someone is asking us to release it all,
to go beyond it, is suggesting that in the pursuit of the
Divine, it is not to be trusted. It is frightening to learn how to
walk again!

To find God—or, better, to make a place for God in our
lives—we have to go beyond the limitations of self.
Moreover, we have to find a way to transcend the vehicles of
perception that make us human. Although this quest seems
somewhat self-contradictory, through our understanding of
God, even at a very basic level, we can begin to discern the
tools necessary to help us go beyond the self. And once we do
that, we will interface with more of God. In turn, that interaction will enable us to leave still more of the self behind in
our journey toward further divine encounter. And so it goes
this evening, tomorrow, and beyond.   KO

The Immediacy of Torah

26 FEBRUARY

*Torah is not even as old as a decree issued two or three days
ago but it is a decree issued each and every day.*

MIDRASH[34]

Just how old is the Torah? While we may not be able to date
it perfectly, there is no doubt that it is ancient. How, then,
can Ben Azzai, the rabbinic scholar and author of the above
quote, say it is not old?

We take pride that our sacred and central text is, indeed,
thousands of years old. Yet, if we revered it only because of
its age, then we could easily treat it as just another antiquity
to display in a museum and point to as an interesting archeo-
logical find. We might say, "Oh, the Torah—we read that
once upon a time." But the Torah never became a museum
piece. For these thousands of years it has remained a living
document, one that we read week in and week out. This
ongoing experience of reading Torah brings an immediacy to
its words but makes us reflect on their message for us today.
Our children learn to read Torah as part of their bar or bat
mitzvah preparation, and hopefully they will have more than
one experience of reading from the Torah, more than one
opportunity to hold the *yad*, the pointer, and hear their voice
chant these ancient words for an entire congregation. No previous generation has relegated the Torah to a shelf to collect
dust. Let us not be the first generation to allow this to happen. Rather, we can rise to the challenge and experience
Torah as if we receive it anew—tomorrow and each and
every day.   LF

The Flames of Hope

27 February

*My God, help me become a giver. Help me give and go on
giving. You've called on us to be charitable. Show me how.
Show me how to live with a pure heart. An open heart.
With a heart filled with joy. Lead me to those who are truly
deserving. For giving is so holy an act. Help me to find the
truly needy. And help them find me.*

RABBI NACHMAN OF BRESLOV

February. Short days, long month. For some reason, I have
always felt that winter comes to a crashing halt during these
twenty-eight (or twenty-nine) days.

Some years even the frivolous festival of Purim comes later
than usual and does not warm these persistently cold days. I
know I write living in the snow belt. But even for those in
warmer climes, what is there to give us hope besides the fact
that baseball pitchers report to spring training this month?
We Jews hope. We are a people of hope. It's what we do. I
know that it is easier to look at the world, particularly at the
end of a difficult day, and despair. It is February, after all.
Gray skies, slate clouds, day after day. But even if you can't
see the sun during the day or the brilliance of the moon at
night, look up anyway. That is the glory and burden, the
responsibility and obligation, the thrill and ecstasy of being
alive and being Jewish. Look into the hearts of your neighbors—on the street, at work, at the shopping mall, in the synagogue, wherever you go—and you will see the divine fire
burning, warm enough to melt away any despair.

We call that divine fire the *neshamah,* the soul. If their fire
seems to burn with more intensity than does yours, ask them
to share it with you. If theirs is reduced to barely glowing
embers, blow on the coals yourself. By sharing our warmth,

we will illumine the parts of our world still plagued by darkness. That is my hope every single day, especially in February. Make it yours as well. RABBI JAMES A. GIBSON

Partnering

28 FEBRUARY

The world is not all danger, and the human is not alone. . . .
The earth is the Lord's, and God is in search of humanity.
God endowed humanity with power to conquer the earth,
and God's honor is upon our faith. . . . God may become a
partner to our deeds.

ADAPTED FROM RABBI ABRAHAM JOSHUA HESCHEL[35]

We usually look upon ourselves as searching out God. It seems like our responsibility. After all, it is we who have to seek the Divine. So some of us look to prayer, others to study and to ritual. Still others simply connect with nature—perhaps taking a hike or watching a sunset—in order to interact with the Creator. In all of these cases, it is we who try to find the holy in our lives, especially amid all that is unholy that threatens to overwhelm us. But Rabbi Heschel wants to teach us something contrary to what we may assume or even have been taught: God is in search of us. It may sound presumptuous, but God cannot be God without us. And in order for God to maintain the divine reputation and be consistent with what God did in the Bible, God has to search for us and make us a partner with the Divine.

What is the connection between the state of the world and our own sense of isolation, alienation, and despair? When we feel discouraged, then we use this prism in order to view the entire world: everything and everyone.

But after a long and difficult day, we have to stop and think. If God is seeking us out, then maybe the world is not so bad off as we thought. Maybe the world is not in danger, and neither are we.   KO

Body and Soul

29 FEBRUARY

Just as the Holy One provides food for the entire world, so does the soul nourish the entire body.

TALMUD[36]

This extra leap year day happens every four years in the secular calendar. In the soli-lunar calendar that governs Jewish time, we add an extra month every two or three years (three times every seven years, to be precise), according to a specific calculation. While leap year gives the Jewish calendar an extra month of joy (since Adar is the month of joy because it ushers in the frivolous festival of Purim), there is not a special designation for this day in the secular calendar. But whenever there is something out of the ordinary such as the extra day in leap year, we have to think extraordinarily.

This time of year, as the month draws to a close and the end of winter is near, we begin to pay more attention to the ordinariness and the extraordinariness of our bodies—all in anticipation of spring that is right around the corner. So we might start working out a little more and eating less.

We might think that our physical well-being comes solely from the food we eat. For those of us who are conscious of our diet, we may spend a good deal of time counting the fat content, calories, sugar, and carbohydrates that we find in our food. We may know exactly how much to consume at each meal to ensure that we lower our cholesterol or calorie intake. At this time of year we all know how difficult it is to be mindful of what we eat. But our physical well-being is also intimately connected to our souls. As the Talmud reminds us, food is crucial, but so too is a healthy soul.

When we understand that our souls and bodies are connected, it is much more likely that we will experience both physical and spiritual well-being. It is, of course, much easier to focus on our food intake than to check on our souls. Checking our souls on a regular basis takes a willingness to look inward and search the many dimensions of our inner being. We can't check calories or fat content, but we can evaluate how we respond to the events of the day and decide how we can pursue healthier attitudes tomorrow. If we put the same effort into maintaining our souls as we put into maintaining or losing our weight, then truly our entire being will be nourished at its deepest levels.   LF

MARCH

For the Love of Reading

1 MARCH

The real question is what changes will be made in you as a result of really reading a book.

LEO STEIN[37]

When I was a young girl I loved going to the library to choose my books for the week. When I was old enough to get a library card of my own, I felt truly grown up. Today I wonder how many children still have that exhilarating experience of going to their local library, checking out a book, and being entrusted to return it for the next borrower. Now we most likely go to the local super bookstore or log on to our favorite Internet site to buy a book. These are always new; we no longer finger the pages of a book lovingly turned by many others. Nonetheless, reading transports us to another world. For a moment we forget our own troubles and enter into the lives of other characters. We identify with their joys and commiserate with their troubles.

Some books remain a part of our emotional life for the long run. These are more than mere stories. They speak to our inner core in a profound manner. These are the books that can change us by causing us to see ourselves differently, by giving us new ways to view the world, our place in it, even

A "good read"—especially before going to
—can be truly life changing. What are your
? How have they changed your life? Have you
ith others?   LF

Monthly Renewal
2 March

*Although the Holy One of Blessing is not visible to the
human eye, God is discernible by virtue of mighty acts and
wonders. . . . By virtue of the renewal of the months, God
is revealed to humanity; it is as though they were greeting
the Divine presence, the Shekhinah.*

Rabbi Jonah Gerondi

Whenever the calendar slips into the next month, it causes
me to think about the passage of time, my life's accomplishments, what work there is yet for me to do. A simple flip of
the calendar from one page to another affords me the opportunity to engage in serious life review. I consider my blessings
and my achievements, as well as my failures and disappoint-
ments. Sometimes I am cognizant of the change of months
and begin this process on the first. At other times I don't realize that another month has passed until a day or more into
the new month. Sometimes it is the change of my quarterly
parking pass that makes me realize that we have entered a
new month. Often it is not until I write a check and am
forced to think about writing down the name of a new
month. Others take their cue from similar common activities:
a monthly paycheck, a new production goal, a change in the
cycle of medication, a rotation of new students or new staff.

This monthly opportunity for introspection is part of my
own spiritual rhythm, but I suspect there are others who
react the same way I do. It is the best way for me to measure

my spiritual growth from month to month. One month passes into the next, and though there are many changes, there
are many things that remain the same that we have learned to
count on.

Rabbi Gerondi helps us to understand that God's presence
is made manifest even in the change of months. It is as if God
is revealed to us anew. Rabbi Gerondi was most probably
referring to the Hebrew months—which are primarily gov-
erned by the cycle and the appearance of the moon. However,
the same can be said of secular months, where God is also
made manifest, where "mighty acts and wonders" abound.
We have only to open our eyes (even before we close them for
the night) so that we can see them.   KO

The Voice of God Has Never Stopped
3 MARCH
Hear, O Israel, the Eternal, our God, the Eternal is One.
DEUTERONOMY 6:4

At the end of the day, you may feel tired in a number of
ways. After hours of work or study, you undoubtedly feel
physical and mental fatigue. And after dealing with demanding colleagues, family members, or friends, you will certainly
feel emotionally exhausted. You may also feel *spiritually*
tired, particularly if you are in the midst of confronting
something very difficult, such as severe illness, death, or
another type of loss.

However, the last prayer that you recite before you go to
bed—the "Hear, O Israel" *(Shema)*—can reinvigorate you
even as you sleep. While sleep restores your physical strength,
the message of the *Shema* will bring you renewed emotional
and spiritual energy. Its essence is very simple: God's voice
continues from Mount Sinai. Listen for it and hear it. The

"Hear, O Israel" is a statement of faith, love, and commitment to listen to God's voice. And to live that belief means bringing oneness and wholeness into the world. It means bringing people together, bringing unity and peace into the lives we touch.

If you hear the call from Sinai and its quiet, daily echoes, you will act upon that divine message in a Godly, ethical fashion. So make yourself receptive to God's message. Listen. Open your heart to receive it. Then it will come. You will hear it. And if you have truly heard it, the voice of God will enter your mind and your heart, and your actions will testify to the fact that God dwells here, now, in your room, watching over you as you gain the strength to face tomorrow.

RABBI LEVI MEIER

The Quality of Humility

4 MARCH

The more true wisdom an individual has,
the greater will be one's humility.

RABBI SIMCHA ZISSEL ZIV

Humility is not a quality that is touted much these days. Instead we hear that we must stand up for ourselves and "toot our own horn." This attitude, however, can easily lead to self-aggrandizement, and no one likes someone who is constantly speaking about his or her own successes. So why is humility out of favor? Perhaps it is because we think that our accomplishments will be overlooked if we ourselves don't highlight them. We also may equate humility with the lack of, or low, self-esteem. After attending workshops and reading self-help books on strengthening our self-esteem, who would want to embrace a quality that would seem to diminish it in any way? None of us, I suggest.

So, let's understand humility differently. Humility means that we don't see ourselves or our actions in either greater or smaller proportion than they truly are. It means we keep in mind the midrash that relates that in one pocket we have a slip of paper that says, "The world was created for my sake," and in the other pocket a slip of paper that says, "From dust I was created and to dust I will return." When we become too enamored with our uniqueness, we take out the one that reminds us that we will ultimately return to the earth, and when we become too despairing, we take out the slip that reminds us that we are God's partners in the world. Let us strive to live our lives in this balance and neither belittle nor aggrandize how we see ourselves, our accomplishments, or our efforts.   LF

Night Calls

5 MARCH

Watchman, what of the night?
ISAIAH 21:11

Night frightens many people. Perhaps it is the darkness. Perhaps it is the way the cacophony of sound travels at night. Or perhaps it is a lingering childhood memory. It could be that loneliness is often intensified after the workday, when many go their own way—especially without a close friend or life partner with whom to face the impending gloom.

There is something about the night that I find alluring and engaging. I do most of my best thinking at night, or at least, that is the time when I initiate the process of recollecting data that will help inform a decision that I have to make. I know that I am probably fresher in the morning—especially when I have the rare benefit of a good night's sleep, something rather unusual with the schedule that I keep. I also know that I am probably most vulnerable in the late evening. I am tired, spent from various encounters of the day. But I find that having the experience of the day—with its ups and downs behind me—provides me with the kind of perspective I need for major decisions; I am open to things that I might not be so open to at an earlier hour. I let down the emotional guards of not being vulnerable that I have erected. It helps me to think more clearly. Then I lie down for the night, knowing that God will help to refresh and renew my soul and thereby participate in the decision that I have to make.

The world may change as it is illuminated by street lights and neon. But divine light illumines even a moonless sky on the darkest of nights. So when I ask, along with the prophet Isaiah, "What of the night?" I am able to respond with eager anticipation: The night is what we make of it. We can fear the darkness. Or we can embrace the light of the Divine and emblazon a pathway through the night. Then we can more readily make our way through it.   KO

Homecoming

6 MARCH

Judaism comes up from the roots and stays with you all your life.

BARBARA MYERHOFF[38]

When Moses was born, his mother Yocheved declared that he was a good child, using the same language God uses to declare that the world, God's creation, is good. The Talmud teaches us (*Sotah* 12a) that upon Moses' birth, Yocheved's whole house—her *bayit*—was filled with light.

This should remind us of a fact we know both intuitively and intellectually. The Jewish home, the place we start from, has the capacity to be filled up with the light of blessing, liveliness, protection, sustenance, individuality, and connectedness.

The notion of a Jewish home has, unfortunately, suffered from sentimentalization in the United States. In the 1940s, Jewish women were advised, "With woman as priestess to tend to its altars; each home is a Temple, each hearth a shrine." In the current age, we have wised up. The reality of filling a Jewish home with light calls upon the full creative and emotional energies of more than a domestic high priestess. A team of people united in relationship to each other, to all other Jews, and to God is required to create a space from which sufficient light will flow.

An elderly participant in the work of the late anthropologist Barbara Myerhoff describes the Judaism that emanates from a home in this way: "It makes the adrenaline flow. It changes your entire view on things. . . . You could not just put it aside when you don't agree anymore. When it goes in this way I describe, Judaism comes up in you from the roots and stays with you all your life."[39]   VANESSA L. OCHS[40]

Purim and Human Agency
7 MARCH
*Wear masks, get drunk, for meaning
is hidden beneath the visible.*
ELLIOT YAGOD[41]

This month we celebrate the holiday of Purim, while some of our neighbors celebrate Mardi Gras (which probably shares some of the same festive roots). While many of us may think of Purim as a children's holiday and enjoy the merrymaking that surrounds this holiday, Purim is really about the redemption of our people. Unlike the story of Passover, when God's presence is front and center, in the story of Purim God's name is not mentioned once. God's presence is indeed hidden from the plot of this dramatic narrative featuring Queen Esther and King Ahashuerus. Instead, redemption is brought about through human agency; namely, the acts of both Esther and her uncle, Mordecai. At the end of the megillah, there is a horrible massacre. However, we do not reenact this blood-bath. Instead, we dress in costumes and make noise to drown out the name of Haman each time we hear it read during the megillah reading. What could have been a re-creation of violence is thus transformed into a raucous, though peaceful, celebration. We, too, can find creative ways to transform our anger, frustration, and even hatred into harmless though powerful rituals.   LF

Loving Reproval
8 MARCH

Reprove a wise person and he (or she) will love you for it.
PROVERBS 9:8

I have always found it difficult to reprove an individual, especially someone who is under my guidance and care. Sure, I can tell anyone off in a fit of anger. Who can't? I can scold a child. I can complain to a clerk in a local store for doing something incorrectly. But to genuinely reprove or rebuke, as the prophets understood the idea, takes a great deal of sensitivity and compassion. It also means that we cannot share what the person has done or what we have said with anyone else. Then it would become gossip, something our tradition strongly warns against. Perhaps refraining from that is even harder.

It is not an easy task to reprove, either for the "reprover" or for the "reprovee." If we are reproving someone, we have to keep in mind many things. First, we have to want the individual to succeed. We have to care about that person. We have to want that person to learn from the mistakes that he or she made. All of this has to come out of love. And if we are the one who is on the receiving end of the reproof, we have to believe that the other person is really trying to help us, to show us the mistakes we have made so that we—rather than he or she—can continue to grow. It make take days or weeks or even years, but eventually, both can understand their part in perfecting the world through personal repair.   KO

Escaping the Tempter
9 MARCH
Remove the Tempter from before us—and from behind us.
LITURGY[42]

In the evening service, we ask God to remove that temptation before us. That makes sense. But why did the Rabbis who constructed the liturgy add the phrase "from behind us" as well? A Hasidic rabbi explains it this way: First, the Tempter comes and tries to dissuade us from doing a mitzvah. Why should we give *tzedakah* to the poor? There are plenty of people who have more money to give than do we. Why should we get up early in order to join in a prayer minyan? It's cold outside and we could easily stay in bed a little longer. Why should we not engage in gossip? After all, the person about whom we are gossiping will never know about it. The Tempter uses all his tricks to get us not to do what is right. He recognizes that there are a thousand reasons why we might not want to do good. All he has to do is find the right one.

But when we resist and do the right thing, then the Tempter approaches us from behind, taps us on the shoulder and says, "Oh, what a pious person you are!" And that approach may be even more insidious than a frontal attack, for if we are not careful, we may actually believe him. And when that happens, God takes the good deed we have done and throws it away. The sages in the Talmud put it this way: "God withdraws from the world because of the arrogant."

So each night we ask God to help us in the struggle to do what is right and not be smug for having done it.

RABBI JACK RIEMER

Your Ultimate Sacrifice
10 MARCH

There are events without which one's life becomes unimportant, a worthless toy; and there are times when one is commanded to do something, even at the price of one's life.

HANNAH SENESH[43]

Hannah Senesh was a young paratrooper who jumped behind enemy lines during World War II. After being captured, she refused to speak and reveal any secret. She was executed. Her passion and concerns come to us from the pages of her diary. This quote comes from a letter she wrote to her brother before leaving for paratrooper training. In our lives, we have probably not faced such life-and-death choices as Hannah faced. Do you betray your compatriots or give your life? Living in Palestine before the war, Hannah volunteered to join the British paratroopers to show her support for the Allied troops. For Hannah, her decision to fight the Nazis was paramount. In fact, it did not feel like a choice but rather like a command.

What are the values, the paramount principles, for which you would leave everything and dedicate your very life? Is there anything for which you are willing to sacrifice all? We each make small sacrifices in raising our children, in negotiating with our partners, and in our workplaces. But what, if anything, are we willing to give our lives for? Judaism does not teach martyrdom. In fact, there are only three situations in which traditionally Jews are allowed to martyr themselves: if one is forced to commit a sexual violation, practice idolatry, or commit murder. What are your core values for which you would give all, for which you are prepared to lay down your life?   LF

My Shepherd
11 MARCH
Because God is my shepherd, I have everything I want, and, more, everything I need.
PSALM 23:1[44]

There is a big difference between what we need and what we want—even though our everyday vocabulary seems not to be able to help us make the distinction. We use the words *I need* interchangeably with *I want*. Perhaps the difficulty comes from being accustomed—as most of us are—to acquiring what we want, so it is hard to determine what we really need. We become surprised when, after years of watching their parents amass large quantities of "stuff," our children are unable to discern what they need from what they want. By helping us to understand the insight of the psalmist with his translation of this well-known text, one of the Jewish people's poets, Danny Siegel, teaches us why the distinction is so hard to make. When we accept God into our lives and thereby acknowledge the divine presence in our midst, our needs and wants converge and we are satisfied. Just as it is difficult to tell the dark from the light at twilight, indeed there is no need to make the distinction between our needs and our wants, because there is none.   KO

Effort Is Good Fortune

12 MARCH

Perseverance prevails, even against Heaven.

TALMUD[45]

I admire Wile E. Coyote and his never-ending pursuit of the Road Runner. He is inventive and persistent and has an inexhaustible source of funding. He never hesitates to buy the newest Acme gizmo, though why he continues to patronize this obviously substandard producer I don't understand. Maybe he is loyal to a fault. His serious cartoon humor makes me think that he is a perfect character for Purim, although we don't see him much at the synagogue, and he certainly did not make an appearance in any megillah that I have seen.

Wile E. Coyote gets blown up, beaten up, burned up, and smashed up, but he never gives up.

Is Wile E. Coyote a failure at life? Is he unhappy with his chosen lifestyle? He certainly has his painful moments, but he doesn't seem unhappy. He really seems to enjoy the challenge. What makes him so content? It can't be success. He has none. Perhaps it is the effort alone that matters.

Effort is good fortune. Yes, we get smashed up, blown up, beaten up, and burned up, and we get up and get going again. All we are is doing. Doing well or doing poorly. We are what we do. Doing is what makes life meaningful. Success may come, failure may come, but nothing will come if you do not *do*.

RABBI RAMI SHAPIRO

Shattering False Gods
13 MARCH

Teach me, God, to have eyes to see all that is false and destructive. Help me to stay far from the forces that can lead me astray. Remind me that I have the power to shatter false gods that lead me far away from You. . . . May I learn to choose wisely, even when in pain, to choose not the path of false comfort but the path that will lead me back to You.

RABBI NAOMI LEVY[46]

Throughout our lives we face many distractions and temptations. Some of the things this world offers loom so large that we begin to worship them. False gods abound. Money, power, status, are each some of the first that come to mind. Certainly these things are not inherently evil. When we use them wisely we can bring holiness into the world. Indeed, we can use our resources to do good, effect change, and use our status to influence others. Yet money, power, and status often lead us astray, for we forget that they are not ends in and of themselves, nor are they a measure of our true being. It is a spiritual challenge to avert our eyes from intoxicating false gods that we meet on our path. Let us say this prayer tonight, and any other time we feel the tug and pull of all that is false and destructive, so that we maintain our divine connection.   LF

Wisdom
14 MARCH

Humans were created to learn wisdom.
RABBI ABRAHAM IBN EZRA[47]

The Rabbis teach that we are created anew each day. This idea reflects the notion that while we sleep (an activity that mimics death), our souls are refreshed and renewed. After we awake in the morning, we are ready to confront the world again—even if we went to bed the previous night spent from our interactions with it. But what is the point of this "re-creative process"? In his teaching, Rabbi Ibn Ezra suggests that we are newly created each day—as we were at the beginning of creation and the onset of our lives—to gain wisdom. The experience of life is a great teacher, often far more important than what we may gain in any classroom.

Wisdom comes when we take an experience, reflect on it, and grow in understanding as a result. We gain wisdom when we can apply what we have learned to the experience of living that still lies before us in the days ahead. While we tend to learn only from things that we have experienced ourselves and are too often unwilling to take advantage of the experience of others (this is especially true with parents and their children), wisdom is achieved when we can effectively share what we have learned with others.

So what did you learn today?   KO

The Mystery of God's Presence
15 MARCH

For the commandment that I enjoin upon you this day is not hidden from you, nor is it far away. It is not in the heavens. . . . Nor is it beyond the sea. . . . No, the word is very close to you, in your mouth, in your heart. . . .

DEUTERONOMY 30:11–15

It is time for us to reclaim the centrality of love in our tradition, to proclaim by the lives we lead that law *is* love, not its opposite. We know that love partakes of the divine. We know that at wordless moments of love our soul expands beyond our mortal frame to reflect the One in whose image we are formed. We know it from the lives of our bodies and from the associations we have been taught—the extra soul of the Sabbath, the Song of Songs.

When I was young, my repertoire was limited. I knew the exaltation of romantic love. I knew the irreplaceable love of a great friend. But I did not understand God's unmediated love. Now, further along my journey, I have been granted the ability to reflect God's image by my own creating of life. Motherhood has allowed me to be loved past my faults and has provided an immeasurable augmenting of my own ability to love. Motherhood has allowed me to return to my parents, return as *teshuvah* and return to them a portion of the love I now know they had for me all along.

What have I learned? That God is with us not only in celebration, which I always knew, but in sorrow, in the dark solitary places where we continue to wrestle with our angel, where, alongside the harsh decree, we all live in God's generous bounty, gift after gift after gift.   NESSA RAPOPORT

Finding Our Center
16 MARCH

An ignorant person believes that the whole universe exists only for him. . . . If therefore, anything happens contrary to his expectations he at once concludes that the whole universe is evil.

MOSES MAIMONIDES[48]

Children believe the world revolves around them. This is the nature of childhood. However, as we mature, hopefully we learn that this is far from true. Otherwise we run the risk of becoming overly self-centered, an alienating trait if ever there was one. We learn that our concerns, worries, and anxieties cannot always take center stage. Of course, we may know people who have never realized this important truth. They talk incessantly about themselves. They still blame the whole world if things do not go the way they expect.

If we find ourselves finding fault with the whole world, our entire community, or our family members, let us step back and take a "reality check." For the reality is, life fulfills some of our expectations and not others; that's just the way it goes. We struggle to stay on our spiritual path and be in relationship with God even when we are deeply disappointed or aggrieved. It takes faith to keep our place in the world in perspective and not cast blame blindly.   LF

Overcoming an Angry Spirit
17 MARCH

One who is slow to anger is better than the mighty, and one who rules that spirit is better than the one who conquers a city.
PROVERBS 16:32

One would think that it is more difficult to conquer one's own proclivity toward anger than it is to conquer an entire city. After all, everyone gets angry, but not everyone is in a position to take over a city or competent to do so. The author of Proverbs recognizes that the most difficult person to control is the self, and yet it is the self that we are in the best position to control. Self-control shows real strength and moral courage. And anger can be its most virulent challenger.

But what do we do when we feel anger creeping slowly to the surface, threatening to overwhelm us? And what can we do to prevent anger from taking over suddenly, unexpectedly, when there is little or no time to prevent it? It is surely not enough for the writer of Proverbs to write down this statement and then expect readers of the Bible to follow its guidance by implicit suggestion. Perhaps it is the engagement of sacred text that is enough to calm the spirit. Continued study, particularly when it is practiced with a partner, has a pervasive calming influence and provides the opportunity for us to learn how to control our anger. And we know that the master teacher of text is mightier than all.

Get yourself a study partner and start learning. Okay, you're tired now—so start first thing in the morning!   KO

Listening for the Whispers of God
18 MARCH

Everything is organically, seamlessly joined to everything else. We have all been players in a divine scheme, neither marionettes nor zombies but waves in an ocean, dancers in a ballet, colors on a canvas, words in a story. Discrete and probably autonomous, but never entirely independent. Of course, it is preposterous. Of course, it makes no rational sense. But for just a moment, it is as if we encounter our destiny. Everything is within God.

RABBI LAWRENCE KUSHNER[49]

We must stop living as if God does not exist except at funerals, weddings, and baby namings. We humans come equipped to perceive, but not prove, God in the universe. We are possessed of souls that sense God as a presence, like an electrical field. There are spiritual paths to choose, paths that can attach our lives to that field, to electrify our spirits. That spiritual force coursing through us gives life meaning, direction, purpose. God is like a background radiation to the universe: hardly perceptible, eternally present and available, affecting much but in ways we cannot fathom. Rationality may be our great intellectual gift. It has certainly been our spiritual curse, as it denies a reality we often perceive but cannot prove.

Yet there are souls aflame around us. You don't have to prove them. You know they are there by being in their presence.

They are the Geiger counters of the holy. These are lives making an enormous difference. Humble and courageous, these souls take risks to be close to God. They aggressively pursue *mitzvot*. Their vision is a tunnel vision, asking simply what God requires of them and then running after it. Let us examine our souls passionately. Let us repent our compromises with evil sincerely to discover God in goodness. Let us pray introspectively, prepared to meet the God who underlies all reality and who put us here. God is ever present. But will we allow ourselves to be available to meet the spiritual? That is the question for these days. Are we ready for real spirituality, to dedicate our lives to something ultimate, to discover our calling in the whisper of God?   RABBI MARK H. LEVIN

Being Focused

19 MARCH

You cannot be everything if you want to be anything.
RABBI SOLOMON SCHECHTER[50]

How many of us know how to focus on what is truly important and meaningful in our lives? It is easy to be pulled in many directions while trying to fulfill the wishes and expectations of others. What happens, though, is that we start to forget, or push aside, our inner core. We find ourselves doing mental and emotional gymnastics, especially if we already have the tendency to want to please others. Before we know it we no longer know who we are, what we want, or where we are going. No wonder we often find the saying "Know before Whom you stand" hanging over the *aron hakodesh*, the holy ark, at the front of many synagogues. We must constantly be reminded of our place in the world.

Take a moment before going to sleep tonight to clarify what is most essential to you. How do you wish to be remembered by your family, friends, or coworkers? Are your actions focused and your priorities clear? Or do you tend to be diffuse so that it is hard for others—or even for yourself—to discern the principles by which you live? It is an ongoing challenge to stay on course and have our purpose front and center. Yet, since we cannot be "everything to everyone," we need to meet the challenge and start being, simply, focused on our chosen priorities, and on the One. LF

Parental Advice

20 MARCH

A soft answer turns away wrath.

PROVERBS 15:1

We know this advice to be true. A soft answer does diminish anger, particularly when mistakes are acknowledged and apologies are made. There is no benefit to always being right in the context of relations between people. People can't hear when they are angry. And when you are angry, you'll say nothing worth listening to, either! So even if you have something important and correct to say, be kind, be gentle, be soft. As a matter of fact, if you do not respond softly to anger, you run the risk of increasing the anger or its intensity, and then the nasty circularity of an ill-fated interaction continues.

If it is the end of the day, and you think that this advice comes a little too late, know that it is never too late to reengage the conversation. Sometimes it is even better to wait until the anger has subsided before you respond. Remember: God is not to be found in the thundering of the heavens. Rather, God is to be found in the still, small voice—but only if we listen carefully for it. KO

The Light of God
21 MARCH

You are my lamp, O God. You turn darkness into light.
2 SAMUEL 22:29

The philosopher/theologian Martin Buber wrote of the eclipse of God, the turning away of God's face and God's light. Then the world becomes a terrifying place and sinks into evil. Our hearts grow dark as we sink into darkness. Yet there is a curious and telling fact about eclipses. The sun never completely grows dark. Even in a total eclipse there is a corona, a halo of light that remains. A scientist friend tells me that the corona is actually light we would never have seen, except for the sun's being blocked. I don't know if that is true, but the image works for me. Only in the dark of the eclipse do we see new light; only in the darkness of the soul can we see the *or chadash*, a new light for our redemption.

Is it possible to believe that light surrounds us? Is it possible to believe that embedded in the darkness there is a ray of pure light, a pearl? Are we willing to believe that a light glows deep in the recesses of our own being, a light so bright it has the power to roll away the darkness? God is the pillar of fire that led the way for the Israelites at night in the wilderness. The children of Israel learned to trust in the fire and follow it. Can we, too, learn to trust the light that guides us, even in the dark wilderness of life? Can we learn from the idea that the dawning of a new day begins at nightfall? Perhaps God's face is hidden sometimes so that we must try a little harder to break through and find the light.

RABBI LAVEY DERBY

Respecting the Little

22 MARCH

Piety, especially Jewish piety, respects the little: the little person, the little matter, the little task, the little duty. Through the little, religion meets the greatness that lies behind.

RABBI LEO BAECK[51]

How do we apportion our attention? Are we attracted to those things that are large in size, status, or emotion? It is certainly easy to become obsessed with the notion "bigger is better." Think about it. Do you yearn for a larger house, a larger car, a bigger job? However, if we think about the spiritual truths of piety, then we also have to pay attention to the details. As an interpretation of the popular saying goes, "Real Torah is learned in the details." And often, noticing the details means attending to the smaller, more subdued moments in life. It means taking the time to share our daydreams with our loved ones, remembering the birthdays and special occasions of our friends and relatives, and bringing a meal to a sick friend. Sometimes it just means picking up the phone and expressing care and concern to someone. It also means extending kindness to those who cross our paths no matter where they work or live. Let us not confuse size or status with significance, for significance and meaning come in all forms, shapes, and sizes.   LF

Self-Exaltation

23 MARCH

One who does not exalt oneself will be exalted by others.

TALMUD[52]

We all have to look out for ourselves. It is part of our survival plan. It is what our parents taught us as key to our navigating our way through life and the world. And they were most likely correct. But when we attempt to raise ourselves up in the eyes of others, sometimes at the expense of others, we actually lower ourselves through the process. Sometimes things just work in the reverse order of our intentions. But we should not be motivated by this (the same "reverse psychology" that parents of young children are familiar with). Instead, we should maintain a humble posture because it is the right thing to do. Let the words of others—and not of ourselves—raise us up. This is also the only posture that affords us the opportunity to "walk with God," at least, that is, according to the prophet Micah. (What does God require of you? Only to do justice, love mercy, and walk humbly with God.) Something to guide us, even while we are sleeping.   KO

Understanding Obedience
24 MARCH

Moses came and told the people all the words of God and all the judgments, and all the people answered with one voice, and said, "All the words that God has said, we will do!"

EXODUS 24:3

After all of the moral laws and civil statutes were presented, the people pronounced their acceptance of these laws with an emphatic, "All that God has said, we will do and we will understand." Commenting on the Israelites' peculiar response (note the word order), Rabbi Menachem Mendl of Kotzk, also known as the Kotzker Rebbe, notes: "There are many wise men, scholars, and philosophers in the world, all of them pondering, investigating, delving into the mystery of

God. And why do they misuse their wisdom? They only mis-use it because they are limited by their intellectual level and their perceptual capacity. But the people of Israel are a holy people. They possess special instruments that elevate their perceptual capacity to transcend the level of their intellect and attain the level of the ministering angels themselves. And their instruments are the performance of *mitzvot*. This is just what Israel said when the people stood at Mount Sinai. 'We will do and we will understand.'"

To many, the Kotzker's claim is positively scandalous. Ours is an age that enshrines reason and the power of science and scientific methodology to arrive at all that is knowable. And yet the Kotzker Rebbe believes that this is absolutely wrong. While certain things can be pierced and comprehended by reason and philosophic reflection, God is not one of them. Rather, the only way to come to know God is through the sacred acts of *mitzvot*.

We may spend lots of time reading and studying, expanding what we know in important areas of science, medicine, and law. We may have a stack of books on the nightstand next to our bed for our evening reading. But if we want to know God, we must leave the books and engage with people and rituals that move us beyond the intellect and take us into the realm of action. And perhaps that is why when Moses asks for God's name, God replies, *"Ehyeh asher ehyeh,"* a rather difficult phrase to translate, which is based on the construction of the verb "to be." Yet, the name implies that God is not to be found in books. Rather, God is to be found in the simple process of being present and attentive to the world around us and engaging it through sacred activity. Look and begin to listen in the morning. You'll find the divine in each and every thing you do. RABBI JONATHAN JAFFE BERNHARD

Do Not Take Revenge or Bear a Grudge
25 MARCH

A person is very sensitive to being insulted and his only comfort from this anguish may be taking revenge, which is to him sweeter than honey. . . . Yet the mitzvah is explicit, "Do not take revenge or bear a grudge."
MOSES HAYYIM LUZATTO[53]

Holding grudges and taking revenge can certainly complicate our spiritual lives. They weigh us down. As one saying has it, "Harboring resentments is allowing someone whom you don't like to live inside your head rent-free." Here Rabbi Luzatto, who taught about the moral and ethical developments behind the *mitzvot* and is best known for his writings on the laws that discuss *lashon hara*, gossip and slander, starts out by saying up front that we are not angels. We are human beings and, as such, have a very real human tendency to "get back" at those who offend us. Yet, at the same time, we must be ever mindful of the commandment in the book of Leviticus (19:18) that teaches, "Do not take revenge or bear a grudge." How can we fulfill this mitzvah? Holding grudges and resentments is in the end self-defeating. One time-proven method of overcoming such urges is to force ourselves to do an act of kindness for the person we resent, or say a prayer on his or her behalf without any fanfare. As hard as it sounds, try it. Acts of kindness can reduce these very potent, and destructive, feelings. LF

Happiness

26 MARCH

The joy of God is your strength.

NEHEMIAH 8:10

According to the Hebrew calendar, which uses the seasons to balance the progress of time marked by the moon, the month of Adar (around February-March) is ushered in by unmitigated joy. This attitude is generally ascribed to the spirit of Purim that shapes the entire month. So, through the frivolous celebration of the festival of Purim, we turn everything in our religious life upside down and inside out. The festive meal that we expect to usher in a holiday is held at the end of the festival rather than at the beginning of it. And we put on masks that allow us for a short period of time to pretend to be someone else and, at the same time, take ourselves less seriously. Even the teachers whose words we usually respect are subject to loving ridicule. Having survived the challenge of Haman, we are thrilled just to be alive.

We are also nearing the end of winter and the beginning of spring. For similar reasons, such change helps to raise the spirit. We get just a hint of what is around the corner: singing birds, blossoming flowers, and the buzz of neighborhood lawn mowers. Just the refreshing breath of fresh air reminds us of how lucky we are to be alive. So, maybe tonight we should work a little less and play a little more. There will be more time to do our work tomorrow.   KO

The Masks of Sinai

27 March

*May God make the divine face shine upon you
and be gracious to you.*

Numbers 6:25

There is an ever-so-fine line between what is holy and what is profane, between worshiping God and worshiping idols, between seeing God's presence in our lives and cursing the darkness. The delicate dance of wanting to know God and simultaneously fearing God's demands and intensity was beyond the theological capability of the generation of Israelite slaves. And perhaps every generation since.

It takes Moses three attempts to successfully deliver the Ten Commandments to his people. First he speaks the words. But they need it in writing. So Moses climbs Sinai again and returns with the two tablets, only to find the Israelites dancing before the golden calf. After severe punishments, Moses climbs Sinai yet again and finally delivers the tablets to the people. The process itself is imperfect, bearing the very sins it seeks to prevent.

But imagine you are an Israelite, freed from slavery by God, but it is only Moses' face you see. You have experienced miracles and liberation. You have crossed the Sea of Reeds. You have stood at Sinai. Following Moses each step of the way, you see manifestations of the divine presence in your midst. Moses ascends the mountain and comes down and verbally delivers the Law. Then your leader, who is aging, is summoned back to the holy mountain alone, with no food or water. You wait for him. And wait. And wait.

You have waited for your leader for forty days and you are anxious. You call to Aaron to do something, and he asks for your gold and makes a calf. Aaron, too, is anxious to see his younger brother return. And so, in a move that is both rebellious and empowering, this apparent sin forces Moses to return to the people—much like a child who tries to get a parent's attention by breaking a rule.

When Moses descends, he goes into a rage, furious that the people would worship an idol after all they had experienced of God. Their rebellious act was also a challenge to Moses' stewardship and a plea for him to spend more time with them, in the camp, than with God on the mountain.

We each need some intensity, some ongoing reminder of God's presence in our world, in our biography. But we don't need it in the form of golden calves. Instead, we ask that God's face shine on us all, so that we may sleep soundly through the night and awaken to do holy work in the world.

YOSEF I. ABRAMOWITZ[54]

Being Sincere

28 MARCH

The essential ingredient for being effective is to be sincere.
VILNA GAON

Sincerity is not always as easy to come by as it seems. We are often put in difficult situations where we may respond insincerely despite our best intentions. We may give faint praise to someone who doesn't meet our standards or compliment others to feign friendliness or pursue the work of networking. Yet, if we do this too often, others will see through us, and our words will no longer be taken seriously. We have all come across someone whose words of praise just don't ring true. It is much more challenging to be sincere with our words, offering praise when deserved and evenhanded criticism when called for. If we find ourselves in a situation where we are unable to act in this manner, then perhaps the fallback position is to keep quiet. Our effectiveness in the world is a reflection of our character, and how we express ourselves—whether with sincerity or insincerity—speaks to others in a loud and clear way. How we are effective in a spiritual way, however, comes from deep within our souls, the place that is often most accessible to us at the end of the day rather than at its beginning. So find that place now and prepare to put it into use tomorrow.   LF

Fulfilling Our Dreams with Passion

29 MARCH

To realize the impossible is the passion of the adventurer.
RABBI ISAAC MAYER WISE[55]

As one who is not big on mountain climbing or skydiving, preferring instead to limit my mountain adventures to those akin to Sinai, the spirit of the outdoor adventurer is sometimes hard for me to understand. It seems that dances with the angel of death should be uninvited rather than welcomed or sought after. What motivates a person to risk his or her life to climb a mountain or to run river rapids or jump out of an airplane? It is more than simply "It is there." Nevertheless, the *passion* of the adventurer is something with which I readily resonate, for I believe that it is passion that fuels our progress, even or especially in the spiritual realm. Judaism is not something about which we can be lukewarm or undisciplined. Without passion our people would not have made their way through the desert or settled the Promised Land. Nor would they have found their way through the world amid incredible odds. Moreover, without a significant measure of passion we would not have been able to shape the North American Jewish community—even acknowledging its current challenges—or have founded the State of Israel. This passion was the result of one individual joining with another to literally change the world or, at least, our path in it. As individuals, we can make a difference, one person at a time!

At the end of the day, when passion often wanes as the result of battles and burdens encountered during the day, we have to look to those who have come before us, look at what they have done, and then strive onward. Their dreams become ours, as we carry them forward.   KO

The Clouded Presence
30 MARCH

The cloud covered the Tent of Meeting, and the Presence of God filled the mishkan *(sanctuary). Moses could not enter the Tent of Meeting, because the cloud had settled on it and the Presence of God filled the* mishkan. *When the cloud lifted from the* mishkan, *the Israelites would set out on their various journeys; but if the cloud did not lift, they would not set out until it did lift. For the cloud of God was over the* mishkan *by day, and fire would appear in it by night, in the view of all the house of Israel throughout their journeys.*

EXODUS 40:34 38

Most of the Torah is set in the wilderness.

Living well in the wilderness—any wilderness, at any time in history—depends on one's ability to live out this complex teaching: When times are dark, one must remember that this is not forever, that the sun will shine again. In good times, one must know just as clearly that this, too, shall pass. In this view, it is essential not to base one's sense of well-being, or one's orientation to life, on anything as ephemeral as the specific events of life, one's desires or attachments. Neither the blessings of happy times nor the sorrows of dark times are permanent and ultimately dependable. The only place that is ultimately reliable in the threatening world of wilderness life, real life, is the connection with the sanctuary within, the place where God's Presence lives. "The person who is whole is himself/herself a kind of *mishkan*."

We must find our way without unequivocal signs. We must discern for ourselves when it is time to stop and wait, when it is time to move forward, when to shift direction. May we nonetheless find the guidance we need, finding our way to the place within where God's presence lives.

RABBI AMY EILBERG[56]

Living for Others
31 MARCH

Life is not meaningful . . . unless it is serving an end beyond itself, unless it is of value to someone else.

RABBI ABRAHAM JOSHUA HESCHEL[57]

These words make us think about just how much we extend ourselves for others and how much time we spend worrying about our own concerns. Certainly, we each have to take care of ourselves; yet there are individuals who think only about themselves to the exclusion of anyone else. When we are in the presence of a self-centered person, we may want to flee. However, let us try to extend some compassion his or her way, for it is a painful existence when someone is so self-focused—and all of us are, at some time or another. Many of us do go out of our way to extend ourselves to others. We aid friends and neighbors, make sacrifices for our family members, and volunteer in communal organizations. While we do not seek to ignore or obliterate our own needs entirely, our lives are greatly enriched when our actions are bound up in a web of relationships. Connections are what give meaning to our lives—they are, by their nature, of value to us *and* to someone else. Rest comfortably tonight in the web of connections that surrounds you.   LF

APRIL

Listening for the Voice

1 APRIL

The voice of my beloved! Here you come, leaping across the mountains, bounding over the hills! My beloved is like a gazelle, like a young deer; here my beloved stands, behind a wall, gazing through the windows, peering through the lattice.

SONG OF SONGS 2:8–9

It may be April Fool's Day for many. But the day is no foolish thing for those who seek love. The poetry of the Bible—even its songs of love, which we particularly welcome in the spring—is sometimes hard for us to fully grasp. Whether in Hebrew or in English, the metaphors seem foreign to modern suburbanites and city dwellers. While the verse alone may be captivating for those who enjoy poetic verse, the images are more appealing to those who have seen the wild goats of Ein Gedi in Israel or who have spent time walking Jerusalem's hilly neighborhoods. And if you are like me, you can just close your eyes, take a deep breath, and you are there. The poetry of the Song of Songs, which Jewish tradition attributes to Solomon in the prime of his youth, is the poetry of young love as much as it is the poetry of a more mature sustaining love that grows over time. It reflects the love of human romance as it does the love formed in the relationship between the individual and God. That is its lasting power.

As you walk through your neighborhood, or as you are carried back to the land of Israel in your mind's travels or in your dreams this evening, listen carefully for the voice of your lover, beckoning you to come forth. But don't wait. Watch for your lover, peering through the lattice, looking for you to approach. Reach out a hand to him or her.   KO

Asking Questions
2 APRIL

There is an old adage that says: For the believer there are no questions and for the unbeliever there are no answers. I have come to know many unbelievers with deep yearnings for serious questions.
RABBI HAROLD M. SCHULWEIS[58]

We are embarking on a time period of inquiry, since questions are an integral part of the holiday of Passover. Even as we prepare for the holiday, there are plenty of questions to ask. Is this kosher for Pesach? Why can't we eat that? How do we do this, again? And, of course, What should I wear and whom should we invite? Traditionally, the youngest child asks the designated "four questions" at the seder table. If you are a parent, you probably hope that your children will ask many more questions—as exasperating as they often can be. Questions lead to knowledge. Questions begin a discussion.

As Jews we understand that questioning is not a sign of disbelief. Rather, questioning is an expression of one's commitment and concern. We might even rewrite Rabbi Schulweis's statement to read, *For the unbeliever there are no questions.* When we stop asking questions, it is then that we should worry. Our questions themselves matter—even if we are not always comforted by the answers we receive. What are the serious questions on your mind as you approach Passover? What arises from your heart and soul? How can you bring these questions to your seder tables and to your life, to begin a new chapter in your life this year?   LF

The Time for Decision

3 APRIL

My stream became a river and my river became a sea.

APOCRYPHA[59]

This is the time of year when high school seniors find out whether they were accepted into their college of choice (unless they received early acceptance notices). They agonize over that decision as if their very lives depended on it. I am sympathetic to their dilemmas, but perhaps they may be missing the main point.

What is most important is not which one of the fine universities one attends, but in what spirit one enters any of the "schools" of life. Not *where* you go, but *how* you go is the name of the game. Sure, one needs *mazel* for anything (even the *Sefer Torah* in the ark needs luck, according to our tradition), but the crucial decision is always what to do about your luck, about the opportunities that life presents.

My friend Steven Schwarzschild began his career as the rabbi of both Berlins and ended it as an internationally famous scholar and teacher. But he remembered with most pleasure his five years in—of all places—Fargo, North Dakota. With all due apologies to the residents of Fargo, we all have our Fargos. The question is what we will become while we are there.

Consider where you are now and what you are making of it.   RABBI ARNOLD JACOB WOLF

The End of Illness

4 APRIL

When the sun lifts up, the sickness lifts off.
TALMUD[60]

When my children were young, our pediatrician had "calling hours." The physician was available during certain periods during the day for advice on parenting or even for simple diagnoses over the phone—which were usually more for the parents than for the children. Many times we were told by our doctor after describing a minor headache, toothache, or low fever, "Give him two aspirins and call me in the morning." By the time my wife and I entered parenthood, this had already become a truism in family-centered medicine. How did this statement become so familiar to so many people? Did doctors simply feel that most illnesses were minor and that they would run their course rather quickly and without major trauma, especially with children? Were we consulting our family physicians more frequently—and unnecessarily—than had our parents' generation? Or perhaps doctors had discovered something that the Rabbis also knew many years ago. The body often heals itself—if we give it a little time and care. So by the next morning, what was troubling you the previous night will often go the way of the darkness.

But there is more to this statement than a confirmation of the insights of folk medicine. The Rabbis of the Talmud are suggesting that time heals. We may carry the memory of our burdens and illnesses with us, but it slowly gets reabsorbed into our psyches. Our spirit can heal over time, and when it does, night turns into day. KO

The Pain of Being in Exile

5 APRIL

What is exile? What is galut? . . . *Let's go back to the relationship of that word* gal, *"to move"; it means movement, continuous movement. It means that everything is moving, except me; or the other way—I am moving and everything else is standing still; or a third way, we are not moving in the same direction. . . . When a person is in exile, nothing fits.*

ELIE WIESEL[61]

The Hebrew word *galut,* meaning exile, seems to reflect the journey of the Jewish people. Traditionally it is used to describe the experience of living outside the Land of Israel. And for two thousand years our ancestors did live estranged from the Land. Indeed, whether they lived in the Ukraine or in Fez or in Yemen, while acculturating themselves to the surrounding culture, in many ways they lived as if "nothing fit." As we move toward the holiday of Passover, we recall our four hundred years as slaves in Egypt; a time when our ancestors were in ultimate exile.

We may no longer have that feeling of literal exile today. Yet there may be other dimensions of our lives that feel ill fitted. Perhaps we experience displacement when we don't feel comfortable in synagogue or if we feel out of place at work, or even in our own families. All of these experiences of "exile" are painful, and we seek ways to heal our soul, the vessel of our being, to feel whole once again. So, if you are feeling tonight as if "nothing fits," see if you can find one small action that can address your personal sense of exile. It may mean reaching out to a friend or a colleague. Maybe it means taking a break, changing jobs, or seeking a new community. However you proceed, may your way back from exile be blessed.   LF

Baseball: Coming Home

6 APRIL

*Within my home, I am able to walk
with the integrity of my heart.*

PSALM 101:2

I have a real ambivalence toward baseball. My dad loves the game. When I was a kid, he and I would play catch. I'd throw the ball and he'd catch it. He'd throw the ball and I'd catch something else for missing it. He wanted me to play ball in high school. I ended up managing the team instead. Still, baseball has a lot to teach. Especially about coming home. Now's a good time to think about it, since the season is nearly upon us.

In baseball, you win by coming home. Why isn't home called fourth base? Nobody cares about fourth base, but everybody wants to go home. But home is more than a place. Home is a state of mind. Home is where we can realize our uniqueness without having that uniqueness drive us into loneliness. Home in this sense has little to do with our child-hood or our parents; home has everything to do with creating a safe space for ourselves to be ourselves with those we love. Each of us needs this desperately. What do we say of players left on base at the end of an inning? They die on base. Unless we can get home, we die. Without that sense of completion, we die—maybe not physically, but emotionally, spiritually.

Baseball is a metaphor for life. We begin at home. The drive to score sends us out. But all the while we are trying to get home. When we get a hit and leave home, we are applauded. But ultimately it is coming home that counts.

Not everybody makes it home. Most attempts in baseball fail. So too with life. We are always trying to get home, to get to that safe place where we will be welcomed. Sometimes we make it; often we don't. The wonderful thing that baseball teaches us is that failure is not defeat but rather part of the game. We are not expected to make it every time.

The playing of the game of baseball restates the promise that we can all be free, and that we can all matter, even if we fail. Now, that's something to think about tonight and every night.   RABBI RAMI SHAPIRO

Going Beyond Complaints

7 APRIL

Refrain from grumbling. It can lead to other sins.

TALMUD[62]

When we were students, my colleague Rabbi Michael Kagan once gave a sermon whose title was something like this: "Don't impatiently honk your horn at a traffic light. The person in front of you may be turning left when you think he is turning right." It was a long title, but he made his point rather quickly. Sometimes when we are waiting in traffic and in a hurry to get somewhere, we make assumptions about the cars in front of us. So when a person is at a traffic light or a stop sign and it looks like he or she has plenty of time to move into traffic, our knee-jerk reaction is to honk the horn. We are always in a hurry to get somewhere, and we assume that the person in front of us is not. After all, if *we* think there is time to move forward, why shouldn't the person in front of us? But what we did not realize was that the driver needed extra time to make the turn, since she wanted to move quickly into the left lane (in order to make a subsequent left turn) as soon as she moved into traffic. But we wouldn't really know that until after she made the turn.

We often draw conclusions with a limited amount of information and then grow impatient as a result. This impatience is quickly transformed into a complaint, often voiced in unpleasant tones to an unsuspecting person—whether it is someone we know, someone we love, or an anonymous service provider that we encounter in the course of doing everyday business. We don't know why the delivery of something is delayed. We only know that it is delayed. We don't know why we have to wait to be served. We only know that we have to wait. And so we complain. After a while, these complaints give shape to a behavior pattern that we follow in other parts of our lives.

When people complain too much, it is a reflection more of their own state of spirit than of what they are ostensibly complaining about. It is this state of the spirit that leads them to sin. As the Rabbis of *Pirke Avot* aptly remind us, "While one mitzvah leads to another, one sin also leads to another." So stop grumbling and complaining. It drags you down. Plan "now" to do a mitzvah instead. Its performance will help you to soar heavenward tomorrow—and that's where we all want to be.   KO

Dayeinu—That Would Have Been Enough
8 APRIL

If God had only taken us out of Egypt . . . it would have been enough. Dayeinu!

THE HAGGADAH

As we prepare ourselves for Passover, it may be hard for us to relate to the first line of this popular song, which we sing with gusto and passion at our seder tables, with the memory of past seders on our mind. Sometimes the melody plays itself over and over in our minds this time of year, especially when we are trying to fall asleep. *Dayeinu.*

Would it really have been enough only to have been redeemed from Egypt? What about the subsequent steps this song lists: dividing the Red Sea, giving us the Torah, bringing us to the Land of Israel? Would we have been content if the process stopped at any one of these steps? I suggest that we would have wanted more. Who among us would want to get stuck wandering in the desert forever? So might there be another purpose for delineating each of these steps? It is to remind us that freedom does not come in one fell swoop. There are many incremental steps along the way in our quest for freedom. As we take each step, let us pause and express thanks. What would our collective consciousness as Jews be like if we forgot about crossing the Red Sea or climbing Mount Sinai and if we only talked about entering the Land after a forty-year journey? We would be missing some of the central turning points in our ancestors' journey. Remember that freedom didn't really come to our ancestors (or to us) until the completion of the journey. And that takes our entire lives to reach. The steps along the way are the most precious steps of all. So for each one of these steps, we really can say *Dayeinu!* And then we might be able to rest a little better.   LF

Wanting to Hold On

9 APRIL

And Moses led Israel onward from the Red Sea.
EXODUS 15:22

Soon after the Israelites departed from Egypt, they drew near to the edge of the Red Sea (which we all now know is a mistranslation of the Sea of Reeds). The crossing at the Red Sea is one of those rare moments in history when God's presence is clearly manifest. While there were undoubtedly skeptics among the Israelites before the crossing, their criticisms crashed down as quickly as did the far side of the sea as it swallowed the pursuing Egyptian armies.

There is one detail in the narration with far-reaching implications. The Bible tells us that "Moses led Israel onward from the Red Sea" (Exodus 15:22). A more precise translation of the Hebrew verb "to lead" *(vayasa)* suggests that the Israelites were reluctant to leave.

A midrash may help us understand why. The Egyptians had adorned their horses with gold, silver, and precious stones. These were all consumed by the sea. Each morning the Israelites gathered at its shores in order to collect what washed up. Thus the writer of the midrash concludes that the Israelites were reluctant to leave the Red Sea because of what wealth it might yet yield.

Moreover, it's hard to leave moments of great joy or even sadness behind. It's natural to want to hold on.

Perhaps the Israelites were not motivated to linger at the sea out of greed but rather to collect the silver and the gold and the precious stones as tangible reminders of what had taken place, like the mementos that we collect—jewelry from a deceased relative, a photo album, grandmother's wedding ring—that represent significant memories in our lives.

The challenge the Israelites faced is the same challenge that we face: How do we hold on to the memory, especially one so powerful as to yield God's presence in our midst? How do we do so as we are about to enter the wilderness, as did our ancestors? Maybe we have to return to the Red Sea and uncover the precious stones of our experience. As we carry them with us, we carry a tangible reminder of the presence of God in our lives.　　　　　　　　　　　RABBI NEIL KURSHAN

Celebrating for the Self

10 APRIL

Devote half of your festival to yourself and half to God.

TALMUD[63]

We usually think of festivals and holidays as days that celebrate our relationship with God or, at least, the relationship of our ancestors with God. I believe that holiday rituals are designed primarily to enhance that relationship. Many of these are family celebrations, because among family members is the best place to nurture one's relationship with the Divine. Most festivals recapitulate aspects of the biblical narrative and our journey in ancient history. Much of that narrative history traces the evolution of our people's struggle with the Divine in the form of what theologian Rabbi Eugene Borowitz likes to call a covenantal relationship. It all makes sense when you carefully read Rabbi Joshua ben Hananiah's statement above from the Talmud. He suggests that there are two parts to every celebration, that unlike large segments of our liturgy, holidays are not there just to provide another context for us to praise God. If our relationship with God is a partnership, then it makes sense that one half of our festival should be devoted to the self and the other half to God. Thus, in the case of Passover, which occurs every year about this time (depending on the way the soli-lunar Hebrew calendar works during any particular year), we are reminded of our own journey—the one that is reflected in the journey of the Israelites moving from Egyptian slavery through the desert into a land of promise and opportunity. But we are also asked to remember that it was God who mightily brought us out of that Egypt with "a strong arm and an outstretched hand." And that's the relationship that we want to nurture.   KO

Meeting Others

11 APRIL

Mountains do not meet, but people do.
YIDDISH PROVERB

Mountains are beautiful, majestic reminders of God's creation of the world. We often travel great distances to go to the mountains to ski, hike, or just get a glimpse of their awesome size and become transfixed by their inherent power. Many people put their lives at risk to climb the world's highest mountain ranges—"just because they are there." And, of course, we know that Moses ascended Mount Sinai, where he remained for forty days in communion with God before returning to the people with the Torah. While mountains symbolize many things, such as the love of adventure and a closeness to God, they seem static and immovable. But they continue to change every moment, even if in infinitesimal amounts.

While grand, mountains stand alone, set off in nature. We, on the other hand, have the opportunity to meet one another. There is nothing that keeps us alone except our own inertia. As we prepare for a night of rest, may we remember that even mountains, which seem impossible to climb and certainly impossible to move, continue to change. May we do the same, even if in small amounts. We still may not be able to move mountains as a result, but we will certainly be able to move ourselves in order to meet people. They just might be doing the same.   LF

Here Today and Tomorrow
12 APRIL

You stand this day, all of you, before Adonai your God. . . .
I make this covenant, with its sanctions, not with you alone,
but both with those who are standing here with us this
day . . . and with those who are not with us here today.
DEUTERONOMY 29:9A, 13–14

The older I get, and the more ritual acts I engage in, the more I am convinced of the simple, elegant truth: The covenant is about the present. It is certainly about the future.

But the power of the ritual act is that the past is always present as well.

One of the most important, though overlooked, aspects of Jewish ritual is that it removes us from time and space. One of the overlooked hallmarks of Jewish spirituality is the power of imagination—not only to imagine the future but also to imagine the past. At the wedding ceremony, Jews not only imagine that this wedding might bring about the Messianic Age. The couple must also imagine themselves to be Adam and Eve, the primordial wedding couple under a *chuppah* that, for the moment, is the local representation of the Garden of Eden.

At the seder, we imagine ourselves to be slaves in Egypt. Elijah comes to the seder, and also to the *brit* ceremony. Maybe his appearance from the past will mean that the present may be sanctified for the future. Sukkot sees us welcoming *ushpizin*—guests from our mythic past—into the sukkah.

"With those who are not with us here today." I have a responsibility for the future. And I owe a debt to the past. The covenant cannot live with simply one pole. It needs both.

RABBI JEFFREY SALKIN[64]

Raising Up to Holiness
13 APRIL
God is holy, holy, holy.
ISAIAH 6:3

This phrase, usually translated as "Holy, holy, holy is the Lord of Hosts," has found its way into our liturgy. Therefore it is familiar to many people. Taken from the writings of the prophet Isaiah, these words are said to have been spoken by the celestial entourage of angels who constantly surround the Holy One of Blessing. Along with several other texts, the phrase forms part of an antiphonal reading among the angels that we imitate in the midst of formal, community worship (during what is called the Reader's repetition of the core prayer in Jewish worship, the *Amidah*). Standing erect with our feet together (to mimic these angels, who are described as one-legged), we rise up on our toes each time we say the word *holy* (which literally means "separate" in the Hebrew). After saying "holy" (or *kadosh* in Hebrew) three times, we get the point of this exercise in spiritual logic: While this action helps us to physically aspire to reach toward Heaven, it also helps to emphasize that, however intimate our relationship with the Divine, God is also beyond us, in a realm that we can journey toward but never fully reach.

For some of us, this idea of God's holiness being beyond us may be frustrating. Why try to communicate with a God or develop a relationship with the Divine that can never fully actualize? For others of us, this idea is affirming. It suggests that as humans we are limited and God represents something that is wholly other and our task is to aspire to that level of holiness. But when we sleep, God seems to reach out to us, and thus we feel the divine presence in our very midst.   KO

The Need for Jewish Human Beings
14 APRIL

Books are not now the prime need of the day. What we need more than ever are human beings—Jewish human beings.

FRANZ ROSENZWEIG[65]

Sometimes I walk into the local megabookstore to check out their section on Judaism—and it's amazing. In these large stores, Jewish books usually span an entire wall of bookcases. There are more books being published today about Judaism than ever before. Only a few decades ago, there were only a small number of books to choose from; today we are inundated. While I think reading Jewish books and becoming a literate Jew is essential, I do not think it is enough just to read. For Judaism is much more than the words we find printed on the pages of a book. I know you are probably saying to yourself, "But we are the People of the Book! How can she be suggesting this?" Yes, we are; yet, we are also a people who has always cherished the dialogue that we have with the words on the page. We read them, discuss them, and then offer our own interpretations. In this way we are constantly renewing Judaism. Many people read before they go to sleep at night. If you are reading a Jewish book now (besides this one), make a commitment to yourself to find someone else who is also reading it tomorrow and then discuss it together. In this way you can become engaged as a Jewish human being who can lift the words off the pages of many books— both ancient and contemporary—and make them live for yourself and others.   LF

Finding Our Spiritual Space
15 APRIL

Suppose there is something going on in the universe which is to ordinary, everyday reality as our unconscious is to our daily lives? Softly, but unmistakably guiding it?
RABBI LAWRENCE S. KUSHNER[66]

The search for the spiritual is a constant river flowing through the American cultural desert. Rabbi Larry Kushner asks the question cogently. Suppose something spiritual does underlie *everything*.

Spirituality attaches to our lives something of higher value than the mundane, something worthy of giving our lives to or dying for. It is no wonder that American culture, so fleeting, so denying of eternality, a culture of "buy today, dispose of tomorrow," so grounded in the twin sirens of sexuality and greed, often leaves us hollow and seeking something ultimate. Spirituality is like a laser beam in the overwhelming darkness of cultural nothingness.

Acting as God commands us to act helps us to unite our lives with God. The only God to be worshiped is the true God of might, the God of Heaven and Earth. That is the spirituality of unifying the human and divine soul. As the Rabbis in *Pirke Avot* direct us, "Make your will God's will, in order that God will make the divine will your will."[67] And start first thing in the morning.   RABBI MARK H. LEVIN

Seeking the Truth
16 APRIL

We naturally like the things to which we have become accustomed. . . . This is one of the causes that prevents us from seeking the truth.

MOSES MAIMONIDES[68]

The status quo is comforting—even when we do not like it— just because we are used to it. That's why most of us are reluctant to change it or leave it behind. In any context in which the status quo is challenged, those who maintain it work feverishly to bring it back to equilibrium, often at the expense of the group who is seeking to change it. This is often ironic, because it makes temporary colleagues out of competitors. And this is deceiving. It is what makes changing institutions so difficult.

It is also what makes changing the self so hard. After so many years, it is difficult to change the self that we have grown accustomed to—even when there are parts of that self that we do not like, that we would prefer to change. So we're stuck with paralysis or, at least, inertia. And truth cannot be found in such a state. We can find the truth in our engagement with the holy. Start with a sacred text. Let it guide you as you engage it.

What is it about the truth that frightens us? Are we afraid to see ourselves clearly? In seeking the truth, will we learn something about ourselves that we would prefer not facing? Are there times when truth should not be sought?

As a medieval philosopher/theologian, Maimonides would argue that our goal should always be to seek the truth. Because he was a spiritual seeker like us, his goal would be the same, for in searching for truth we can find the pathway to the Divine. And that truth sustains the self and the world.   KO

The Gold in Our Hearts
17 APRIL

You are rich though you do not know it. You have wells of kindness within your heart. At times people will bless you more for a smile, a kindly glance, a gesture of forgiveness than for a treasure of gold.

ABRAHAM KABAK[69]

So often we get caught up in measuring our wealth purely by our assets. We may listen to the financial reports before going to bed and anxiously awaken waiting to see what happens the next day. While this may cause us some anxiety, when we pause to reflect, our real wealth lies within. The economy is sure to go up and down, yet our inner wealth—consisting of our memories, the ways we love others, and the bonds we make within the communities we live in—can sustain us forever. When we touch this well of kindness within us and give it away to others, we can go to sleep each night content that the day that is parting was a success. We might even want to say "the market is up" on those days when we find it particularly easy to extend a word or gesture of kindness to others, or when someone extends a gesture of kindness to us. For in essence, the true barometer of our humanity is our inner wealth, the kind that will pay for our way to eternity.   LF

Becoming One with Ourselves

18 APRIL

The Israelites enjoy light in their dwellings.
EXODUS 10:23B

I am fascinated by the eighth plague, locusts, which was brought in by an east wind and carried away by a west wind. The wind blows both east and west for us, the children of Israel.

The east wind. We call it *chokhmah,* wisdom, the heart's deep wisdom.

The west wind is the self-conscious spirit of inquiry and ideation, identification, conceptualization, and language. It is called *binah.*

The west wind is conscious, linear, practical, and rational. The east wind is intuitive, lateral, and mystical.

Both winds blow through our camp, then as now. We are an east/west people, perched on our western branches, recovering our eastern roots, tentative in the tree itself.

Our goal is always integration, union, to be *shalem* (whole) when the terrible twos of existence—west wind and east wind—fold into the One, as they do on Shabbat.

The nemesis is Pharaoh, in Hebrew *Par'oh,* the disintegrator, the one who insists on separation, from the word *peh-resh-ayin,* separated, rent, split. *Par'oh* is the great separator. And that's why we have to leave Pharaoh tonight—so that we can become one, with ourselves.

RABBI JAMES STONE GOODMAN

Living a Significant Life

19 APRIL

People are not afraid of dying; they are afraid of not having lived. We can handle mortality. What we cannot accept is anonymity, insignificance.

RABBI HAROLD KUSHNER[70]

We all want our lives to count, our actions to be taken seriously. We are particularly mindful of this idea as we consider the fact that this day marks the anniversary of the onset of the Warsaw Ghetto Uprising in 1943. While anonymity can, at times, be what we seek, in the long run, we have a deep desire to be known, visible, and counted. We want our lives to have a meaningful impact. Meaning comes in many guises. It does not mean that we have to seek out any particular fame or amass a fortune. It means that we seek out what speaks to the truths in our lives and makes them come alive. Some of us give time and energy to causes that are close to our hearts in order to create meaning. We infuse our lives with holiness and connection by working on projects, developing hobbies, creating warm communities. When we live anonymous lives we run the risk of feeling cut off and alone in this world. Judaism is an antidote for anonymity: To live as a Jew means to live a connected life. Be holy. Seek out community. Make connections. Live fully. Anonymity does not get high marks in the Book of Life. Find ways to make a difference tomorrow. We need to banish anonymity and meaninglessness from our lives so that at the end of our days—and at the end of this day—we can each say, "I have lived a significant, full life." LF

Thinking and Doing
20 April

If you can't think with your heart, then think with your head.
Rabbi Kerry M. Olitzky

This seems like an odd notion—thinking with our *hearts*. We would expect someone to tell us to think with our heads— which seems like something that our parents or teachers might tell us just after we had done something without thinking. But in ancient Israel, the heart *(lev)* was considered to be the seat of the mind. There was even a period of time in which emotions were said to be seated in the kidneys! Rather than an anatomy lesson, the statement quoted above is what might be considered by some as *musar,* ethical guidance for the everyday.

In all of our human encounters, we should be guided by our hearts, saying and doing what is sensitive, supportive, and understanding. But we cannot always *feel* our way in relationships or through life. Things become too complicated for us to be able to feel in our hearts what is the right thing to do. That's when we call our minds into service. Having this dual resource, it is part of our survival mechanism. So think with heart and head. Use both in your service to your neighbor and to yourself.   KO

The Night of Anxious Watching
21 April

That was for God a night of anxious watching to bring them out of the land of Egypt; that same night is God's night of vigil for all Israelites throughout the ages.
Exodus 12:42

The night before the Israelites left Egypt is called *leil shimurim,* the night of anxious watching. You plan and you plan and you plan, you think you know how to leave, you have turned it every which way, and the day is finally coming when all your preparations come due . . . tomorrow.

What happens on the night before? It is the night of anxious watching.

You know you are going (don't you?), but the night before you leave you enter another mind, where you have not lived before. It is the night of anxious watching, *leil shimurim,* because in spite of your fear, in spite of the draw of the journey, in spite of the residue of *mitzrayim* [Egypt, the "narrow place"] that you realize will take you generations to work out of, in spite of all your plans, there is a hesitation. You realize that there is something you haven't accounted for, something you haven't planned for, something you didn't realize in the detail work you have given yourself to up till now.

This is it, you are thinking, the night of anxious watching, something yet left undone. You stop and realize that though you canceled the newspaper, told the neighbors you were going, had the mail forwarded, called ahead to arrange your welcome, still you realize that something in you wants to stay, or something that stays goes with you. You know this to be true on the night of anxious watching, but because you are connected to the spiritual necessity of freedom, because you know all real freedom is earned through the blood, through the bone, you give yourself over to the ambiguity of leaving, loss, staying, going, being—freedom, freedom, freedom.

When you have lived in a narrow place, no matter how much you plan your liberation, when you finally break out, you run away like a jackrabbit into the night.

RABBI JAMES STONE GOODMAN[71]

Visionary Leadership

22 April

Where there is no vision, the people perish.

Proverbs 29:18

It was about this time of year that Moses led our people out of Egypt—around 1250 B.C.E. That's why Passover is celebrated each year in the spring. Just as the world experiences regeneration, renewal, and rebirth, so did the Jewish people when they gained their freedom. It took Moses a long time to persuade Pharaoh to let the Jewish people go. After all, they were his laborers, heavily involved in building his store cities. But just as the plagues convinced the Egyptians to let go of the Israelites, the plagues served to convince the Israelites of the power supporting Moses' leadership.

But why had the people really been willing to follow Moses? Classical commentators on the text argue that the people followed Moses because he was God's emissary. But Moses was able to lead the people—and the people were willing to follow—only because he had a vision. He knew that they had to leave the "narrow places" of Egypt before they could venture into the desert. Moses knew that they would have to journey through the desert before they would be ready to enter the Promised Land. And he saw the future prosperity of the Jewish people once they settled the Land. Had he not known where to take the people and how to lead them, they would have perished, and as a result, so would we. To paraphrase pop culture's approach to this idea regarding Moses' visionary leadership: He got vision!

Where does our vision come from? From opening our hearts to God tonight, tomorrow, and the next day.   KO

Why Complain?

23 April

And they called the name of the place Massah *(Trying)* and
Meribah *(Strife)* because of the striving of the children
of Israel, and because they tried the Lord saying,
"Is the Lord in our midst or not?"

EXODUS 17:7

During this part of the year, we celebrate Passover, the holiday of our freedom. But as this text shows, it doesn't take
long before the Israelites begin to complain. They complain
that Moses has brought them out of the desert to die for lack
of graves in Egypt. They complain that the manna, the desert
food that God provided for them, is tasteless. They complain
that there is no water. Today we might exclaim, "Wow. They
certainly were an ungrateful bunch. What a short memory
they seem to have had." But are we so different? How quick
are we to complain? Do we hold on to, or quickly forget, the
miracles that happen in our own lives? Complaining can
sometimes become an automatic response. If things don't
work out as we expected or as we had hoped, we complain.
However, such a response is never really constructive. It
depletes our spirit. The next time you feel like complaining,
consider turning the situation around. See if there is something for which to express thanks. Let us try to find ways to
be grateful and ask for God's guidance to help us through
those moments of trying and strife without complaining or
losing our faith.   LF

Dwelling Within

24 APRIL

Let them build Me a sanctuary so that
I may dwell among them.

EXODUS 25:8

God is, at once, everywhere and no "where." God is everything and no "thing." That challenging, abstract statement can help to bring the statement above into focus. In the Torah, the Israelites are given detailed instructions for building the *mishkan,* the portable, wilderness sanctuary. But how can any physical space, especially a space constructed by human hands, contain God? What does God mean when instructing Moses "Let them build Me a sanctuary that I may dwell among them"? Can human beings actually build a dwelling place for God?

A long time ago, I remember going to a carnival where they stamped my hand to show that I had paid the admission fee. The ink they used was invisible except under ultraviolet light. As I walked around the carnival, I remember trying to see the stamp on my hand. But try as I would, there was no sign of the mark and I quickly forgot it as I got caught up in the excitement of the rides and the crowd. Only when we returned to that particular spot again did I remember the stamp and put my hand under the special light to see what had been there all along.

The *mishkan* is like a spiritual ultraviolet light that God instructed us to create. It is as though God said to Moses, "Build this tabernacle so you'll have a place to come back to and remember that you bear My stamp, even if it gets so dark that you can't see the mark, even if you forget that it is there. Build this place so that in its light, you'll be able to see what often seems invisible to you." It's not so much that the tabernacle gives God a place to be. Rather, the *mishkan* provides us with a place to be with God, a place to remember the mark and to see that it is always there—even when we forget or can't see it.

The real purpose of building the *mishkan* is to create a space for God inside our hearts, to remind us of the holy, precious mark we bear and to help us see it again. We can't create a dwelling to contain God. But we can create a place that helps us to recognize and nurture that part of God that we contain, the mark that defines our humanity. God wants to "dwell" within us. Understanding that, we learn that a holy place—a place for God's dwelling—certainly can be portable, can be built by us, and can be set up any place and any time. So let's get to work!   RABBI JONATHAN KRAUS

Visibility

25 APRIL

A person sees only what is visible. But God sees into the heart.
I SAMUEL 16:7

As someone classically trained in rational philosophy, schooled in institutions that prided themselves on a "scientific approach" to knowledge, I was taught not to trust what anyone else observed and even to doubt what I myself saw and heard. It is all part of what may be technically called Cartesian doubt, emerging out of the work of the philosopher Descartes. This was always a hard lesson to accept even in the midst of rebellious adolescence, when I was prepared to reject the establishment and to challenge its status quo. How could I not be persuaded by the sights and sounds of the material world when I was just growing to enjoy them and find meaning and comfort in them? I came to realize that what I see and hear are not illusory even though I am limited by the perception of my eyes and ears.

It was Martin Buber—who spun this idea about perception a little differently—who helped me find my way through it. He suggested that we have to navigate our way through the knowledge that we have inherited and, in equal measure, what we have reasoned on our own. Surely our portal to the world is severely limited. That's why the classic question "If a tree falls in the forest and you do not hear it, does it make a sound?" is unanswerable. As the prophet Samuel taught, we can see only what is visible to us. That stands up to the test of reason. If something is not visible, how can we see it? Can it be seen at all? But that is the point. Only God can see what is not visible, what may be hidden in the heart. Perhaps we would do better by looking in God's direction.   KO

Combating Fear

26 APRIL

All the world is a narrow bridge and the main thing is not to be afraid.

RABBI NACHMAN OF BRESLOV[72]

To what degree does fear rule your life? There are so many things in this world that can cause us trepidation and even out-and-out panic. Whether we fear sickness or the paths our children will take or the unexplained violence that plagues our society, there is enough uncertainty in life to paralyze us if we were to allow it. When fear consumes us, we become too scared to take risks and we begin to live in very confining ways. Yet the spiritual principle that Rabbi Nachman teaches us here is not to let fear immobilize or overwhelm us. Sometimes the most courageous people are those who over-come their internal, deep-seated fears. Ever speak to someone who overcame a fear of flying or of heights? It is truly amaz-ing to hear about the strength it takes to battle such unex-

plainable, though real, fears. While fear is a part of living—
we cannot totally escape it—we can keep it at bay by infusing
our lives with hope, prayer, and action. This doesn't mean
that our lives will be free of suffering or pain, yet we will
become better equipped to face fearful moments.   LF

The Place
27 APRIL

*A giant ladder was set up on the ground, the top of it
reaching up to heaven. Angels of God were going up and
down on it, while God was standing right beside him.*
GENESIS 28:12

Did you ever have one of those restless nights where you
just couldn't sleep? No matter what you do, you just cannot
get comfortable. Your pillow feels like a rock and the mat-
tress is as lumpy as if you were lying outside on the ground
someplace. Counting sheep doesn't work. It never does when
you start to think about the day you've just experienced. You
let your mind wander a bit, to see where it might lead you.
And usually, before long, you're fast asleep, resting peaceful-
ly, off on a journey. But sometimes your mind takes you to
places you're not sure you want to be. Some nights, the
dream seems to keep us more awake than if we had never
fallen asleep.

Jacob had one of those nights. Weary after a hard day's
running in the desert, in need of some shut-eye, he stretched
out on the ground to get a good night's sleep. Using the closest thing available, a rock, for a pillow, he lets his mind wander a bit. And this is where it leads him: "A giant ladder was
set upon the ground, the top of it reaching up to heaven
Angels of God were going up and down on it, while God was
standing right beside him" (Genesis 28:12).

If there was one thing he didn't need, it was a moving-escalator dream. This was sure to disrupt his rest, with all of these angels running up and down. This was not the nice, quiet dream he had hoped for. And then, as if that weren't enough, God had the chutzpah to suggest that Jacob hop on the heaven-bound escalator/ladder himself. What in the world would make God think that the sleepy patriarch was in the mood for a ride or a little climb?

Just then a pair of angels on their way home from Sodom stepped on the ladder. Glancing down at Jacob, they couldn't believe their eyes. As they ascended, they called out to their friends upstairs, "Hey, take a look down here at this guy's face. It's Jacob, the one whose image is engraved on God's throne of glory!"

Overhearing the angels, Jacob turned to God, standing beside him, and was shocked to see the Holy One a few yards away making another ladder. "What are you doing?" Jacob asked. "The same thing that I have been doing since the finish of creation. I'm making ladders for people like you to climb. I set them down, here upon earth, hoping that someone will see them and understand.

"The task is to climb, to bring Heaven and Earth together, until there is no distinction. Each rung holds the opportunity for making the world a bit more human, a bit more holy. Every new step is a challenge, to let a little more Divine into the world, into yourself. And, reaching the top, you can see the image engraved upon the divine throne . . . the likeness of the Holy One, which lies within you. The problem is," God continued, sitting next to Jacob on his rocky bed, "many people, just like you, think that it is all a dream. They will not climb. They cannot, for they don't see or realize that the ladders are real."

Jacob awoke, not sure if he had been dreaming, uncertain whether he had slept that night at all. Wiping the tears from his eyes, he could see the ladder, which God had set out for him to ascend. If you close your eyes, as you drift off to sleep, you may be able to see Jacob beckoning to you to join him.   RABBI JEFFREY SIRKMAN

The Direction of Torah
28 APRIL

As water flows to the lowest level, so Torah finds its way to the lowly of spirit.
TALMUD[73]

The Rabbis repeatedly liken Torah to water. Like water, Torah is abundant and vast. But that alone is not what persuaded them. The Rabbis understood that water sustains life and so does the Torah. Thus we speak in the metaphor of the redemptive waters of Torah. Although each plant or animal has to find its way to water, Torah finds its way to us. It speaks in a language that all can understand. In fact, according to Jewish tradition, Torah was revealed in the seventy languages of the world so that everyone would be able to understand its message. Usually we think of these seventy languages as emerging from the cultures of different peoples around the world. Perhaps when the Rabbis described this aspect of Torah revelation, they were speaking of seventy *levels* of language as well as seventy different languages. Each "language" expressed Torah in terms that some individual group or groups of people could understand. Thus the message of Torah could find its way to all—extending also to the lowly of spirit. Maybe it is when we are "lowly in spirit," particularly at the end of a long frustrating day, that the sacred text becomes Torah, raising our spirits to the mountaintop, where its message can be revealed to us.   KO

Influencing Others

29 APRIL

*When you try to influence someone, it is important
that the message he hears is that you love
him and care about his welfare.*

VILNA GAON

All of us have ways we influence others. Certainly we have great influence on our family members and, at times, on our friends. Many of us are even engaged in influencing others in the course of our work. However, whether we intuit it or not, it is futile to attempt to influence someone if we do so in a way that is uncaring or perfunctory. This is why a good salesperson first establishes relationships: Everyone wants to feel cared for (even if the person is just buying a new piece of clothing). It doesn't matter if we are trying to influence someone to vote for a particular candidate, convincing a loved one to make a decision, or soliciting a *tzedakah* contribution. In these situations, and many others, it is wise to be mindful of how we go about exerting our influence. Do our tone and message convey a sense of concern about the listener and his or her needs? If so, then we have the opportunity to touch his or her heart. If not, our words will easily be tuned out. Influence is a powerful thing. When we seek to exert it, let us do so responsibly, with due sincerity and concern for the well-being of the one who is sharing the interaction with us.   LF

Breakthrough

30 APRIL

We have seen the day when God speaks to humanity.
DEUTERONOMY 5:21

There are times when we are drowning in despair, when we feel that we are swimming just below the surface of the water but do not have the strength to break through for a life-giving breath of air. When our lives are overwhelmed by the pressures of the day and we seem unable to resolve the problems that we face, it is easy to question the existence of God. It is easy to lose our faith. We may feel that we are alone, unsupported, alienated, and isolated. Certainly our ancestors, who faced far worse times, had reason to doubt the existence of God. Yet many of them continued to believe.

In times of utter despair, we may find our strength in the words of the psalmist who instructs us, "I turn my eyes to the mountains. Where will my help come from? My help comes from God, creator of Heaven and Earth" (Psalms 121:1–2). Even as the world affirms God's continuing presence in it, many things that occur in it are far beyond our comprehension. There is the cruelty to which one human subjects another. There are diseases for which there are not yet cures. And there are many acts of nature that defy our understanding. With all these things, *we* are proof of God's presence in the world—when we reach out to others in time of need, when we offer words of healing, when we comfort those who have fallen, when we give of ourselves. It is this faith that has sustained those who have come before us and will continue to sustain us today. MARCIA COHN SPIEGEL

MAY

Communal Life

1 MAY

At a time when the community is in need one should not say, "I will go home and peace be to you," but rather one should participate in alleviating the community's troubles.

MIDRASH[74]

Judaism is especially cognizant of the relationship between individuals and the community. In our highly individualized society, it is all too easy to remove ourselves from the community. After all, our days are busy, and dealing with our individual needs as well as the needs of our close friends and family (often a whole "community" in themselves) takes a lot of energy. Yet when we work together with others to solve a communal problem, we commit ourselves to being part of something grander than ourselves and our personal problems. Granted, this takes time, patience, and creative thinking. Often it means making compromises and even sacrifices. Especially when the going gets tough, some of us might choose to walk away. However, the benefits of being part of all the internal and, yes, political dynamics that take place in most communities outweigh the disadvantages. We rejoice when we collectively come up with new ways to solve nagging problems or when we find solutions to new situations.

We build lasting friendships that will be with us in times of personal sorrow and rejoicing. And most important, we break our sense of isolation, the malaise of contemporary life. So tonight, in the spirit of Jewish tradition, let us focus on the inner strength we need to become fully participating members of a community.   LF

Sinai Echoes

2 MAY

If one hears the call from Sinai and its quiet, daily echoes,
one is obligated to act upon that divine message
in a godly, ethical fashion.
RABBI LEVI MEIER[75]

Toward the end of the spring, several occasions make their mark on the Jewish holiday calendar. They all represent stops that we have made along our historical journey: *Yom Hashoah* (Holocaust Memorial Day), *Yom Hazikaron* (Israeli Memorial Day), *Yom Ha'atzmaut* (Israeli Independence Day), and Shavuot (Festival of Weeks, which celebrates the revelation of the Torah). Since the second day of the Passover holiday, we have actively marked each day on the calendar and recalled this passage each day during the evening prayer service.

Jewish tradition calls this period from Passover to Shavuot *sefirat ha-omer*. This is an ancient way of counting down to the harvest season that has been raised up to a more spiritual level in more recent times. While the special days that almost immediately precede Shavuot entered the calendar during the modern period, they all point toward the timeless revelation of Torah and its message of optimism that continues to drive Jewish history into the future. This is what makes Rabbi Meier's teaching particularly relevant to this season of the year. We must listen for the echoes of Sinai in our daily lives.

Once we hear them, then we have no choice but to respond to them. It is our obligation. This response is transformed into ethical actions; as a result, others will hear the voice of Sinai through the words and the works—ours—of Torah.

So get a good night's sleep. There is much work to be done in the morning. KO

Teamwork

3 May

How good and how pleasant it is that brothers (and sisters) dwell together.

Psalm 133:1

This marks the end of the track season at my daughter's high school. I know this because I have been asked to throw a salad together for the team's year-end picnic. I suggest to my daughter that she might not want to stay too long, considering that she has finals coming up. "Oh," she tells me, "it's the last time we'll be together as a team."

Her strong feelings about being on a team remind me of a favorite television program in childhood, one that featured a different international circus each week. I particularly loved to watch the trapeze artists. It was not so much their individual skill and daring that impressed me, though both were awesome; it was the trust that they had in each other as teammates. If you were the one flying on the trapeze, you allowed one member of the team to push you off the platform with just the right force and at just the right time. And when you swung out and let go, you trusted that you would be caught by another member of the team who was swinging toward you.

Most of my own professional life has been spent working alone, teamless. Editors were phone calls and then faxes away in distant cities; and my young students, though close to my heart, have been on the other side of the learning and generational divides: I teach, they learn; I am older, they are younger. So the times I have been part of team projects—in work or in the community—have really stood out. They make me think about whom I can really trust and depend on; they make me think about who will always go the extra mile for the sake of the team. And so, in the spirit bringing many team endeavors to closure as summer approaches, I offer this *kavannah,* a meditation for all kinds of team players who celebrate the blessing of their being together as a team:

Our teamwork has been a blessing. We have learned that people working together may accomplish what individuals working alone may not. If we are blessed to be a team again, may we be like trapeze artists—pushing each other in the right amount at and the right time, and always being there to catch each other, especially when we are flying through the air. May the divine presence be our safety net, when despite our skill and good intentions, we inadvertently slip or disappoint each other. VANESSA L. OCHS[76]

The Journey from Passover to Shavuot
4 MAY

From Passover we learn that we are not slaves; from Shavuot, that we are not gods. From Passover we learn what to stand against; from Shavuot, what to stand for. From Passover we learn about our rights; from Shavuot, about our responsibilities.
RABBI ARNOLD RESNICOFF[77]

At this time of year, regardless of where on the secular calendar Passover and Shavuot fall, we are in the middle of the *omer* period during which we count forty-nine days from

Passover (starting with the second night) to Shavuot. The journey from Passover to Shavuot is primarily one in which we transform ourselves from a just-freed band of slaves into a covenanted people. On Passover we celebrate our liberation; on Shavuot we celebrate receiving the Torah, the culmination of that freedom—though it is early in our historical journey in the desert. As Rabbi Resnicoff suggests above, Shavuot teaches us that though we are free, we are not gods. Freedom does not give us the right to think of ourselves as all-powerful or omniscient. Rather, we are a human community that seeks an ongoing relationship with the one God. We are not to confuse our new freedom with a belief that there is no effort involved in this relationship. Rather, through our covenant with the Holy One, we learn that with freedom come responsibilities. In Judaism we call these *mitzvot*. As we near Shavuot this night, let us reaffirm the responsibilities that come with being Jewish; in so doing, we strengthen our connection with God and our community.   LF

Happiness through Doing Deeds

5 MAY

Happy is the one whose deeds are greater than one's learning.
MIDRASH[78]

Jewish tradition has always emphasized learning. For many, learning sacred text is both the gateway and the context for Jewish spirituality. Unlike the temple priesthood that historically preceded it, which gained its community authority through ancestry, throughout its various iterations the entire institution of the rabbinate is based on knowledge. Today, particularly in the liberal community, the contemporary rabbi's authority emerges from his or her learning.

Nevertheless, knowledge—whoever "owns" it—is of little consequence to the historical and contemporary rabbis if the learning does not lead the individual to the performance of good deeds. Some rabbis will go so far as to argue that the sole purpose of learning *is* the doing of good deeds. In one classic example from the Mishnah, in the midst of a discussion concerning a certain set of behaviors that each individual is obligated to undertake, without specifying the specific amount or duration (which is clearly indicated in most other contexts), the rabbis of the Mishnah add that "the study of Torah equals them all" because it leads to them all.[79]

You could probably make your own list of deeds that will lead you to Torah. As you try to do so this evening, just remember: learning may make you happy, but doing good deeds will make you smile.   KO

Counting the Days
6 MAY

And from the day on which you bring the sheaf of the offering . . . you shall count off seven weeks. . . . You must count until the day after the seventh week, fifty days. You shall bring an offering of new grain to Adonai.
LEVITICUS 23:15–16

For some odd reason, each time I read any biblical commandment about the counting of days, I remember "Zoo Day" in Cincinnati, Ohio, from my childhood. Because Zoo Day came near summer vacation, it was the first light at the end of the tunnel. When Zoo Day finally arrived, groups of children from different streets, carrying packed lunches in shoe boxes, would set forth early in the morning as if on a great pilgrimage, into one flow walking happily toward a wonderful day at the zoo. So, as soon as the date of Zoo Day was announced by the teacher, we were counting the days. I even remember a big plain calendar on which each school day between us and Zoo Day was, at the end of the day, x-ed off.

Counting the days is not, of course, limited to children. Everywhere in the world, multitudes of all ages are counting the days; counting the days to weddings, celebrations, retirement. Even the prisoner who is confined to a cell looks forward to the day of release, as does the high achiever awaiting a big promotion.

From a different perspective entirely, when we stand at the grave of those we love, we are reminded of the relentless count: to the last of our own days. Then I think of the words of the psalmist: "Teach us to number our days with wisdom" (Psalms 90:12). But how to count the days with wisdom? Here I believe that the practice that follows the biblical ordinance of counting the Omer, the sheaf offering, offers us guidance.

There is wisdom in the setting aside of a period of time regularly to stop and actually count off each day, reflecting the wisdom of Rabbi Bachya ibn Pakuda: "Each of your days is like a scroll. Write on it only what you want remembered."

After the Jerusalem Temple was destroyed, Jews could no longer bring the daily offerings, or in its season, the Omersheaf. Instead, according to our sages, daily study of the sacred text, daily worship, daily deeds of lovingkindness, became the daily offerings to God. Every day is a day of celebration of the possibility of offering our own growth, like the sheaves; celebration of the improvement in strengthening of the best in our souls. Each day there is the possibility of the deepening of our capacity to give and to love.

When we remember to count the days, to take them seriously, to take note of the infinite value of each day, and to make each day a receptacle of offering and praise to God—to make them count for good—we neither have to worry about the passing of our days nor any longer *dis*count them; because each one of them is a seed of eternity, each day a flowering promise of immortality, bearing the sweetest fruit for our hungry spirits, each day a blessing from God.

RABBI HERBERT BRONSTEIN[80]

For the Sake of Heaven

7 MAY

If God had explicitly stated the reward for doing each of the mitzvot, *they would not be performed for the sake of Heaven. . . . People would do only those offering great benefits and neglect others, leaving some of them undone.*

YECHIEL BEN YEKUTIEL[81]

What motivates our actions? Are we spurred on primarily by the promise of reward or the fear of punishment? Or are we motivated by the intrinsic value of our actions? Traditionally, we are taught there are 613 *mitzvot* in the Torah. In fact, many of these are not applicable to our lives today because they have to do with Temple sacrifices, which we no longer practice, or they are limited to those who live in the land of Israel. Nonetheless, the question that has been asked for centuries—namely, Why?—is one we also ask. Why observe the commandments? Are there rational explanations? As modernists, we would feel most comfortable if a rabbi would only delineate the rational explanations for each and every commandment. But instead, faith requires us to take a leap and to fulfill *mitzvot* even when explanations do not come easily. Often the action involved in fulfilling the mitzvah itself is the best teacher.   LF

Holy Submission

8 May

To each wave that approaches me, I bend my head.
TALMUD[82]

Rabbi Akiva made this statement when retelling his colleagues about how he survived a shipwreck. But he was also suggesting to them a spiritual posture for living. Although most of the time we are taught to stand erect and hold our heads up even in the face of the oppressor, Akiva advises us that there are times—particularly in our relationship with God—that we must submit. Perhaps it was his encounter at sea that provoked this idea. Or perhaps his commitment to this idea saved him when the sea threatened to take his life. It is the kind of wisdom that emerges out of the experience of living.

There is a Yiddish expression that offers a similar perspective on the world: Only a pliant reed can sustain strong winds. But Akiva maintains an even stronger position. He is not advising us just to be flexible when it comes to our relationship with God. Akiva wants us to submit to the will of the Divine, and we can only discover that will when we are willing to be subject to it. It is the same reasoning that is implicit in the choice that many liberal, rational Jews are making to voluntarily take on the obligation of *mitzvot*. Some might even say that this is showing leadership through submission. This is the spiritual logic behind Akiva's advice. We may be engaged in a covenant, a partnership with the Divine; however, Akiva would probably argue that we are the *very* junior partners.   KO

See This Day
9 MAY

See, this day I set before you blessing and curse . . .
DEUTERONOMY 11:26

See this day. This very day, today. Most of us spend our time rehashing yesterday or anticipating tomorrow. Most of us would do anything to avoid having to see this day, to pay attention to what is happening now. Even when we think we are seeing this day, we are looking through lenses so colored by past experience and cultural conditioning that all we see is a reflection of what we expect based on what we have been taught in the past. What Moses is asking of us in this passage from Deuteronomy is to see this day as it is, new, unique, open to possibility.

"I set before you blessing and curse." If we truly see this day as it is, then we will see that it contains both blessing and curse, light and shadow, good and bad, suffering and joy. Most of us are conditioned to hope for the former and anticipate the latter. We call this being realistic. It isn't. It is conditioned thinking that has nothing to do with reality. Reality is both blessing and curse. You cannot have one without the other. One makes no sense without the other. They are dependent one on the other. This is why Moses did not say "blessing *or* curse." He said "blessing *and* curse." You cannot escape from both, though many of us try to do so. Blessing and curse are given to us by life, and how we respond to them is what we give to life. We cannot control the former and are not morally accountable for what we encounter. We *can* control the latter, and for that we are indeed accountable. This is the lesson of the message: We can only experience the blessing when we are prepared to accept the curse.

RABBI RAMI SHAPIRO

The Gift of Life

10 MAY

The years of one's life are not a bequest, guaranteed for an extended period of time. Rather, each and every breath is a gift from God.

COMMENTARY ON THE TORAH[83]

How often do we slow down to really consider the span and scope of our years? It's true that today many people are living healthy, active lives for longer and longer periods of time. Though retirement officially begins at sixty-five, today this marks a new period of life for many people. Nonetheless, even with an expanded life span, the years of our lives are not infinite. Each day, each season, is a gift to cherish. Each day that we grow older—with wrinkles and growing waist-lines—is a gift, a blessing. And birthdays themselves are indeed days to celebrate, not dread: ask any cancer survivor.

We need to savor our life now to the fullest extent possible. This may be easy to say, but it is certainly not always easy to fulfill. We all tend to say, for example, "Oh, I'll pursue my dreams when I retire." We all get up some days on the wrong side of the bed, as the saying goes, or perhaps we are dealing with a tense work situation or have financial concerns. It is hard to remember, much less focus on, the value of each of our moments when we are in the thick of life's stresses. Thanking God for each breath of life may be the last thing on our minds. We are worried about who's going to pick up the kids from school and how to complete the latest project on time. Nonetheless, the spiritual path is to recognize that life is a gift. As we drift off to sleep tonight, let us recommit ourselves to cherishing life—each breath of it.   LF

God's Role

11 MAY

God has made me fruitful in the land of my affliction.
GENESIS 41:52

As arduous as it is to "make lemonade from lemons"—as the truism goes—it is much more difficult to acknowledge and affirm God's role in our suffering. After all, although we all encounter challenges in our lives—some life threatening and spiritually demanding—we want to attribute only blessing to the Divine and never tragedy, curse, or affliction. So we blame tragedy and suffering on the vagaries of life. Then God gets reduced to being able to offer only profound solace and support but little else. This theological and existential challenge is what motivates many to suggest that God's impact on the world and our lives is rather limited, because by limiting God's power to punish, we may unintentionally also be limiting the power of the Divine to bestow blessing. This is a tough call for religious people who believe in God. Philosophers and theologians, as well as the rest of us, have been debating this notion for a long time.

Not surprisingly, the Torah text is not satisfied with leaving the question alone. It implies that God can work with the individual to take a curse and transform it into blessing—a more sophisticated, religious spin on making lemons into lemonade. This text from Genesis offers us a testimony and a promise so that we can rest easier.   KO

Principles for Living
12 MAY

*Rabbi Ishmael said, ". . . and one of the principles of
interpretation is* klal u-frat u-klal: *the general,
the particular, the general."*

LITURGY[84]

It seems strange that this should be included in our morning
prayers. Actually, it is a prelude to the study of sacred texts
that is included in the morning liturgy. But this teaching of
Rabbi Ishmael's is more than just a study tool that is of benefit to us in the classroom. It also represents a profound lesson
for living. Perhaps it should be included in the evening liturgy
as well, in order to help us make our way through the night,
in order to help us understand what we have just experienced
through the day.

This teaching emerges from the Talmud. It is a way of
interpretation, one of thirteen rules of interpreting sacred
text, given in the name of Rabbi Ishmael. It is called *klal u-
frat u-klal:* the general, then the particular, then the general. I
found this rather curious. I thought about it like I do my
crossword puzzle, trying to figure out at the end of the day
what did not occur to me first thing in the morning (when
I first work on the puzzle). Was Rabbi Ishmael offering a
formal clue to the puzzle of life or just a contextual clue or
perhaps both? There is a door in and out of the particular,
coming and going, that leads to the universal. The particular
opens on all sides to the universal, coming and going.

Some time ago, I was sitting in Jerusalem with an Israeli
man having dinner. He had just returned from the United
States, where he studied for his Ph.D. in Indian philosophy.

"So what are you doing in Israel for such a long time?" he
asked me over fish.

I was learning how to play an ancient Middle Eastern musical instrument with a master teacher in a small Arab village in the north of Israel. I had learned to keep the explanations of such activities brief. Not everyone would understand. So I asked him, "How interested are you?"

"When you love something," he said, "every particular reflects the whole. It's the multijeweled net. Every facet reflects the whole. Every something becomes everything."

Something to think about. Something to learn. From the general to the particular to the general. From the day to the night and then back to the day again.

RABBI JAMES STONE GOODMAN

Chesed

13 MAY

Kindness is the overflowing of one's self into the lives of others.
ANONYMOUS

In Hebrew the word for kindness is *chesed*. This word, *chesed,* connotes the original unconditional love that flows from God to humanity. We, in turn, tap into this divine *chesed* and extend it to others. Many of us do acts of kindness. We might do so in order to fulfill certain *mitzvot*. Or it may just feel like the natural thing to do. Others of us may have to exert ourselves in order to extend lovingkindness to those beyond our most intimate circle of friends and family. Reflect for a moment about how you extend kindness to others. For example, are you someone who says yes when asked to do a favor? Do you look for ways to help others who are in need? Do you organize others, perhaps through a synagogue, federation, or community center, into *chesed*-providing groups so that systems are in place and can be easily activated when a need arises? Throughout the former Soviet Union there are now *chesed* groups working to provide food staples for the elderly and sick. This is one way that Jews of all ages are reconnecting with one another and with our tradition. The giving of *chesed,* whether to those closest to us or to others whom we may never meet, is not limited by any boundaries. It is only limited by the size and strength of our hearts. So get some sleep. There is plenty of work that God wants us to do in the morning.   LF

From Old to New
14 MAY

You have to clear out the old to make room for the new.
LEVITICUS 26:10

Is this Torah's way of saying that we have to let go of the past in order to embrace the future? For a people who is sustained by memory, this would be an odd posture for its most sacred text to assume. Memory and the past inform who we are and what we can become. We do not want to break from it, as much as we might want to grow beyond it, particularly points in the Jewish past that have been marked by suffering and martyrdom.

The modern State of Israel was built out of the ruins of the Holocaust. So the Torah must be trying to teach us something else, something that transcends any one time period in the Jewish journey. Perhaps the lesson is not in actually letting go of the past but, rather, in the activity of "clearing out the past": getting rid of the accumulated debris that weighs heavily on our spirit. By making a place for the new in this way, we are able to cleanse the past. Maybe just a simple change in our attitude opens us up to the possibility of taking hold of the past and transforming it for the future. And the best time to start is now.   KO

The Uniqueness of Being
15 MAY

Let us bless the Source of Life in its infinite variety.
That creates all of us whole, none of us perfect.

JUDITH GLASS[85]

It may sound like a cliché, but it's true: Each of us is unique. Many of us have heard this idea since we were children. But few of us have taken the time to probe what it really means. Obviously, we share a great deal in common with everyone else. It is what makes us all human. Yet the complex of who we are and how we got this way is what makes us unique, the combination of what some people have come to call nurture *and* nature. As a result, none of us can be measured by the attributes of another or even his or her strengths or weaknesses, since we are all our own standards of measurement. While we might share similar characteristics with another or bear resemblance to someone else, and even be mistaken for another, not one of us can really be taken for another—though it makes for some successful movie themes. Since that is the case, one would think that the presence of God is unique to each individual as well. But spiritual logic is often counterintuitive. So in the midst of this endless human variety, God is consistently present in every soul. What makes it sometimes seem different is the individual's acknowledgment and application of that spark of divinity. And that factor is what brings our uniqueness into the realm of similarity. This may be a difficult idea to keep in mind as we are bombarded with products that promise perfection, products that compare us with and promise to transform us into another. We let ourselves become deceived into believing that just by the purchase of a particular product—let alone its application—we can attain someone else's measure of beauty, strength, or potent sexuality. And we buy the product because we want to believe it is possible. In one way or another, we just don't believe that our uniqueness is a divine gift. Instead, we have taken a blessing and shaped it into a curse.

The Torah teaches us that we are made in God's image. While the individual stories take different twists and turns, we are actually told this twice in the sacred text for the sake of emphasis. In this divine image is the potential for infinite application of this uniqueness, no matter how many people are born, generation after generation, just as there is no finite measurement that has any relevance to God.

Before you consider yourself any more or less than your neighbor: Take a good look at yourself and then at your neighbor. Can you see the spark of the Divine as it ignites your soul? Perhaps in the divine light that it sheds you are able to see how you are different from your neighbor. And that's something to celebrate—now, tomorrow, and the day after.

Marcia Cohn Spiegel

Silent Screams
16 May

Know that it is possible to let out a very great scream
in a voice no one will hear. No sound actually emerges—
the scream takes place within the silence.
Everyone is capable of such a cry.

Rabbi Nachman of Breslov[86]

Part of our culture is our love of words. We speak, write, and express ourselves through the art of crafting words into sentences, and then sentences into paragraphs, and even, at times, paragraphs into essays. Yet there are times in our lives when even the most poetically expressive of words cannot convey what we feel, whether it be pain, despair, or anguish.

When this happens, our verbal sophistication can fail us. We may be screaming on the inside and unable to give voice to our emotional troubles. No one hears us. We may feel imprisoned within ourselves. We can only hope that there is someone close at hand who sees our anguish—despite our muteness—and comes to our help. This "scream within the silence" that Reb Nachman describes can also happen to those we love—our spouses, friends, children, and colleagues. How can we be there for others when there is no out-and-out communication of a need? Can we be sensitive to each other to a degree that we can extend ourselves when others cannot reach out to ask for help for themselves? This is a level of awareness that takes great compassion and care. Yet when we work to do so, we are truly doing God's work. Tonight, contemplate how you might do it, then tomorrow, be a good listener.   LF

Hiding

17 MAY

You cannot hide anything from God—or your neighbor.
LADINO FOLK SAYING

We have all learned since childhood that nothing is hidden from God. Some of us even count on it! Early in the book of Genesis, we read of Adam and Eve trying to hide from God after they ate of the fruit of the tree of good and evil. The Torah text then goes on to say that God went looking for them, as if God did not know where to find them. However, it is clear that God's question to Adam, "*Ayeka?* Where are you?" is rhetorical. God wants Adam and Eve to take note of what they had done and *where* it had taken them. And in the Book of Jonah, which we read at the beginning of each year on Yom Kippur, we encounter the prophet Jonah trying to run away from God—as if he can elude the task that God has assigned to him. Perhaps some of us have attempted to hide from God—or hoped that God did not take notice of something that we had done.

What is remarkable about this Ladino folk saying about hiding, from a culture that emerges among those who can trace their ancestry to Spain, is the relationship that is placed between God and our neighbors. Perhaps the folk understanding is that our neighbors are, in a sense, messengers of God. Neighbors have an uncanny way of seeing everything. So instead of reading the common ethic of don't do anything in public that you don't want to be seen, those who penned the folk saying above are trying to suggest: don't do anything in private that you are not prepared to do in public. God and your neighbors will know. Sleep on it. There may be something you'll want to do in the morning.   KO

The Question of Existence
18 MAY
On the day I stop asking questions, I will stop existing.
JEWISH FOLK SAYING

Now one can read this as a provocative statement. This folk saying uses the Hebrew word *l'hiyot,* which means "existing," and not the Hebrew word *lichiyot,* which means "living." These two words are very similar. But there is a difference.

Somehow, asking questions is a matter of existence on a level that goes beyond our physical survival. To live, we might say we need water, food, shelter. But when we think about our souls, not just our bodies, we need certain emotional and spiritual experiences for them to thrive, and one of these seems to be the very act of asking questions. Our existence, both as individuals and as a community, rests on the asking of questions. People who stop asking questions may be living—but are they experiencing the full spectrum of existence?

In English we would say, "I'm just existing, not really living." But in Hebrew, the words' meanings are reversed; we would say instead, "I am just living, not fully existing." This is much more than a matter of semantics. Let us set our resolve to ask questions so we will not stop existing.　　LF

Kindling the Spark
19 MAY

A young man once wanted to be a blacksmith. So he became an apprentice and learned all the necessary techniques of the trade. Having finished his apprenticeship, he was chosen to be employed at the smithy of the royal palace. However, the young man's delight soon ended when he discovered that he had failed to learn how to kindle a spark. All his skill and knowledge in handling the tools were of no avail; without a spark he could not proceed.

HASIDIC STORY[87]

Many of us have probably spent years gaining education or training and may even have served as an apprentice or intern before beginning our life's work. We may have learned fundamental theory along with cutting-edge techniques. However, all this knowledge and firsthand experience will do us good only if we have a spark within that we can call upon to get things started. In order to have vision and implement our new ideas, we need to locate that spark within. Without it we, like the blacksmith, will be unable to proceed.

Where is your spark? How do you call it forth? Sometimes life's complexities can cause it to be diminished and it can be hard for us to locate. Yet Judaism teaches us that we are created in God's image. That image is always within us, and when we stay in touch with our divine core, then we can nurture our inner spark so that it becomes the inspiration that allows our work to occur. No matter where you are in your life, take this time to reflect on how you use your spark. Take care not to let this spark become extinguished. It is vital to our existence, to renewing our spirit, and to being passionate about the life and work to which we are committed.   LF

Strong and Swift

20 MAY

The race is not to the swift, nor the battle to the strong.
ECCLESIASTES 9:11

Most of us are in a hurry. We rush to work and then rush home. We hurry our meals so that we can do other things—or get back to work. We rush through childhood or may push our children into adulthood. No matter where we turn, we feel this accelerated pace, especially in the cities and on the highways. Rushing has become part of our culture, exacerbated by the onslaught of computers and electronic devices that are increasingly faster. They actually invade our private lives and blur the lines between home and work. Yet no matter how fast we go, it is never fast enough. With the introduction of each machine, we still want our communication to be even faster.

Similarly, in the sports arena, which has replaced the battlefield as a place where strength is celebrated, we look for those who are the strongest to lead our favored teams into victory. There, where violence is permitted within the parameters of a set of agreed-upon rules, we encourage our team members to display their strength.

But as Ecclesiastes has learned in his own life—and thereby wants to teach all of us who are prepared to listen to this text—the race is not won by the fastest runner, nor is the battle won by the strongest warrior. There are other things to consider. Stamina. Determination. Passion. Commitment. Faith. The race can be won by the one who refuses to give up, and the battle by the one who fights for what he or she believes in the heart.   KO

Seeing God's Voice

21 MAY

And the people saw the sounds.

EXODUS 20:15

How are we to reexperience Sinai? How can we attain the ability to hear the voice of God and to stand before the presence? According to one tradition, the voice of Sinai goes forth every day, not just at one moment long ago. Even so, how can we achieve the ability to hear it?

One possibility is suggested by this puzzling verse about the people seeing rather than hearing the sounds. Imagine if a deaf person walked into a room where there was music playing and people dancing. At first they might assume that the dancers are crazy. Yet, with some awareness, they will realize that there is music even though they cannot hear it.

We are all hard of hearing when it comes to the voice at Sinai. The key to being able to hear it is to realize that the music is playing—that is, that God calls out to us every day. With that awareness, when we look at the world we can see the "effects" of that voice—in nature, in acts of lovingkindness. At those times, at least, we remember we should strive to hear the voice. The first step, then, is to "see the sounds"—that is, to see the effect of God's voice and to remember its existence long before we can actually hear it.

This is the beginning of the road to Sinai.

RABBI MICHAEL STRASSFELD

Practical Spirituality

22 MAY

Spirituality is really and intensely practical. It is the ordered discipline of the spirit that enables people to meet any fate and rise above the hazards of fortune.

REBEKAH KOHUT[88]

How can spirituality be practical, as Kohut would have it? Judaism teaches that the rituals that make up our daily religious lives, such as lighting Shabbat candles, praying, and giving *tzedakah,* have practical implications. For they, indeed, are guiding forces behind the way we present ourselves in the world and how we relate to others. They are concrete demonstrations of what we believe. If we believe that we are God's partners to better this world, then we must take action to implement what we believe. Our rituals give us a strong foundation upon which we can rely when we are faced with difficult life moments. Spirituality is about living in relationship with God and with others so that the web of our lives becomes tightly woven. This will sustain us today and prepare us for meeting the difficult, trying moments that we have yet to face tomorrow.   LF

Acquisitions

23 MAY

With all your getting, get understanding.

PROVERBS 4:7

This is a simple text from a source that is known for its simple advice for daily living. The authors of the Book of Proverbs have drawn conclusions from their own experience of living and are sharing those experiences with us, the readers. We can imagine that they hope, as those of us who are parents hope for our own children, that they can help others learn from their own experiences.

It seems that the more we own, the more important we think we are, especially if what we own is bigger and therefore better than what our neighbors have—bigger house, bigger car, more stuff. While we may too often fall into the thinking that everything is for sale and can be acquired for a price, there are certain things that we cannot just purchase and add to our personal stockpile. Some things can be acquired only by learning through our experience with living. And these things are not acquired overnight. They take time, as we take hold of them little by little.

So the writers of the Book of Proverbs advise us to change our focus. Stop buying things. Instead, get understanding. It's good advice to sleep on.   KO

Let Your Light Shine
24 MAY

Note well, and follow the patterns that are being shown you on the mountain.

EXODUS 25:40

For most of Jewish history, the preeminent symbol of Judaism has been the menorah, a seven-branched candlestick that was found in the desert tabernacle and later in the ancient temple in Jerusalem. That menorah is mentioned in the Torah when God tells Moses to "make a lampstand of pure gold . . . its base and its shaft, its cups, calyxes, and petals should be made of one piece. Six branches should issue from its sides."

In reading this description of the menorah, the confusion is overwhelming. The details are so complex that it is easy to despair of ever visualizing it correctly. That same confusion must have gotten the better of Moses. But why were the details so difficult to retain? Perhaps it was so the Torah can teach us about human beings and about being human. After all, Moses was able to remember the entire (written and oral) Torah, according to Jewish tradition. How could such a gifted mind have trouble remembering the details of the menorah? Perhaps the Torah is telling us that even the most gifted of minds is stronger in some areas and weaker in others.

Each of us has some special talent or gift that is our unique strength. No matter how special other people may seem, you are able to bring your unique perspective and insight and talents to bear in a combination that no one else can reproduce. Each of us, in our own way, can add something irreplaceable to the luxurious weave of humanity. Every individual person, like each glistening thread, makes the cloth that much more shimmering and durable. No one can replace you. Perhaps that is also why the menorah has so many lights. Each one of the seven lights shines in its own way. In fact, the only thing that can make a menorah *treif* (unfit for use) is if the lights are not all on the same level—precisely even—so that no two lights can be confused as one. Also, the Talmud instructs that no replicas of the Temple menorah can be made or displayed anymore. Perhaps this is another assertion of the importance of each individual. Just as the Temple menorah cannot simply be replaced, so too no human being can simply be replaced. Instead, those seven burning flames testify to the shining light within each human being: "The human soul is a lamp of God."

The light of God's love, justice, and concern can only illumine the world through the individual light that we shine through our deeds. Like the menorah of old, we can illumine the world. So shine on, and shine brightly.

RABBI BRADLEY SHAVIT ARTSON

For Whom We Work

25 MAY

Reb Naftali was walking home when he saw a man patrolling the grounds of a magnificent estate. He asked the man whom he worked for. The guard replied and then asked Reb Naftali, "And for whom do you work?" That question hit the rebbe so hard that he said to the man, "Will you come work for me?" The man replied, "What will be my duties?" Reb Naftali answered, "To ask me that question daily so that I do not forget."

HASIDIC STORY[89]

For Whom do we work? On one level, we can each answer that question by giving a straightforward answer—naming our supervisor or leader or board of directors, or the president of the organization where we work. Those of us who are self-employed may respond by saying we work for ourselves. How many of us, though, would respond by saying we work for God? For indeed, the moral of the story above does not refer to our everyday work. Rather, the rabbi asks to hear the question "For whom do you work?" daily because he wants to be reminded that he is in the service of God. Even as a rabbi, he realizes that he can forget this basic fact, so he seeks to hire the guard to be his daily reminder. Such a reminder may be more important and more necessary for those whose jobs do not seem to permit them such frequent spiritual reflection. But we are all in God's service, not just those of us who are rabbis. Can you think of a reminder of this central truth that will work for you tomorrow? It might just change how you perceive the work you take on in the world.   LF

Divine Thunder

26 MAY

Who can understand the thunder of God's mighty deeds?
JOB 26:14

In the midst of his pain, the biblical Job wondered what had happened to him. He and members of his family seemed to suffer without cause. As a result, Job has become the Western paradigm for unexplained suffering. Yet Job responded to his situation without giving in to his despair. Instead, he pondered aloud as many of us do: "Who can understand the thunder of God's mighty deeds?" Job understood that even God's simple acts were mighty and thunderous. His question implied a profound understanding of God's interaction with the world. As hard as we try to do so, we just don't understand much of what God does. Nor, as humans, are we fully able to do so.

I once heard Teddy Kollek, former mayor of Jerusalem, quip that Westerners have to learn what Israelis have learned: Not everything can be solved or resolved—particularly not with money. "Sometimes we just have to learn to live with our problems." This is particularly true when it comes to God. Learning to live means entering into a covenant with the Almighty and thereby developing a relationship with the Divine.   KO

The Light That Dwells in Darkness

27 MAY

Let us walk in the light of God.
ISAIAH 2:5

The fear that arises in the darkness seems to be deeply ingrained in human consciousness, there from the beginning of time. We comfort our little ones with little night-lights—that are often adorned with cartoon characters to make them feel even more comfortable. My son, as his big sister before him, pulls the covers all the way over his head to fall asleep. The fear of the night, the fear of the enveloping dark, is too great. Who knows what fright inhabits the dark? Our children know! They give their fears names: witches, ghosts, monsters, bigger children, parents. Most of the time, they grow out of their childhood fears. No monsters under the bed tonight. Yet as we grow older, strangely, we might find ourselves afraid again. We, too, know what hides in the cold darkness. There is death there. There is the pathetic vulnerability of life there. There is uncertainly there. There is the icy cold of our life's meaninglessness there. If we are at all self-conscious, how can we not be terrified?

In the nighttime of your soul do you call upon God for help? Many no longer believe. After all, it is all irrational, superstitious. Or, perhaps, in the dark you feel alone, like the child, waiting for comfort to come. God, you think, has long since abandoned you. God is nowhere to be found, and certainly not in the dark. Or, perhaps like Adam, you think that you are unworthy, that because of some unspeakable sin God has turned away from you, that God could not care about you, not you.

Fear and loneliness are children of the night. But so is faith, and God, though it may not seem so, is intimately tied to the night. As Rabbi David Wolpe writes: "In the greatest dark, the dark of Egypt, redemption occurs. In the ultimate night, that of the future, redemption is promised. God moves between the poles of night, danger and promise." In our own darkness, in our own fears and pains, is the place to seek for the God who waits within. Freed from the burden of light, we see inside.   RABBI LAVEY DERBY

154 · RESTFUL REFLECTIONS

Drawing Aside the Curtains
28 MAY

*When the young Rabbi Eleazar of Knoznitz was a guest in the
house of Rabbi Naftali he once cast a glance at the window
where the curtains had been drawn. When his host asked him
why, he said, "If you want people to look in, then why the
curtains? And if you do not want them to, then why the
window?" "And what explanation have you found for this?"
asked Rabbi Naftali. "When you want someone you love to
look in," said the young rabbi, "you draw aside the curtain."*

HASIDIC STORY[90]

Each of us has entrances into our soul that are at times accessible and at other times less so. We need these doorways and windows because, otherwise, the potential for living rich spiritual lives would be contained in a vacuum, accessible only to ourselves. And our spiritual lives thrive when we experience the holy with others, sharing with them our reflections, our hopes, and even our doubts. Yet we make choices about with whom we share the deepest spiritual parts of ourselves.

Learning when "to drawn aside the curtains" is not about whom to let in. Instead, it is about making sure that the strictly rational does not get in our way, so that the spiritual can come through. This is particularly important in the evening hours when thoughts from our day clamor for attention. Set them aside so that the spiritual moments of our day can take hold and we can rest more calmly.   LF

Torah Light
29 MAY

Those who study Torah give light wherever they are.
MIDRASH[91]

This is a simple statement about the incredible power inherent in Torah. Many people read this text from the Midrash and think the Rabbis were making a statement about their colleagues, or even themselves. After all, those of us who study Torah regularly do feel strongly about it—as we should. But it is the light of Torah that draws us to it. And it is the light of Torah that transcends its students and shines beyond them. The Rabbis wrote from their own experience, emphasizing how the light of Torah provides illumination for anyone who comes to study its sacred writ. Moreover, those who study Torah carry its light with them, for it blazes a path in the darkness for those who carry its torch even as it provides light for others.

It is an easy approach to driving out the darkness in the soul. Study the text of Torah and light up the world.   KO

Secure Nights
30 MAY

When my cares are many, . . . Your comfort delights my soul.
PSALM 94:19

When I was a child, my mother taught me to say the *Shema* at night before I went to bed. When she sang it to me, it was an extraordinary moment of closeness, unfettered by any of the day's frustrations or difficulties. That evening ritual touched my heart so that for years, even as a teenager, I said *Shema* to myself each night. Each time I said it, it evoked the memory of a mother caressing her child to sleep, which continued to be a comfort to me at times of adolescent anger and disappointment. I still say it most every night.

At some level, all forms of prayer express a longing for the closeness that many of us felt as children. While we pray as a means of connecting to God, we also long for a closeness to one another as well. When we read, pray, and sing together, we realize that we are not alone, that we matter to more than just ourselves.

As technology increasingly isolates us from one another, it is natural that we would seek connection through the coming together in prayer. No image on the World Wide Web can replace the picture of a community of individual souls coming together in prayer. No click of a mouse can ever replace the touch of another's hand or the brush of a kiss as we greet each other. So extend a hand to the other and you may find one reaching out to you. To touch is to be touched in return.

RABBI JAMES A. GIBSON

Protecting Us from Bad Neighbors
31 MAY

May it be Your will, Lord my God, to protect me this day and every day from insolence in others and from arrogance in myself. Save me from vicious people, from bad neighbors, and from corrupt companions. Preserve me from misfortune and from powers of destruction. Save me from harsh judgments and spare me from ruthless opponents.

LITURGY[92]

The traditional prayer book, called the *siddur* in Hebrew, is filled with many surprises. Many of us may be familiar with the central prayers, such as the *Shema* or the *Amidah*. Here, though, is an example of a daily meditation that is said in a section of the morning service that is little known. I imagine that if we could make it a practice to say this each day, we could instill within ourselves a new consciousness toward how we treat others. When we realize our own vulnerabilities, then it becomes less difficult for us to acknowledge that everyone is vulnerable in one way or another. It comes with being human. We turn to God to guide us and to keep us from making decisions that will play on our vulnerabilities. That is why we ask for the strength and wisdom to stay away from people who can cause us harm. Whom we spend time with does matter, for we tend to share similar attitudes and perspectives with those we "hang with." So we ask God to help us discern when we find ourselves in "bad company," so to say. We also ask God to help us keep our own arrogance within bounds. For if we are too arrogant, we can drive others away and end up isolated and cut off from those whom we so desperately need. Try saying this each day—you can even alter it slightly to recite at night—and see if a new dimension develops in your life.   LF

JUNE

Judgment
1 JUNE

*God judges us not according to what we start
with but what we end with.*

RABBI LEVI MEIER[93]

Although my attention is usually focused on God's judgments more intensely in the fall as we approach the observance of Yom Kippur than it is at the beginning of the summer, God's observance of my behavior is something that is constantly on my mind. I am always conscious of it even as I struggle with what it means to be judged and evaluated by the Holy One of Blessing. This idea helps me to form a standard for my interactions with people, as it provides a means for me to reflect on things that I have done. The process of reflection is indispensable. As I review each day at its end, I admit to myself where I went wrong and how I might change for the future. This daily practice of *cheshbon hanefesh,* introspection and self-assessment, helps me to grow. Here Rabbi Meier's guidance really helps. He continues, "God judges us on the basis of how deeply we struggle with the challenges that have been set before us. And only God knows and understands the depths of the struggles of each human being, the secret recesses of the heart which no human being can judge."[94]

We all err and make mistakes. It is part of being human. But the process of growth can be described as part of the process of *becoming* human. Our goal—and God's evaluation of it—is where we end in the process, rather than where we began.   KO

Giving What Is Needed
2 JUNE

Nurturing involves learning that what one gives must suit the recipient's need rather than one's emotional need to give.
TZIPPORAH HELLER[95]

Our motivation for giving is more complex than we often acknowledge. We give to receive love, respect, and honor as well as to be of service and meet real needs. In our personal relationships we run into trouble when we give someone what we think they want when, in fact, we are giving what we want. We can pause to ask ourselves, "On whose terms am I giving this gift?" When our own desires and emotional needs become entangled in the act of giving, we are headed for a collision. We have each probably given our friend or spouse or child a gift we thought they would love only to receive a disappointing response. When we give, it is always wise to try to put aside our desires and listen deeply to what the other person needs. This is also true in our commitment to give *tzedakah*. For many of us this may be a central way we connect with the larger Jewish community. We may be involved in raising funds for important organizations and causes. In this arena, too, it is wise to give pause in order to identify the real hurts, pains, and needs and try to alleviate them even when they may not always resonate with us personally. If we can discipline ourselves in these ways, we will truly be giving in a fully selfless, respectful, and nurturing manner.   LF

The Privilege of Learning and Doing

3 JUNE

Your laws are a source of strength to me wherever I dwell.

PSALM 119:54

I once knew a man who wanted to make Shavuot a national holiday throughout the United States. Not a bad idea! This holiday celebrates the giving of the (Ten) Commandments, the basic document of civilization itself, the foundation text of humanity, as such. It offers us the world's first glimpse of what it means to be obedient to that duty, what could be otherwise assigned to practical reason.

But for Jewish people, it means even more than that, more than brute ethics and simple (if also far-reaching) obligation. It represents God's reaching down to us and favoring us with Love that binds, with commandments that prove how profoundly we are loved.

Shavuot is also the time to celebrate the Confirmation of our youth, when we bring our best young people to the altar to mark their introduction, as a group, into the life and Torah of Israel. It is a solemn moment but a very joyful one. It brings back our own youth and our own memories.

May this Shavuot be a true festival of joy in which we express our gratitude for all that we have been given and, most of all, for the privilege of learning and doing that Torah which is symbolized and renewed by Shavuot.

RABBI ARNOLD JACOB WOLF

Searching for Love

4 JUNE

In the night
From the place where I reclined
I have sought the one I love.
I sought, but I found not!
I shall arise now and go around the city,
In the streets and in the squares,
To seek the one I love.
I sought, but I found not!

SONG OF SONGS 3:1–2

According to the liturgical calendar of the synagogue, the Song of Songs—what clearer statement of personal feelings?—is read during the holiday of Shavuot. While it is a poem about human love, the rabbis have taken it as an allegory for the love between God and the people of Israel. While that may be a stretch, the love expressed by one person for another should mirror God's love for the people.

Many people particularly resonate with this section of the poem. It reflects the yearning for love that goes unfulfilled, something we all experience during our life. We may try to fill this empty space in many ways—through obsession with our appearance, unhealthy relationships, and destructive habits. So we go to sleep at night, momentarily fulfilled, and then awaken in the morning recognizing that we have become even more malnourished.

So what do we do? We continue the journey, richer in understanding and buoyed by the love of God, which transcends the loneliness of the night and alienation of the day that precedes it. KO

Pursuing Peace

5 JUNE

*We should think how far we would travel in order to see
our sons or daughters when we want to see them,
or the lengths we would go in order to see our loved one.
Then we may realize how much more we should pursue
peace within our actual ability to do so.*

SEFER HASIDIM, 954

Many of us travel great distances to see our children and grandchildren. Since so many families no longer live in close proximity to one another, travel has become routine. We zealously collect frequent flyer miles, often to visit dear relatives. And if we have a beloved who lives far away, we know intimately the beck and call of the plane or train schedule that bridges the geographic distance that separates us. We all know of examples when we exert much effort and go to great lengths.

So, too, we are taught that we need to extend ourselves when it comes to pursuing peace. Interestingly, the Hebrew verb "to pursue" is most often used when it comes to securing peace. There is an understanding that peace does not come easily: Effort and exertion are needed. But how many of us do go out of our way to heal broken relationships or discordant community relations? How many do what we can to pressure our lawmakers to establish peace between warring nations? Let us commit ourselves to pursuing peace "within our actual ability to do so"—in our homes and communities and among our neighbors.   LF

A Home Run

6 JUNE

*In the direction one follows in this world will
one be led in the world of eternity.*
ZOHAR I, 100A

I hit a home run once. The excitement of the race between Mark McGwire and Sammy Sosa paled in comparison with my own moment of triumph. I think I was about twelve years old at the time. During that summer, I took part in a public-school-sponsored woodworking and sports program. We would build shelves and model sailboats for an hour or two each morning and then troop from the shop to the ball field for a choose-up-sides baseball game. The diamond was painted on a huge (as I recall from my perspective as a young boy) blacktop playing field, so there were lots of scraped knees every day.

Though I was a pretty good shortstop, my value in the batting lineup was minimal. I couldn't hit worth a darn. That's why that one shot stands out as if it happened yesterday.

I walked up to the plate carrying a relatively small, worn, light bat that I always used. The bases were loaded, end of the last inning, our team behind. And yes, on the first pitch I hit my home run.

Now I must be clear that the ball did not go over any fence, wall, or other barrier demarcating the field. In fact, it never got off the ground. It was only a grounder, but it went between the pitcher's feet and the second baseman's legs, and the center fielder fell down trying to get to it. So the ball rolled and rolled until it reached the gutter at the edge of the field and disappeared. Since no one had laid a glove on it, the hit was proclaimed a home run.

Because it was the end of the season, the coach let us choose bats to keep from the collection that had accumulated during the summer. The choosing order was based on performance that day, so I got first choice. I picked the best-looking, biggest, nicest, newest bat from the pile, clearly the most desirable. I was the envy of everyone.

For the rest of the summer I proudly used that bat in all the games I could find to play in. But I never got a hit. The bat was too big and too heavy. With each strikeout, I longed for that smaller, chipped old Louisville Slugger that had fit me just fine.

I think of that old bat whenever I want something that doesn't quite match the person that I am. It's a good remembrance at times of "overreaching." As we begin the summer, may this be a time for all of us in which we discover joy in the things best known to us.   RABBI JEROME K. DAVIDSON

The Age of Wisdom

7 JUNE

With age comes wisdom, and length of
days brings understanding.

JOB 12:12

This is the day that Jerusalem was united in the year 1967. It was a triumphant day in the midst of the Six Day War, where Israel's survival was constantly threatened. Today many of us take Israel for granted. As we grow older, we remember that day very differently than when we experienced it firsthand.

It is amazing that as we get older, our parents get smarter. Or, at least, that's how it seems. Maybe as we gain understanding, we become aware of the wisdom that our parents and those of a previous generation have gained and attempt to impart to us. In some cases, they want to give us the benefit of their experience so that we do not have to encounter the same difficulties they did. However, each generation seems to have to learn on its own.

Time changes our perspective on most things. But age alone does not bring wisdom, nor do life's experiences necessarily bring understanding along with them.

By apprising us of his story, Job wanted to advise us to take note of the import of each day, or what he calls "the length of days." In doing so, we have the potential to gain understanding from each day that draws to a close. After suffering terrible loss, Job came to understand that we must value each day—something that many of us do not come to understand until we have faced major trauma in our lives. If we simply allow time to pass by, then we pass by along with it. As a result, we will be unable to gain wisdom.

Grow older and grow wiser. And just grow.   KO

Full Rights

8 June

Not toleration, but the unrestricted exercise of all their rights shall be demanded for your coreligionists.

COUNT BERNARD ERNST VON BÜLOW[96]

On this day in 1815, Napoleon was defeated at Waterloo. For many of us, this may be an incidental footnote in history. What does this have to do with us today? Let us remember that an immediate consequence of Napoleon's defeat was the diminishment of the increased rights that Jews had obtained under his rule. We forget that less than two hundred years ago the question of granting Jews citizenship was *the* political question throughout Europe. Even as late as 1878 there was still heated debate over toleration versus full citizenship. Today we take our political status as full citizens for granted.

Yet our ancestors would be shocked to see the extent to which we are integrated into American society. In thinking about this tonight, we should express our thanks to God—but then, tomorrow, we must exercise our right to be different and stand out from among the crowd. In doing so, we will go a long way toward knowing why God placed us here and now to do our work—and not at Waterloo.   LF

Up All Night
9 JUNE

When I pass by someone in the street, I'll try always to give them something, even if it's only a little; and I'll trust that giving will be good for me too; and each year at this time I'll try to renew that decision.

NIGEL SAVAGE

It is only about fifteen years since I went to my first *tikkun leil Shavuot*. I was a graduate student and the theme for the evening was *tzedakah*, a theme that always seems to make its way through the Jewish community, particularly during holidays. People usually translate *tzedakah* as "charity," but it is rooted in the Hebrew word for "justice," for doing that which is right. *Tikkun leil* is an old tradition, which has been enjoying a rebirth, of staying up all night and learning Torah before the morning of Shavuot, the festival which celebrates the giving of the Torah—and our receiving it.

As the night wore on, and as I began to tire, my mind began to wander. I found myself thinking about all the people in the neighborhood who were up all night because they were homeless, who did not have the opportunity to luxuriate in an all-night study of Torah, though many of them may have been among those who received it according to the way we understand the text.

Since then, I don't pass people by without giving them something. Advice, guidance, some food, information, a little Torah—but always money. Maybe I have not helped that much, but here's my thinking: I've helped a little. I feel a little better, and I am more comfortable engaging the people I encounter on the street. And I rest easier, hoping that I will not be up all night worrying, on another night. NIGEL SAVAGE

True Friendship

10 JUNE

Honor thy friends, for thou art an accumulation of them.
E. M. BRONER[97]

Many of us recognize that we are indebted to those who came before us—parents, grandparents, great-grandparents—and are a summary of many of their attributes and values. Some of us even share our names with these relatives as a way of keeping their memory alive among family members. However, few of us think this way when it comes to friends and acquaintances. How can who we are and what we have become be dependent on others who are not related to us? Unlike our relationships with the family into which we are born, we choose our friends, those with whom we want to spend leisure time. We learn a great deal about who we are and what we have the potential to become through our interactions with friends. After all, who will tell us more honestly the impact of what we have said or done? Family members want to love and support us and are generally reticent to offer such criticism. Often the very love that draws us together prevents them from being able to help us in that way. However, Jewish tradition admonishes friends to offer *tokhecha,* rebuke, when necessary. It is a requirement of friendship. In turn, we must thank them for their *tokhecha*—

as difficult as it may be to do so—and then, as E. M. Broner suggests, give them honor. Or, to take a cue from a contemporary truism, "we only take compliments from an enemy and criticisms from a friend." KO

Separating Good from Evil

11 JUNE

All of history is a sphere where good is mixed with evil. The supreme task of man, his share in redeeming the world of creation, consists of separating good from evil and evil from good.

RABBI ABRAHAM JOSHUA HESCHEL[98]

On the surface, this can sound so easy: Just separate the good from the bad—what's so hard about that? Yet we know that distinguishing the good from the bad and the bad from the good can be filled with complications. The ethical situations that we face are rarely clear-cut. Life is just not a black-and-white movie. It is filled with inconsistencies and the many shades of gray that often make the ethical path cluttered with unforeseen obstacles. Nevertheless, it is still our supreme task, as Heschel suggests, to do this moral work, and thereby redeem the world, even if we attend to only one small corner. We cannot sidestep the hard issues because they are too complicated or complex. Rather, we must do our best to discern just how evil finds its way into the good. We must call it by its name and uproot it from our midst. We can do it by ourselves, but we cannot do it alone. We gain the strength necessary through our relationship with the Divine. By joining forces with the Holy One of Blessing, we can do holy work in the world, starting tonight, and continuing in the morning. LF

Negotiating with God
12 JUNE

*[The sacred text says:] Love God and serve God with all
your heart and soul (Deuteronomy 11:13). But what
is the service of the heart? It is prayer.*

TALMUD[99]

When troubles hit or we want something badly, whether or
not we believe in the existence of God, most of us find ourselves in a plea-bargaining mode.

If the initial request doesn't pan out, we often go back to
the negotiating table with a new deal. "Okay, I'll retake the
chem exam, but let me pass this time and I'll promise to go to
the synagogue every week," the student says. "Okay," the
mother says. "I'll get through the surgery, but let the lymph
nodes be clear, and I promise not to ask for another thing."

We plead and bargain, yet we often believe we've had no
response or that the response is "No."

But is it? The response may not be direct or easily discernible, but if we examine the arguing, bargaining, and dis-
cussing, we may find the answers we seek are there for the
taking. For in the process itself we begin to clarify our
thoughts and cope with our fears and uncertainties.

Few of us can maintain indefinitely all the perspectives
acquired in moments of crisis or stress. But as we negotiate
with God, we do gain some powerful personal insights that
don't necessarily leave us. We learn to know ourselves,
understand our values, and eventually find ways to handle
the realities, difficult as they may be.

Often when we think the response to our request is "No,"
it really is "Yes." We have only to recognize it.

Here's hoping that this makes you rest a little easier tonight.

FRANCINE KLAGSBRUN[100]

Memory

13 JUNE

Remembrance—both our own and God's—is a divine gift.

RABBI DEBRA ORENSTEIN[101]

There are some things, like where we parked the car, that we remember for just a little while. Then the memory is gone and we are usually unable to recapture it, but we generally have no need or desire to do so. This is often referred to as flash memory. We do not fully appreciate its importance until it diminishes somewhat and we hear ourselves or others saying, "Where did I put my car keys?" or "Where did I leave my purse?" or "Have you seen my briefcase?" Sometimes we attribute its diminution to age. Often it is a result of distraction. We are trying to do too many things at one time, what computer science has termed multitasking, so one message to our brain eclipses another. These are all aspects of our "flash memory," indispensable to daily living.

But what we like to call Memory, intentionally distinguished with a capital M, is different altogether. Unlike history, which is the recording of events over time that are then interpreted by the recorder or historian, this kind of Memory forms an essential core part of our being. From the time we are born, memory helps to shape our character and our personality. And accumulated Jewish memory shapes our identity as Jews, even as we add to it through the experience of our own lives.

We remember our past. We ask God to remember it as well, so that we can together march into the future.   KO

Seeking Balance
14 JUNE

This is how our good inclinations should rule over our character traits. We need to learn how to be proud and not proud; how to be angry and not be angry; how to speak and how to remain quiet; how to be quiet and when to speak.

RABBI DOV BAER OF MEZERITCH[102]

When we think of our character traits we realize that we each have good traits along with some other ones that may trip us up and get in our way. Perhaps we think it is a spiritually worthy goal to completely obliterate these problematic characteristics. But no. What we seek is not to completely eradicate them but to know when these traits become our strengths. There are times when we need to be proud, to get angry, to speak out. Tradition teaches that these qualities should not dominate, though; we also need to learn when to have humility, contain our anger, and be quiet. It is a balance that we seek. Consider for a moment which traits you need to temper. What would it mean for you to rein in these traits and gain balance in this realm of your life?   LF

The Essential Commandments
15 JUNE

The commandments were given to purify humanity.

MIDRASH[103]

Rabbi Lawrence Kushner tells of the time he brought a nursery school class into the synagogue sanctuary for a tour. He showed them the *bima,* the *ner tamid,* the cantor's and rabbi's lecterns. Finally, the tiny kids stood before the huge doors of the holy ark.

"What do you suppose is in there?" he asked them.

"Nothing!" one child answered. "It's empty."

"A new car!" another shouted.

"An old, old Torah!" responded another.

"I know! I know!" one child insisted. "It's a mirror!"

Each of the kids was right. For Jews distant and disconnected from Judaism, the first child was right: The ark is empty. Judaism is alien and barren of meaning and substance.

For others, Judaism holds only a superficial, aesthetic appeal. It's all bar mitzvah parties, bagels and lox on Sunday morning, and what we'll be wearing to Yom Kippur services this year. Religion as cultural entertainment—a warm, ethnic sentimentality without ethical or spiritual demands.

But for those who are prepared to look deeply and imaginatively, the ark contains a mirror, reflecting the truth about ourselves, our values, our accomplishments, and our limitations.

During the season of Shavuot, we celebrate receiving the gift of Torah, the mirror of our souls. It is ours, but only if we are brave enough to look deeply and honestly within.

After a good night's sleep, try listening to God's voice with a different ear, then try looking inside for yourself.

RABBI EDWARD FEINSTEIN

Heavenly Hospitality

16 JUNE

Hospitality is even more important than encountering the Shekhinah, God's intimate presence.

TALMUD[104]

At various times of the year, mostly during holiday periods, hospitality is woven into the fabric of Jewish life. On some occasions, such as Sukkot in the fall, we even invite ancestral guests to join us in the sukkah in a mystical, metaphysical sort of way. We call this practice *ushpizin*. And each Shabbat, it is not unusual for newcomers to the synagogue to receive invitations for lunch in various households in the community. Even the original practice of saying kiddush over wine in the synagogue on Friday evenings for the Sabbath—even when it was said at home—evolved as a way of synagogues extending themselves to travelers who may have been staying overnight at the synagogue. In nearly all other cases, any recitation of prayers a second time was discouraged or even prohibited.

I once encountered the staff of a local conference center who went so much out of their way for guests that they called it aggressive hospitality. Perhaps this philosophy is what we should champion in contemporary Jewish life. Many of my friends set their Sabbath and holiday tables with extra place settings before they leave for the synagogue, because they intend to meet guests in the synagogue and invite them home for a meal and a little local hospitality. We might call it aggressive Shabbat and holiday hospitality. As tired as we are from a week of work, there is something renewing about inviting guests to enjoy Shabbat with our family. And when we do, we indeed feel God's presence in our midst.   KO

Vacations and Holiness

17 June

Entrances to holiness are everywhere.
The possibility of ascent is all the time.
Even at unlikely times and through unlikely places
There is no place on earth without the presence of God.

MIDRASH[105]

During the summer we find time to go away, experience new vistas, and refresh our perspectives. We may think of vacations as a chance to get away from our responsibilities and the day-in, day-out pressures that make up our lives. Some of us may even use our vacations to take a break from our spiritual path. Okay, 351 days of the year, we may figure, we can pursue a disciplined spirituality, but for 14 days a year, we need a break from this, too! But no. Vacations are a prime time to reconnect with our inner selves and our spiritual path. A change of venue helps us to reassess our priorities. We may have a renewed clarity of mind while we hike a mountain, whitewater down a rapid, or walk down the streets of a foreign city. Since doors and passage to the Holy One might open at any time, let us use this time to become more aware of our spiritual nature. Let us use our time away to open ourselves to holy experiences even as we pursue fun, relaxation, and adventure. Whether you find yourself watching a sunset from a mountain's height or exploring the ocean's bottom, experience the awe as a passage to your soul—as an entrance to holiness.   LF

To Dance and to Sing

18 JUNE

I call out to You, Adonai, and to You, Adonai, I plead. . . .
Change my mourning into dancing.

PSALM 30:9, 12

This psalm text takes on an additional level of meaning each time I encounter the death of another. Though the death diminishes me, the psalm replenishes my spirit while it helps to bring me calm before resting at night. Since I first recited this psalm during my teen years, the passing of each additional soul from this life into the next fills me with anxious grief. "I call out to You, Adonai, and to You, Adonai, I plead." How could I keep silent now? What is the true depth of my grief and anguish? Do I hurt just for me? For You? For him?

For her? "Help"—my soul cries out, as the words emerge uncontrollably from my lips. Just this one word, "help"—because I don't even know how else to respond, what kind of specific assistance to ask for. Please God, just listen to my cry. Hear me and be kind to me. Respond. React. I plead with you to "change my mourning into dancing" and let me once again experience joy. And then I can put my head to rest this evening, knowing that "joy will come in the mourning."

Maybe I can't find joy right now, today, as the sadness continues to make its way through my soul. But perhaps by starting today, I will gain the strength to continue tomorrow. Maybe by just repeating these words, I will find the inner resources to continue to sing Your praise, as I long to do.

STUART KELMAN

Neighborly Love

19 JUNE

You should love your neighbor as much as yourself, because you were strangers in the land of Egypt.

LEVITICUS 19:34B

We have heard the instruction contained in the first part of this verse from Leviticus. We know that we have to welcome strangers, reach out a helping hand to newcomers, and extend ourselves to neighbors. But why does the Torah join our experience in Egypt to this directive? Is it because of the way we were treated in Egypt that we should treat others more kindly?

Very little of the Torah actually talks about our experience in Egypt, except that we were slaves and that God brought us out under Moses' leadership. And with the exception of the heroism of Shifrah and Puah, two midwives assigned to assist in delivering Israelite babies who refused to destroy male children as they were told to do, we know little about the interaction of our brethren with the native Egyptian people. Perhaps if the Egyptian people had treated the Israelites differently, Pharaoh would have done so as well.

Love yourself. Then love your neighbor. Then remember how it felt to leave the narrow places of Egypt for the wide expanse of the desert, so that you can love your neighbor a little more, as much as you should love yourself.   KO

The Power of Naming

20 JUNE

People's names fall into four classifications. Some have fair names but have done foul deeds; others have ugly names but have done good deeds; some have ugly names to which their deeds correspond; and others have the good deeds to match their lovely names.

MIDRASH[106]

As the midrash above suggests, we have to look beyond a person's given name to discern the person's true character. However, names do have spiritual significance in Jewish tradition. In choosing a name for our daughter or son, we bring this newborn into relationship with the Jewish people for the first time. It is a tradition to name a child after a relative who has passed away. We do so with the hope that that person's memory will live on through this new life. We say *zichrono l'vrachah,* which means "May the name be for a blessing," but it is much more than just the name that we hope will be carried on from one generation to the next. It is the person's good deeds and values and the name he or she made during the years the namesake was alive. We hope that the new child will continue on with these, and also become one more link in the chain of tradition that holds together our personal families and the Jewish people as a whole.

On the first day of summer, as many of us take to the beach and leave our footprints in the sand, we should remember that what is of importance is the name we create for ourselves and the spiritual connections we express by continuing in the footprints of our ancestors.   LF

The Gift of Boredom
21 JUNE

Desire fulfilled is a tree of life.
PROVERBS 13:12

The more aware we become, the more prone we are to stumble on the obstacle of boredom and restlessness. Boredom is the place where we begin to hate the sameness in our lives. It is that place where we feel that consciousness has been chewed on by someone else and then put before us. Everything becomes tasteless. Nothing satisfies.

Restlessness arises from that boredom. A *yetzer*—an impulse—develops to push us away from what we find is so boring. We want to run to some new experience, some new relationship, some new perception of how we should be. Then, for an instant, it seems like the boredom has disappeared. But in truth, the boredom has not disappeared. It is like the table that is very dusty. You can wipe away the dust, but the table, the place where the dust collects, remains unchanged. The truth is that our constant chasing after what is new does not change the place within us where the dissatisfaction arises.

There are basically two ways to deal with our boredom. The first is to shut down our minds. It is to turn away from the anger and pain we are wrestling with. It is to change our jobs, where we live, our relationships with lovers and friends. Sometimes that is indeed what we need to do. But the danger is that we can shut down for too long and begin to live in the memory of those moments when we were truly alive. We forget that the miracle we once cherished is still possible in every second, in every minute, in every hour—if only we go to the source of our satisfaction.

The Torah path prefers that we take a second approach to dealing with boredom and restlessness. The Torah encourages us to personalize our daily experiences. Each moment can be incredible. Each moment even of washing dishes or of fighting gridlock traffic can be a new opportunity for greater passion in our lives. To this kind of mind, even watching grass grow is exciting.

The deepest heart yearns for that alive state. The mind is dynamic. If we experience boredom, that is an opportunity for a renewed awareness of what the Torah tells us: that every day, every moment, we may be made new.

Avram Davis

Long Life
22 June

For keeping God's commandments, statutes, and ordinances, one's days are prolonged.

Deuteronomy 6:2

People have been searching for the key to long life since the beginning of human creation. Part of North American lore includes the travels of the explorer Ponce de Leon, who "found" the fountain of youth near Saint Augustine, Florida. Perhaps that is the reason so many of our relatives have moved south as they have gotten older! A traditional reading of the story of Adam and Eve in the Garden suggests that they were given immortality and could live forever in Eden, but when they decided to taste the forbidden fruit, things changed. They may have gained knowledge of good and evil, but they got mortality along with it. As a result, they were thrown out of paradise.

In the Torah, in the verse cited here from Deuteronomy, we learn that God did not take away everything from Adam and Eve when they were thrown out of the Garden. Even though it was not the immortality that they originally enjoyed, God gave them the opportunity for long life. And the only thing that they—and we—have to do is keep "God's commandments, statutes, and ordinances." As a result, we may not always achieve long life, but we will gain immortality through proper living. Seems like a pretty good deal to me.

KO

Gifts from the Home

23 JUNE

Be happy with the gifts that come from your home.
TALMUD[107]

Sometimes we can't see the gifts that are closest to us. Our gaze wanders and we look far afield, missing what is standing before our very eyes. Intimacy breeds not only love and familiarity but also, at times, a sense of blindness. In the worst case, we become contemptuous and ungrateful. Since families are forever, we can easily take them for granted; it takes skill and wisdom to be able to see the gifts those closest to us give us in both big and small ways. While we probably spend much time caring for our children, they also give us gifts of love, smiles, awe, and wonder. Our spouses, with whom we are partners and soul mates, also give us gifts when they support us in our work or share with us our—and their—dreams and hopes for the future. When was the last time you stopped to show gratitude to your children and spouse? Tonight, stop and open your eyes to that which is near at hand. Take a moment to reflect on all the wonderful gifts that our family members give us through both their words and their actions. In a multitude of ways our families hold together our world. They are our lifeline. And their presence enriches our lives with their smiles, hugs, and loving glances. Let our eyes not stray but rather let us truly see the gifts that emanate from our homes.   LF

A Blessing

24 June

Blessed are You, Adonai our God, Sovereign of the Universe . . .
Liturgy[108]

A blessing, a *berakhah,* is an invitation to see the world from God's perspective. *Berakhot,* blessings, transform ordinary moments into significant happenings. *Berakhot* interpret our experiences and uncover the deeper dimensions of our actions. *Berakhot* are antidotes to boredom. They infuse surprise into the mundane, provoke us to think, thank, take notice, and exclaim. *Berakhot* keep us alert to the richness of even the most daily activities—eating, washing, seeing a sunset, smelling a spice—and transform them into opportunities to experience meaning and transcendence. *Berakhot* are reminders that there are no neutral human activities. Everything we do has cosmic significance, moving us either closer to or further from the Jewish dream of a perfect world.

    Berakhot are not words we have to say but openings to shape, name, and define what we are doing in a different light. Too often, *berakhot* have been disconnected from the very experiences they were intended to shape. *Berakhot* such as those at the beginning of *Shacharit* (morning worship service) that speak of opening our eyes, wiping sleep from them, standing up, stretching our backs, getting dressed, and feeling strengthened from a night's sleep ought not to be recited from the siddur. Rather, we should reconnect them to the actions as we do them. In doing so, our morning routines can become a divine-human drama.

The *berakhah* reorients us to see that the really "real" religious activity does not lie in reciting the *berakhah* but in engaging in the activity in the world. At the beginning of the twenty-first century, *berakhot* extend the boundaries of the sacred, ritualize a love of life, and challenge us to build as it has never been done before. The *berakhah* connects us to the Divine at a time when we need it most, though our success would seem to indicate that we need it least. For the *berakhah* is our pathway to the Divine. Say one now, before you sleep. You will sleep more soundly and be able to build your world more securely in the morning.

RABBI IRWIN KULA[109]

Leaping Forward in Faith
25 JUNE

*A Jew is asked to take a leap of action
rather than a leap of thought.*

RABBI ABRAHAM JOSHUA HESCHEL[110]

As hard as it may seem when we are in school, taking a qualifying exam for something, or even trying to figure out the solution to a problem in our work, thinking is a relatively easy process. It is the doing that is so hard. For Rabbi Heschel, doing animates the thought and gives it meaning. He argues that the Jew "is asked to surpass his needs, to do more than he understands in order to understand more than he does. In carrying out the word of the Torah he is ushered into the presence of spiritual meaning. Through the ecstasy of deeds he learns to be certain of the hereness of God. Right living is a way to right thinking." Heschel did not just "talk the talk," as the colloquialism puts it, he also "walked the walk" as he joined civil rights leaders like Martin Luther King Jr. as they marched arm in arm in southern cities in the 1960s to protest the treatment of African Americans.

One of the early-morning blessings that we are instructed to say has to do with the study of Torah. Following the familiar, traditional formula for blessing—which is really a vehicle for entering into dialogue with the Divine *(Barukh ata Adonai, Elohenu Melekh ha-olam asher kidshanu b'mitzvotav vitzivanu . . .)*—the text continues *"la-asok b'divre Torah,"* which is usually translated as "to study the words of Torah." A closer read reveals more specific instruction: "to busy ourselves with the words *and* works of Torah." This is what Rabbi Heschel taught: the words and works of Torah cannot be separated from one another. They are instructions from the same Source. It is our responsibility to join the teachings of Torah by making sure that what we say is joined together and substantiated by what we do.   KO

The Point of Judaism

26 JUNE

The essence of Jewish spiritual practice is living out our highest ethical ideals. The point is not to win a game or even win a case: the point is to be a more compassionate and loving human being, the point is to be more present to the divine light in every moment of creation, the point is to be kinder and more honest with oneself and others.

RABBI SHEILA PELTZ WEINBERG[111]

In our work lives we may be motivated by a "bottom line." How much we produce or how much we sell or how many new clients we engage may be the standard by which we are judged. Evaluation is tied to hard numbers in many professions. Yet, as Jews we have another measure that guides our lives, a measure that does not have hard numbers attached to it. Compassion and kindness cannot be measured in hard and fast ways. If we can show compassion to one person and touch his or her heart in some way, we are batting 1000. It is not easy to simplify Judaism, or any religious ethical system for that matter, into one point. But when push comes to shove, Judaism's point is to be a more compassionate and loving human being. We may have forgotten this message over the years. If we can keep this in focus, then we will be able to sort out all the choices that stand before us. It is when we forget this simple truth that we become confused and have difficulty determining where to put our time, energy, and resources. Tomorrow let us strive to make compassion the centerpiece of living our lives as Jews.   LF

A Balance of Humility

27 JUNE

We do not need to think little of ourselves; we don't need to think of ourselves at all.

HASIDIC SAYING

In Jewish tradition, few character traits are as praised as humility, *anavah*, and a yielding, submissive spirit, *shiflut ruach*. Moses is described as "a very humble man, more so than any person on earth" (Numbers 12:3). Humility is not necessarily connected with self-abnegation or having a poor opinion of oneself. As the modern Jewish sage, the Chafetz Chaim, would ask rhetorically: "How poor an opinion of himself could Moses have had, given that, as giver of Torah, he knew the biblical verse 'Never again did there arise in Israel a prophet like Moses'?" (Deuteronomy 34:10).

Jewish tradition never underrates humility. The Talmud suggests that possessing a submissive character is equal in religious value to bringing every sacrificial offering at the time of the Temple.[112] To the rabbis, only one who is submissive and obedient oneself can serve as a judge over others.[113] However, the talmudic discussion in *Sanhedrin* (38a, b) makes clear, our sense of humility must be balanced by a sense that we are created in the divine image.

Apparently, we are to accept our talents and take full responsibility for their proper use. Wherein, then, lies humility? First, humility and a submissive spirit originate in a consciousness of divine greatness. Compared with the Holy One, what is even the greatest of human beings? Second, in contrast to arrogance, *anavah* and *shiflut ruach* represent a turning away from self-involvement and toward a concern for others and their welfare. In this sense, humility is summed up in the Hasidic dictum: We do not need to think little of ourselves; we don't need to think of ourselves as all.

RABBI TSVI BLANCHARD[114]

Searching for Truth

28 JUNE

The search for truth, about our world and ourselves, must be vigorously pursued. We must be as honest as we are resolute. And when our search is accompanied by faith and simplicity, we have no lingering doubts or paralyzing impasses—only joyous contentment.

RABBI NACHMAN OF BRESLOV[115]

Like other Hasidic rebbes of his generation, Rabbi Nachman believed in the passionate pursuit of truth. It must be unrelenting and all-consuming. And the quest must be undertaken with full disclosure: honestly and openly. This pursuit, and the passion that girds it, should fuel everything we do and should be manifest in a simple, burning faith in God. Not only will such a combination wipe away doubt and inertia, Nachman maintains, but it will also provide us with contentment that is marked by a sense of overwhelming joy. This is the very result for which many of us, the spiritual seekers of this generation, have been pining. If Rabbi Nachman's approach can bring us such ecstasy, what else could we ask for? But first we must sleep, and then, awakening with a replenished spirit, continue our pursuit in the morning.   KO

Affirmation
29 JUNE

*The human wishes to be confirmed in one's being human,
and wishes to have a presence in the being of the other. . . .
Secretly and bashfully the human watches for a "yes" which
allows oneself to be and which can come to oneself only
from one human person to another.*

MARTIN BUBER[116]

It's normal for us to seek affirmation from those around us. Most everyone does it. This behavior pattern usually begins while we are children. And our parents and teachers try to shape our behavior through such activity. As a result, we look for such affirmation from our parents, and then our teachers and our friends. It is one of the ways that we think we learn how to act ethically and morally. No matter how self-assured we may become, this search never completely abates, nor does the need for external guidance. But our desires are often misdirected, as we mistake the loving affirmation and direction of others as solely human acts. They are reflections of the holy, one of the many ways that God channels divine energy into the world. Thus, it is God from whom we really gain approval and seek confirmation for our actions. And it is the only approval that really counts.

As our faith matures—and even wanes at times—our relationship with God changes, as does our need for such constant and overt affirmation. As we offer guidance to another and seek it for ourselves, let us remember the real Source for all of our actions: the One that is ever affirming—who informs and affirms even while we are sleeping.   LF

On the Road to Perfection

30 JUNE

Shalom *is the name of the Holy One, the name of Israel, and the name of the Messiah.*

TALMUD[117]

The Hebrew word for peace, *shalom,* is derived from the root, *sh-l-m,* denoting wholeness or completeness, and its frame of reference throughout Jewish literature is bound up with the notion of *sheleimut,* perfection. Peace is commonly understood as the absence of war, or perhaps as tranquility. But the Jewish understanding of shalom is not so limited. Shalom is both a moral value and a divine attribute.

What can this teach us? What might it mean to us, "Israel," that we share a name with both God and the Messiah? Can we really retain this vision of peace, which lingers on the utopian, while living our deeply flawed lives in this nonmessianic world? The quote above tells us that we can. It seems to teach that we can be the conduit between God and the redemption of the world.

How? Perhaps we must realize that ultimate perfection is a series of smaller moments of completeness and wholeness.

We are on the road to perfection, *sheleimut,* when we nurture loving relationships in our homes, *shalom bayit.* We are on the road to perfection when we resemble the rabbinic portrayal of Aaron, being *rodfei shalom,* pursuers of peace, fostering greater understanding between people as expressed in how they talk to each other or how they treat each other. We are on the road to perfection when we use our strength and power to bring security to individuals and to entire communities. As we realize that there are things worth fighting for and risks worth taking, we emulate God, who can grant both strength, *oz,* and peace, shalom, in the same act.

In our flawed ways, and by incremental steps, we can perfect the world. We can bring the shalom that is so much more than the tranquility or absence of war. Thus, shalom is rightfully our name when our lives, and the peace we create, are the bridges between that peace that is God's name and that is the name of the Messiah.

RABBI BRAD HIRSCHFIELD[118]

JULY

Embracing Vulnerability

1 JULY

*A religious human being must be able to recognize his
vulnerability, must be able to allow himself moments of
surrender, must be able to affirm and to love God, despite
all. . . . Unless the new Jew can overcome the veneer of
toughness toward God that he has taken on as a healthy
defensive pose, he will have lost the only inner core that will
give meaning to his hard-fought struggle for survival.*

RABBI ARTHUR GREEN[119]

It is hard to think about the Jewish community today without
some mention of the Holocaust. Following that unparalleled
experience in human history, many Jews, of all backgrounds,
refused to acknowledge the presence of God in their lives.
They even removed all God language from their vocabulary.
As a result, an entire generation, whose legacy we inherited,
was left with little or no room in which to develop a relationship with the Holy One of Blessing. Vulnerability, the kind
that results from being victimized—and the refusal to be so
ever again—tends to make us less open: to others, to ourselves, and to the Divine. Spiritual practice has the inherent
potential to help us face our deepest fears and transport us to
realms where we more easily drop our everyday defenses—if
we are prepared to be open to such practices. To get to that

place, we have to be willing to open our hearts and allow ourselves to acknowledge and embrace the vulnerabilities that lie within. In this way we can surrender to a relationship with a loving God who will nurture our inner self. So when we open our eyes in the morning, perhaps we can be ready to open our souls as well. LF

Changing the World

2 JULY

It doesn't matter who you are, what you have done or not done in the past. As long as you answer, "I am ready," whenever the call comes, you can begin the process of transformation that will truly allow you to change the world.

RABBI LEVI MEIER[120]

Some people say that success is determined by being "at the right place at the right time," a situation that is generally beyond our control. However, some people are able to seize an opportunity when they see it or hear it: "whenever the call comes." In doing so, they arc able to transform the past by laying claim to the present. Rabbi Levi Meier continues his teaching above by suggesting: "When the call comes, you need only say, '*Hineni*'—I am ready." *Hineni* is a stance for leading. By borrowing from the language of the Torah and by responding with the word *hineni*, we express that we recognize the importance of the task that we are confronting and the need to undertake it.

While the Torah restricts the origin of such a call to God, we know that this call can come in a more indirect way, from a variety of sources. It is not restricted to the voice of God calling from the wilderness, an image taken from the Torah and the journey of our people through the desert. Usually the Bible speaks of a call coming directly from the Divine or mitigated through the prophets or angels. However, humans can give voice to a call from Heaven. Sometimes human beings—even when they do not realize it—are emissaries of the Holy One of Blessing and call us to service. We have to be ready to listen, whenever we are called—and whoever does the calling—to carry on God's work in the world.

The response to the call is the first step toward personal transformation that allows for greater transformation. By changing ourselves, we can begin to change the world. So take the first step, and then keep walking.　　　　KO

Charitable Acts

3 JULY

Even a poor person who lives off charity should perform acts of charity.

TALMUD[121]

Charity holds a dimension in Jewish tradition far beyond giving money or gifts to the poor. That is why even recipients of charity are expected to give some charity themselves. Charity is an attitude: it is something you do, not only something you give. If you celebrate a moment of joy, you invite the needy into your celebration. If you can help someone find a job or lend someone money, you do so before being asked. You extend yourself for those in need in a way that causes the least embarrassment to them and draws the least attention to you. "The rewards of charity," the rabbis said, "depend entirely upon the extent of the kindness in it."

From the words of the prophets to those of medieval moralists, one theme resounds again and again. It doesn't matter how many religious rituals a person observes if that same person cheats in business, mistreats workers, or is too greedy to help the poor. The true measure of ethical behavior is how honest and fair you are, and what your commitment is to the welfare of others. So think about it tonight and then determine what you are going to do in the morning.

FRANCINE KLAGSBRUN[122]

Our Thanks to America

4 JULY

Deprived as we hitherto have been of the invaluable rights of free citizens, we now—with a deep sense of gratitude to the Almighty—behold a government erected by the majesty of the people—a government which to bigotry gives no sanction, to persecution no assistance, but generously affording to all liberty of conscience and immunities of citizenship, deeming everyone of whatever nation, tongue or language, equal parts of the great governmental machine.

MOSES SEIXAS[123]

Today, July 4, we celebrate America's independence. Perhaps we have plans to go outdoors and enjoy a picnic, a parade, or fireworks. In addition to enjoying Independence Day traditions, we can pause and reflect on our experience as American Jews. All in all, the Jewish community in America has prospered and flourished in its short history. For many of us, our families arrived on these shores no more than three or four generations ago, a short time span when we consider the history of the Jewish people. But here we have not experienced anything as intensive and widespread as the anti-Semitism of the Middle Ages, the massacres of the Crusades, or the persecution and exile of the Spanish Inquisition. Here we have flourished as individuals and as a community, and so we cherish the memory of this country's founders who created a nation based on the constitutional right that prohibits the restriction of the freedom of religion. This clause—the

First Amendment of the Bill of Rights—has allowed true pluralism to take root in America so that today we are a nation of many peoples and many faiths. Let us be thankful today, this day of Independence, for the American experience. It is truly unique in the history of the Jewish people.   LF

Comforts

5 JULY

In nakedness I emerged from my mother's womb,
and naked shall I return.

JOB 1:21

As adults, most of us have gotten used to security and shelter—and many of the things that have made our lives more comfortable. While some of our parents and many of our grandparents may not have done so, we actually take most of it for granted. These are things that we expect, to which we feel entitled.

It is hard to imagine ourselves as we once were as infants, totally dependent on others for support, coming into this world with nothing. Those who were poor immigrants like my grandparents, those who arrived in America as children with nothing except the clothes that they wore, may have some notion of what it is to enter the world as infants do.

Job teaches us out of the experience of his life that although he suffered great personal tragedy, he cannot be ungrateful for the blessings he did enjoy—however short-lived they were—for he will leave this world as empty-handed (what he calls "naked") as he was when he came into the world. What he acquired, even the love of his spouse and children, could not accompany him to the grave. This is a powerful and difficult notion of faith that does not resonate for most of us. Thankfully, most of us will not suffer as did Job. Even so, few of us will have the unyielding faith that he had. Nevertheless, his faith in God amid incredible suffering and strife is certainly a goal toward which to strive, however inadequate the religious belief that we achieve may be in comparison.   KO

Garments of Light

6 July

When God finished speaking to Abraham, God departed and Abraham returned to his place.

GENESIS 18:33

Adam sundered the lower worlds from the higher in his search for experience, not the holy. Noah breached the worlds even more in his attempt at repair—it seems that any ulterior search for the holy, even for repair, can disrupt the world of the spirit. The only authentic search, it seems, is to know God. In knowing God, we repair the breaches and nourish the upper worlds. In the *Zohar,* Abraham is the moment of the reversal of bicosmic entropy. The world is no longer empty of meaning because of the breaches; restoration occurs. The *Zohar,* in the portion that tells Abraham to go forth, called *Lekh Lekha,* says that the world was created through covenant, the covenant of fire; the word *bereshit* is rearranged to spell *brit esh,* literally a covenant of fire. Adam dismembered that covenant, Noah violated his. In circumcision, Abraham uncovers himself to God and God uncovers God's divine self to Abraham, as we see in the verse above, words that occur in the Torah right after the circumcision. The holy lights that were the garments of Adam and Eve, until they dressed themselves in the shade of the Tree of Vagaries, were now given to Abraham as his garment. In the midst of our darkness, may we be given the privilege of being clothed in these garments of light as well.

RABBI MORDECAI FINLEY[124]

The Way of Goodness and the Way of Evil

7 JULY

*The way of goodness is at the outset a thicket of thorns, but
after a little distance it emerges into an open clearing.
The way of evil is at first a plain, but eventually
runs into a mess of thorns.*

MIDRASH[125]

It is so easy at times to become confused and not know
which direction will lead us down the path of goodness and
which down the road to evil. This is especially true when the
path of goodness is strewn with obstacles that can frustrate
us and block our progress. To maneuver down this path
requires that we have steadfastness of purpose and vision
along with a good measure of persistence: if we stick to it we
will be rewarded and find ourselves on the path of goodness.
Conversely, it is also true that confusion often sets in when
we find that the path of evil—let us say the path of destruc-
tiveness—is also one that we, at times, find ourselves on, and
the way can seem so easy at first. Only with hindsight, and
when we find ourselves entangled in a "mess of thorns," after
we are already well along this path, do we realize our error.
As the Midrash reminds us, we must not be discouraged if we
encounter some thorns at the start of our path. For we might
be pleasantly surprised to find out that after the initial obstacles we are on the right path after all.   LF

Reflections of Self

8 JULY

*Look into the eyes of those who surround you and you will
see a reflection of yourself.*

RABBI KARYN D. KEDAR[126]

We have all heard this said about children, and those of us
who are parents have experienced it firsthand. We often catch
glimpses of ourselves and what we do and say in our own
children. Some of this "mirroring" is learned as our children
imitate what they see us do. Some behaviors are genetically
transmitted, as well. Regardless of how our children achieve
it, seeing such a reflection often has a sobering effect on us,
especially when the traits that they exhibit are those that we
have worked hard to diminish. On the other hand, when our
children display the behaviors that we have worked hard to
instill and model in our everyday lives, then we feel that we
have done our job as parents.

However, Rabbi Kedar's comment transcends the limits of
our families. She suggests that those who surround us are a
reflection of ourselves. In other words, we tend to spend time
with those whose values are similar to our own, even when
we do not realize it.

Take a look at your friends, at the people with whom you
spend your leisure hours. If they do not reflect the values that
you hold dear, change your friends. Better yet, change yourself. Then go out and make some new friends.   KO

Timeliness

9 JULY

This is the meaning of the Jewish Sabbath, to give to humans peaceful hours, hours completely diverted from everyday life, seclusion from the world in the midst of the world.

RABBI LEO BAECK[127]

Time, as we know it, was invented only in the nineteenth century. A century ago, most people got up and went to bed with the sun and measured their day by the factory whistle or the town clock. Arriving twenty minutes one way or the other didn't much matter. The concept of an "appointment" was invented only in 1880. So was the concept "you're late." Time was local: Two o'clock in San Francisco had no relation to two o'clock in New York. All that changed with the railroad. Railroads run on schedules. And schedules demand standardized time. The country was divided into "time zones" and time was made uniform. The advent of radio brought uniform time into the home as families rushed to finish dinner to hear their favorite program. Relative to human evolution, fifty years is a remarkably short period; but in the fifty years from 1880 through 1930, our sense of time was completely overturned.

And it has turned again. A friend who works as a business lawyer describes his stress this way: Once, a contract, a letter, a proposal, came in the mail. You thought about it, drafted your response, and sent it off. Total turnaround: about a week. Then came express mail. The proposal comes via FedEx by 10:30 A.M. and the response is expected by the next day. Then came fax: The response is expected by day's end. Then came e-mail. Now the response is expected instantaneously.

We live in what writer Michael Ventura describes as "the age of interruption," when "inner time"—our personal sense of the rhythms of time—and the regimented time society imposes upon us don't jibe. What happens to human beings when the rhythm of life speeds up so drastically? The faster we go, the more empty we feel.

Here's a gift for summer (that you can carry into the rest of the year). One extended day a week—twenty-five hours of freedom (one hour longer for Shabbat): to slow down and breathe, to do nothing, to accomplish nothing, except reacquainting yourself with the people you love and the parts of yourself left behind in the rush. To turn your back on the urgent and the pressing, and think about the eternal. To renew your search for what's true, what's beautiful, what's good, what's important. We call it Shabbat. And it is God's gift to you . . . before it's too late.

We count the days of the week in anticipation of Shabbat, and those days start in the evening. So instead of counting sheep tonight as you doze off to sleep, count the days of the week—as you look forward to Shabbat at its end.

RABBI EDWARD FEINSTEIN

Nature as a Pathway to God
10 JULY

Teach our little ones true Judaism. First God. Introduce them to the wonders of plant and animal life. Show them God in the bursting seed, in the budding flower, in the bird-producing egg, the glorious sunshine.

JULIA RICHMOND[128]

There are many wonders in the world that fill us with awe. This is the miracle of creation that is beyond our reach. For while we, too, have creative abilities, we cannot replicate the majesty of the Grand Canyon or the simple beauty of a field of newly blooming flowers or the intricate economy of an ant colony. When we see the beauty of the world through the eyes of a child, we are reminded of the surprises and awe that our world yields. So many of us live such a harried life that we rush past the natural wonders that surround us. It is often the children in our lives who catch hold of an unusual sight—or even an everyday occurrence—and cause us to slow down and marvel. Tomorrow let us draw on their innate wonder at creation's mysteries and remind ourselves that nature is a door through which we can also return to reconnect with God—no matter how many years we have celebrated. Slow down and embrace the wonders of creation as God's handiwork.   LF

Getting Better

11 JULY

Things can go from the very worst to the very best in just the blink of an eye.

RABBI NACHMAN OF BRESLOV[129]

You have heard it said and probably seen it happen in your friends' lives or even your own. By one act an entire life is changed. We hope it is changed for the better. But it is not always so. Too often, tragedy strikes when we least expect it and our lives are indeed changed forever.

In a more everyday example, some people find that the adolescence of their children fits Rabbi Nachman's statement. For years parents and children fight with one another, struggling for control and independence. Then suddenly, often during the first visit home from college, the rebellious adolescent has not only become an adult, he or she has also become a friend.

Rabbi Nachman is an optimist. While he understands the challenge of everyday living, he also wants to teach us about what is always possible. He knows that each individual has the capacity to turn his or her entire life around (I like to call it *teshuvah*-change) with one action. It takes work, but it is often just the decision to change that clears the path for change to occur. All in the time it takes to blink an eye. So what are you waiting for?   KO

A Refreshing Creation
12 JULY
One's feet are one's fate; they lead us where we are wanted.
TALMUD[130]

The following teaching comes from a holy Polish teacher who was called the Sefat Emet. He lived around the turn of the twentieth century and was part of the end-flowering of Polish Jewish mystical thought.

Once, when the king was away, the castle caught fire. The people were in great distress, but they obeyed their king's command never to draw water from the well. When the king returned, he saw that his castle had burned to the ground. "Why didn't you draw water from the well to put out the fire?" he complained. "If the castle's on fire, it's all right to draw water from the well." "Well," said one of the villagers rather sheepishly, "we haven't drawn water from the well in so long that we forgot how to do it." When the king heard that, he sighed and began to teach the people how to draw water from the well.

All of us are in that state of consciousness: the castle is on fire so we have to learn together how to draw water from the well. Perhaps we need to put out the fire of anger, or perhaps we must learn how to put out the fire of the obstacles we put on our own path.

In the Torah, God says to Abraham, "*Lekh lekha*. Get going." And the Sefat Emet taught that a human being is called "one who walks." He said that a human being is filled with the need to go from level to level. But what we do can easily become only a habit. When a thing becomes a habit, we cannot see into its sweet inner nature.

This is true even of the spiritual practice we do. It is so easy for us to do it and do it and do it until we fall asleep and forget the sweet inner thing that we once knew. It is necessary, taught the Sefat Emet, to seek the new in every moment. Even the Infinite One, the Force of the Universe, renews all creation in each new second. Every second the creation is being supercharged with the vitality of its is-ness, of its fresh goodness.

We need to be careful, therefore, that we are not overcome by habit. There is the habit of how we deal with each other. There is the habit of saying, "I hate broccoli so I won't eat it again." From the most mundane to the most profound, a person becomes ruled by habit. Human beings need to permit themselves to be renewed in every moment, in everything they do. Every moment, we should be ready to move to a new place, to a higher level, to seek the new.   AVRAM DAVIS

Bridging Religion and Spirituality
13 JULY

*The spiritual is that realm of human experience which religion
attempts to connect us to through dogma and practice.
Sometimes it succeeds and sometimes it fails. Religion is the
bridge to the spiritual—but the spiritual lies beyond religion.
Unfortunately in seeking the spiritual we may become
attached to the bridge rather than crossing over it.*

RACHEL NAOMI REMEN[131]

The term *spirituality* has become very popular in recent years. We hear people say, "I'm not religious, I'm spiritual." But this statement dismisses religion too quickly, because

when religious practices work best they connect us
beyond our normal everyday consciousness to another
of awareness of something greater than ourselves and
limited perspectives. Traditional forms of practice can lead us
to the spiritual. We are also aware that, at times, some of the
traditional rituals may no longer speak to us. Or we sometimes forget that they are indeed vehicles to another dimension, and we end up, all too often, performing them in a rote
manner. Then religious ritual and tradition can seem deaden-
ing instead of inspiring. In seeking a spiritual path, let us not
discard all rituals or "traditional" ways. Instead, let us reexamine them and use them to cross the bridge to the spiritual
dimension we all seek.   LF

A Caring Heart

14 JULY

*Whatever else God may be, God is primarily and
preeminently a great heart, caring most for what seems to
be important and sacred to us, namely, our loves and
aspirations and sufferings.*

ADAPTED FROM RABBI HENRY SLONIMSKY[132]

The Bible portrays God as tough, often unyielding, and frequently vengeful. For some, this idea fills us with awe and
respect. However, for most, the idea of such a God is frightening and distancing. This is the image of God that many of
us learned as young children and rebelled against as adolescents. As a result, we may have rejected such an idea or, at
least, found such a God difficult to relate to and communicate with. It may even have kept us away from our Judaism
for many of our adult years.

But there are many attributes to God and we have to be
open to a variety of experiences of the Divine. To paraphrase

...hough this aspect of the Holy One might
...y other things, God is primarily a caring
...t of God that offers us comfort, raises us up
...n, and generally supports us in our need. KO

The Context of Life

15 July

To see the true, to love the beautiful,
to desire the good, and to do the best.

Moses Mendelssohn[133]

Is your life just a random string of events, some happy, some sad, some filled with pleasure and others with inexplicable pain? How do you evaluate what unfolds before you: parents, children, work stress, and success? Is there a context for your living?

As Jews we have been given a template that provides an underlying context for our lives. Often we are not aware of the context. We simply make decisions that are guided by the passing of this context from generation to generation. We stand up for justice, even when it is inconvenient. We take care of our parents. We provide the finest possible education for our children. We don't seem to think about these things as being particularly Jewish.

Much of our spirituality, it turns out, is about providing a context for our lives. Who am I and where am I going? This is the question that each of us must ask at varying points on life's journey. What we do with that information, how we make the decisions that both guide our path and enable us to absorb the curveballs that life throws at us, depends on our context. Without a spiritual template, life seems like a jumble of meaningless obstacles with a few high points of pleasure. We reach a certain point where we are forced to ask: Is this all there is?

The Book of Exodus provides us with the context as we tell our story. We repeat the story in the Passover seder, as well as in the regular reading of the Torah, just to remind ourselves and the members of our family. The escape from Egypt is not just about frogs and the Pharaoh, it is the story of a people who escape the lower levels of slavery in order to embrace a context for their lives. Even though we do not understand it all, we accept it. We don't always understand why we should keep Shabbat, or stay out of adulterous relationships or honor our parents, but we evaluate our actions in the context of those principles passed down at Sinai.

Sometimes it is hard to remember how to incorporate this idea into our lives. The more we study, the easier it becomes. So stay up a little later tonight and study. You'll rest a lot easier. RABBI JUDITH HALEVY

On Leading
16 JULY

*I don't know what would have happened if a public
opinion poll was taken when Moses left Egypt!
My impression is that he may not have enjoyed a
majority. . . . Shall we go after the Golden Calf because
it's the will of the majority, or should we go to the
Promised Land because that is our destiny?*

SHIMON PERES[134]

Our society has become expert in opinion polling. In fact, it has become a science used widely by marketers, politicians, and the media. There are leaders who don't make a move without knowing ahead of time through sophisticated polling techniques what the public's response will be. Those of us who seek visionary leadership realize this tool's limits. This kind of research has us looking at all sorts of things but seldom at ourselves. We are too busy looking at others to discover what may lie deep within ourselves.

For leaders to lead often means choosing the path that the majority may not support. It is that much harder when there are concrete numbers and statistics in front of us that go against our position. We lead from vision, not polls. Moses never took a poll of the people. Instead he took risks and pushed people to go forward when they wanted to return to Egypt, the land of slavery. Even as he was guided by God, he looked inside his spiritual self. We, too, can be like Moses: taking risks, using our powers of persuasion, and reiterating our vision in order to gain the trust of those who are around us each day, and in the end, move toward our ultimate goal of discovering our spiritual self so that we may then lead others to their own discovery of a promised land.   LF

Encounters with the Divine

17 JULY

Encounters with God are not always pleasant; they are not always aesthetic; and they often leave you with an injury you bear for the rest of your life.

RABBI ALAN LEW[135]

It may have never occurred to us that encounters with the Divine might be anything less than wonderful. After all, that is why so many of us continue to yearn for them and work toward them. However, if we would only consider Jacob's nighttime struggle with the angel in Genesis, we would realize that while he gained a blessing, he limped away from the encounter permanently injured. This is the lesson of the Torah about which Rabbi Lew is reminding us, something that most of us forget or, at least, choose not to remember.

Why *would* we think that such encounters are only pleasant or aesthetically pleasing? Fear also teaches us about God, as does pain. The bloody sacrifices known to our ancestors were certainly not pleasing to our sight or to our sense of smell. (This is probably one of the reasons why the priests were forced to burn incense so much of the time. It is unclear which smell was worse: the animals being slaughtered or those already burning on the altar.)

It's true that we have come a long way since animal sacrifice—even if it was as much a barbecue picnic as it was a religious rite. Nevertheless, our encounters with God are not necessarily any more pleasant even if they are filled with blessing. And that they are!   KO

A Palace in Time

18 JULY

To observe the Sabbath is to bear witness to the Creator.
MIDRASH[136]

Shabbat, our weekly observance, is not about place. It is only about time. Rabbi Abraham Joshua Heschel called it a "palace in time," a refuge from the mundane and the humdrum. Shabbat is a day that becomes bride and queen, when pauper and prince alike are royalty. Shabbat teaches that what we know, how we act, and how we relate are the yardsticks of our lives. We are not measured by what we have but by how we live. On Shabbat you are royalty, you're majesty—part of a kingdom of priests and a holy people. Savor that concept; relish it; delight in it; do not take it for granted. Welcome Shabbat even if only for an evening, a service, a dinner together, an hour, even if but for a moment before you sleep for the night.

RABBI RAYMOND A. ZWERIN

Being Bearers of Light

19 JULY

Traditionally, when a man or woman became a king or queen, one needed to have a halo that others could recognize in order to call them by their title. So a crown was made that glowed and shone. When they wore the crown on their head, it said, "Look at me, see how I shine." However, as children of God, we are all empowered light bearers. When we touch the Infinite, there is no need to wear the crown. We already radiate light.

RABBI ZALMAN SCHACHTER-SHALOMI

We are all taken at one time or another with the fantasy world of kings and queens. Royalty sparks within us a dream that we, too, could live an enchanted life. How many of us grew up on stories that ended with the well-known sentence, "and they lived happily ever after"? Many of us are enthralled by the pomp and circumstance that surround the status of royalty, and others of us love the idea of beautiful garments, dazzling jewels, and limitless privilege. How some of those jewels sparkle! But for most of us, the world of kings and queens is nowhere within our reach. That is, unless we take to heart the teaching of Reb Zalman, who reminds us that we are all royalty. While we do not wear bejeweled headpieces or royal robes, we can allow our connection to the Holy One to illuminate our own crowns made of light. We do not need the jeweled headpieces, for our divine light is so much stronger. So, as we wind down tonight, let us be aware that each person we met today wears a crown of light, and so do we. While these crowns may not always be visible, their divine spark is as real as ever.   LF

Staying Close
20 JULY

*It's easier to criticize from a distance than
it is to make a positive difference.*

RABBI BRADLEY SHAVIT ARTSON[137]

People like to criticize. Some people even consider it a favorite pastime. We get so used to it that we don't even realize that we are doing it. Then it makes it even more difficult to try to say something affirming and complimentary to a person. The pursuit of truth becomes sacrosanct. It matters not who gets hurt in the process. Obviously, if we make less of others, we have unconsciously deceived ourselves into thinking that we are making more of ourselves. But when we make less of others, we diminish ourselves as well. At the same time, such criticism distances us from people.

This is why the lesson that Rabbi Artson teaches is so important. It is easy to criticize from a distance. But when we get close to a person, such criticism comes with more difficulty.

Here's the spiritual logic implicit in his teaching: Stay close to your friends by staying far from criticism. In doing so, you can continue to keep them close. KO

Dignity
21 JULY

*To be invested with dignity means to represent something
more than oneself.*

RABBI ABRAHAM JOSHUA HESCHEL[138]

Kavod means dignity, honor, weightiness, and it comes from the root *k-b-d*. One can understand a community's values by whom and by what it considers worthy of *kavod*. There is a kind of honor communities bestow that depends on status, power, and wealth that is often tied to a sense of self-importance. This type of honor is considered a limited resource and people fight or vie for it, thinking of it as an award to be acquired or won. But there is another type of honor that is far weightier, one that depends on who we are and what we stand for, an honor that is connected to our deepest selves.

Look at some of the words with which *kavod* is traditionally linked in the Jewish way: *kavod hamakom* (God); *kavod hatzibur* (community); *kavod hatorah* (Torah); *kavod habriyot* (human beings); *kavod morim* (teachers); *kavod hameit* (dead); *kavod harav* (rabbi); *kavod Shabbat* (Sabbath); and *kavod horim* (parents). The range and depth of our tradition's understanding of *kavod* is breathtaking. *Kavod* is a currency that flows back and forth between human beings and between human beings and God. There is an infinite amount of this *kavod*, and *kavod* is of infinite value.

Who is worthy of being treated with *kavod*? One who treats God with *kavod*. Human beings are capable of making *kavod* happen and worthy of receiving *kavod*. God gets *kavod* from us and we get it from each other. *Kavod* only exists if we give it to each other, and only if we give it to each other do we have it from God. RABBI IRWIN KULA[139]

The Unintended Benefit of Forgetting
22 JULY

When you harvest a field and forget a sheaf do not go back and pick it up; it shall go to the stranger, the fatherless, and the widow in order that God will bless all your efforts.
DEUTERONOMY 24:19

This verse refers to the mitzvah of *shichecha*, in English "the forgotten sheaf." It refers to the scenarios wherein the harvesters would forget to pick up a sheaf they had bundled in the field. The Torah says, "Do not go back. Leave it for the poor." So here is a mitzvah that has to do with forgetting. Slightly peculiar, considering that we as a people have made a point of remembering. The Hebrew word *zakhor*, remember, is engraved in our hearts and minds. What can this mitzvah mean for us today, especially since it seems tied to a time when working the land was the principal means of making a living and of giving to those in need?

Most often we are taught that we must be conscious and intentional when we give *tzedakah*. But this mitzvah teaches that there are times when forgetting can produce the same results as our most conscious actions. While we cannot plan to be forgetful, this mitzvah teaches that when we do forget something we can turn it into another opportunity for giving. So the next time you are forgetful, see if you can—just perhaps—find a way to creatively use your unintended forgetfulness to help someone benefit.   LF

The Path of Righteousness
23 JULY

The study of Torah is the path of the chakham *[wise person]. Devotion to God is the path of the* navi *[prophet]. Devotion to others is the way of the* chasid *[pious]. But the path of the* tzaddik *[righteous] is an integration of all three.*

RABBI TERRY A. BOOKMAN[140]

It seems that Rabbi Bookman offers us a history of piety in Judaism, with instructions how to climb on the shoulders of our ancestors and reach even further. If the study of Torah provides the wise person with a path for life, we can assume the same for ourselves. Studying the Torah may even help us make the transition from ignorance to wisdom—if we are prepared to be guided by the teachings of the Torah. In order to do so, we have to be willing to engage the text and become one with it. We have to enter its pages and breathe in its words, submitting ourselves to its will.

The prophets—even those who were at first reluctant—were spokespersons for God. They served as instruments of the divine will in the world. Thus, they devoted themselves to interpreting God's plan for us. While others interpreted world events as political in nature, the prophet tried to help us to understand God's role in them.

The *chasid* is devoted to one's neighbors, conscious of how he or she treats others. This consciousness has become the signature activity of such piety.

But the path of the righteous, the path we strive to discover in our lives, is an integration of the behaviors of *chakham*, *navi*, and *chasid*. This is no easy task. The path may take us on different roads, but they all lead us to the same place. KO

Unconditional, Covenantal Love

24 JULY

Many waters cannot quench love; neither can floods drown it.
SONG OF SONGS 8:7

In the *Shema* we are taught, "And you shall love the Eternal your God with all your heart, all your soul and all your might" (Deuteronomy 6:5). Jewish tradition sets the requirement to love God in the context of the covenant between God and the People Israel. Throughout Jewish history, the loving covenant increasingly became a reciprocal relationship sustained by mutual respect, patience, loyalty, and faithfulness. Despite the strain of modernity and the ordeal of the Holocaust, the covenant remains grounded in what seems to be a shared unconditional love, *ahavah*.

The covenantal relationship has often made taxing demands on both sides. From the perspective of the human participants, love of God endures these covenantal requirements more willingly than fear of God. Perhaps for this reason, the love of God has always been understood as being superior to the fear of God. Indeed, the rabbis imagined the Torah and its requirements as God's marriage contract with Israel, a reflection of divine love. Naturally, they thought that Israel's loyal fulfillment of the commandments should be motivated by a similar love for God.

The love of God must be an undivided commitment, involving the whole person. There is room for only one covenantal partner, only one beloved God. Nothing, neither personal property nor private interest, may be held back. The rabbis even insisted that a Jew love God with "both inclinations," that is, with the urge to do evil as well as the urge to do good. Just as covenantal love brings us toward greater wholeness, it also demands that we commit the entirety of our being to our divine partner.

By living the covenantal life and walking in God's ways, we come to know God profoundly and weave our deepest, most loving intimate attachment.   RABBI TSVI BLANCHARD[141]

The Gift of Hospitality
25 JULY

One who receives his friend with friendliness and hospitality, even if he doesn't give him anything, it is as if he has given him all the gifts of the world.

TALMUD[142]

Hospitality can seem like an old-fashioned value. Today when we are overcommitted and our time seems so limited, it seems unlikely that we will receive others as hospitably as we might like. We may meet our friends for dinner to catch up, but do we invite people into our homes? When you think about it, though, perhaps extending ourselves hospitably is not solely a matter of time but also a matter of attitude. We are hospitable when we give others our attention and act as if their visit is all that matters for the moment. This may mean turning off TVs, not answering the phone, not letting other distractions get in the way. It may mean speaking in a manner that is not rushed. Meetings at work are usually on the clock, but our time with friends and family members is more fluid and free-flowing. As the Talmud reminds us, hospitality goes beyond providing the best food and wine or stimulating conversation. It really addresses our ability to value someone's presence. When we are invited to a friend's home for a summer meal, and we want to buy a gift to express how we feel toward them, it is worth slowing down to give a more precious gift: valuing the presence of those we love.   LF

Worshiping God

26 JULY

Every reason given for the mitzvot *(commandments or sacred tasks and deeds) that bases itself on human needs—from many considerations of the concept of need, whether intellectual, ethical, social, national—voids the* mitzvot *from every religious meaning. If they are meant to benefit society or if they maintain the Jewish people, then the one who performs them does not serve God but oneself, or society or one's people. In any case, such an individual does not serve God but uses the Torah of God for one's own benefit and as a means to satisfy one's needs. The reason for the* mitzvot *is the worship of God.*

ADAPTED FROM YESHAYAHU LEIBOWITZ[143]

Traditional Judaism teaches that *mitzvot* are commandments from God, originating from Sinai—sometimes mediated or interpreted by the rabbis. A more liberal approach suggests that *mitzvot* are key to human self-improvement. Thus they are divine instructions rather than commands. Whether one is heavily involved in the performance of *mitzvot,* or whether one is just starting on the path of a life of *mitzvot,* the question remains the same: Why do them?

The contemporary Israeli philosopher Yeshayahu Leibowitz makes it quite clear. While there are those who seem to use *mitzvot* for a variety of purposes, there is only one reason to do *mitzvot:* the worship of God.

So when you get up in the morning, prepare a day of ritual—and a day of worshiping God. You'll rest better knowing what lies ahead of you.   KO

Living in the Image of God
27 JULY

God created the human being in the divine image; in the image of God, God created the human: male and female God created them.

GENESIS 1:27

With these words, the Torah proclaims three remarkable guiding values for life: that human value is without limit (as is God); that human capacities are God-like; and that we cannot think of God properly without thinking of humans, just as one cannot think of humans without immediately associating them with God.

Human value: Being made in *tzelem Elohim,* in the image of God, a human is endowed with three fundamental dignities: infinite value: "to save one life is equivalent to saving a whole universe"; equality: no one can say that "my parent is of greater value than your parent" because no image of God is intrinsically superior to any other; and uniqueness: "When a human creates many coins from one mold, all resemble each other, but the Sovereign of Sovereigns, that is, the Holy Blessed One, stamped every human in the mold of the first Adam, but each one is unique."[144]

In principle, all these dignities are inalienable, beyond human control or society's authority to take away. In actual fact, the dignities of human beings are not fully honored. Judaism is committed to transform the world so that they can be fully realized and sustained in daily life. This is the promise of the messianic age.

Human capacities: One can define the fundamental divine capacities as six in number: consciousness, power, relationship (love), will, freedom, and life. In each, God's capacity is ultimate.

In the Talmudic understanding, the divine call to Israel "to walk in God's ways" (Deuteronomy 10:12) and "to cling to God" (10:20) is a call to imitate God's qualities, that is, to step up to our God-like quality of love. In Rabbi Joseph B. Soloveitchik's insight, this instruction is extended to every one of the human's God-like capacities; they are to be developed to the fullest to bring us even closer to God. And we are to use these capacities to perfect the world. By inviting humans to join in *tikkun olam* (perfecting the world), God has linked the destiny of the divine creation with human fate.

When Rabbi Akiva said that "love your neighbor" is "the [one] great principle" on which the Torah is based, his colleague Ben Azzai responded that "human beings are created in the image of God" is an even greater principle. Living up to this principle accounts for the whole Torah.

RABBI IRVING GREENBERG[145]

Lamenting

28 JULY

*By the rivers of Babylon, there we sat and
wept as we thought of Zion. . . .
If I forget you, O Jerusalem, let my right hand wither,
let my tongue stick to my palate if I cease to think
about you, if I do not keep Jerusalem in my
memory even at my happiest hour.*

PSALMS 137:1, 5

In the heat of the summer, when many of us take time for vacations, we are confronted with the holiday of Tisha B'Av, the ninth of Av. It is a day on which we mourn the destruction of the First and Second Temples. Today Jerusalem is a thriving city and our capital. We are fortunate to live in a time when the Jewish people once again lives as a sovereign nation, but we still pause to recall the past two times in our history when Jerusalem, the spiritual, cultural, and political center of our people, was destroyed and we began our long journey of being exiles.

This well-known text is from a psalm that, according to tradition, was written following the destruction of the First Temple in 586 B.C.E. by the Babylonians. The exiled Israelites wept as they were forced to relocate to Babylonia, leaving Jerusalem behind. The Second Temple was destroyed by Rome in 70 C.E. after years of war, also on the ninth day of Av. On Tisha B'Av we traditionally fast and hear the book of Lamentations chanted.

Let us pause tonight to cherish Israel as our homeland and pray that the state of exile never again touches the Jewish people. In the spirit of Tisha B'Av, we express our thanks that once again we can live or visit Jerusalem, the eternal spiritual capital of our people.   LF

Fixed Prayer

29 JULY

Rabbi Eliezer says, "When someone makes their prayer fixed [keva]*, their prayer is not prayer.*
MISHNAH[146]

Prayer is dialogue with the Divine. While there is a place for fixed prayer as part of the rhythm of Jewish prayer, Rabbi Eliezer argues that such prayer may not be considered prayer. Perhaps he is saying that fixed prayer must lay the foundation for prayers that are the outpouring of one's heart (what our tradition labels as *kavannah*). My experience with liturgy has persuaded me that fixed prayer may even approximate real prayer but it can never equal it.

The prayer book may be seen as the history of Jewish theology (a fancy word for the way people conceptualize God). The prayer book is a source book for the evolving dialogue that helps forge the relationship between individuals and God. Some have said that while the prayer book helps to link the generations, its real purpose is to occupy the rational side of one's brain, the *keva* side, as it were, in order to allow the other side—the *kavannah* side—to pray.   KO

A Notion of Idolatry

30 JULY

Wherever you find human footprints, there God is before you.
MIDRASH[147]

In the middle of the summer, while we may be far from reading about the episode of the golden calf in the weekly reading cycle of the Torah, we are not far from its message. According to traditional Jewish theology, many of the calamities we experienced as a people were a direct result of straying from the path that God has laid before us. In the Torah, we had just received the Ten Commandments, and Moses was up on the mountain to receive the entire Torah, when our ancestors busied themselves at the foot of the mountain, fashioning a golden calf.

How could the Israelites, who had experienced the Exodus, the splitting of the sea, and the giving of the Torah at Sinai, come to desire a golden calf, we ask? As for us, the sin of idolatry seems very distant from our lives. Yet the worship of the golden calf is a simple mistake and a common desire. It is wanting to hold on to what is. It represents a quest for certainty in an uncertain world. In the face of mortality, we want to fiercely hold on to this moment, to this loved one, to this experience. In other words, we want to freeze time. The calf is the notion that God begins molten and liquid but ends up in one solid form. The mistake is for Israel to say *Eleh Eloheikha Yisrael*—this (and only this) is your God, Israel. That mistake had reduced all of the experience of the Exodus, all of the Torah at Sinai, to this one form.

At the burning bush, God told Moses who God is: *Ehyeh asher ehyeh*—I will be what I will be. God is an ever-changing God. An idol makes a claim on eternity. However, all things pass away. The only "thing" that is eternal is the Eternal One. To worship anything else is to make an idol of the temporal.

Thus, idolatry is not about worshiping a stone image, nor is it a worship of the gods of money or success. Idolatry is a worship of a partial truth, a limited vision of what is rather than a worship of the One whose seal is *emet:* truth.

RABBI MICHAEL STRASSFELD

Overcoming Passivity

31 JULY

Our obligation is to give meaning to life and in doing so to overcome the passive, indifferent life. A person who is indifferent is dead without knowing it. I believe that life has meaning in spite of the meaningless death I have seen.

ELIE WIESEL[148]

The past century was full of meaningless death and horrible violence. Indeed, even today it seems that we have not learned from our past. Ethnic strife, religious hatred, and teenage violence rock the foundation of our very existence. It is all too easy to turn our attention elsewhere so as not to notice the pain and suffering that fills our world. We may turn on the TV and watch shows filled with violence, tuning out reality—the violence that exists just outside our homes.

We cannot let an attitude of indifference rule. It deadens our souls. After the Holocaust and the many other atrocities of the past one hundred years, it is easy to become cynical and claim that life is a meaningless journey. Yet, despite the atrocities we have seen and heard about, we stand up and say, "No!" Life is good and we seek meaning. As Elie Wiesel reminds us, meaning comes in cherishing our every encounter with another human being who reflects God's image back to us. We must not take these meetings lightly. For it is there that we can become inspired and find meaning to carry us through life.

LF

AUGUST

Serving versus Fixing
1 AUGUST

Fundamentally, helping, fixing and serving are ways of seeing life. When you help you see life as weak, when you fix, you see life as broken. When you serve you see life as whole.
RACHEL NAOMI REMEN[149]

The Jewish community often talks about the value *tikkun olam,* which means to fix or to mend the world. It comes from a theology that believes that the world is broken and that as God's partners we have an obligation to mend any small corner of the world we can. Reflecting on this value, I notice that the language we use directs us to fix and mend, thus emphasizing the broken nature of things rather than the wholeness of life. What if we were to change metaphors, and shift our perspective ever so slightly to remember that while there is sorrow and pain to help with, anguish to fix in life, there is also a great and joyful fullness that already exists? Life is a whole cloth that weaves together all our experiences. When we change our viewpoint to one of service, we can begin to see that both brokenness and wholeness exist side by side in our world. When we awaken tomorrow, may the pieces of our brokenness be brought together with the parts of others so that we can all experience whole-i-ness together.   LF

Climbing with God
2 AUGUST

*As I begin to climb, I become aware that God is in that
very place, the space between where I have been and where
I am going. It is where I live. And I do not live alone.*
RABBI KARYN D. KEDAR[150]

Perhaps you are like me: I have been searching for God my
entire life. The search grew from a yearning I felt as a young
child. However, it was not something that I could easily articulate in my youth. It took time to be able to reflect on what I
felt and then give voice to it. Even the vocabulary did not
come easily, but it evolved over time.

Sometimes I have gotten a glimpse of the Divine, much like
Moses did when he was hidden in the cleft of the rock and
experienced God only after God had passed him by. This is
particularly true in my relationships with others, where I see
the Divine manifest in the work of humans. At other times I
have actually felt God's presence more directly, particularly in
moments of great meaning, whether they be during the birth
of my children or the illness of my spouse.

I had not previously thought about the space that Rabbi
Kedar describes. But it is awareness of that space that can
help us to climb to the mountaintop, and as we do, we feel
God's presence between each faltering step.   KO

Where Are You?
3 AUGUST

God called out to Adam and said, "Where are you?"
GENESIS 3:9

The first question asked of the human being in the Torah is
God's question of Adam—*"Where are you?"*

Pay attention to the Torah's questions. Read them as if they were italicized, written in red, or underlined. For the questions capture the essence of the Torah's lesson. *"Am I my brother's keeper?"* *"Shall not the judge of all the earth do justice?"* It is as if the question came first and the narrative was written around it as its supporting commentary.

Of them all, no question is as profound as this first question: *Where are you?* Adam and Eve, having chosen to eat of the forbidden tree, having disobeyed their one commandment in order to gain knowledge, suddenly understand the cold reality of their separation from one another, from nature, and from God, and they feel shame. So they hide. They hide from God, from one another, and from all they should be and could be. *"Where are you?"*

So where are you on your journey? How much closer to wisdom? How much nearer to completing the tasks for which you were created? How much closer to your dreams? How much closer to those you love? How much wider your circle of concern? How much deeper your friendships? What did you do with My gift of a year of life? What have you done with all your years? *Where are you?*

During the Hebrew month of Elul, the month (which generally coincides with August or early September) given to deep reflection about the purposes, the accomplishments, and the failures of life, we search and reflect, study and judge ourselves before the new year begins. It is a time to find a quiet corner of life and ask, with all honesty and courage, God's penetrating question, *Where are you?*

RABBI EDWARD FEINSTEIN

Moral Values in Our Daily Lives
4 AUGUST

The future, like the past of the Jewish community, will be determined by the faith of Jews in the moral and ethical values which are theirs, and the extent to which these values become part of their daily lives.

JUSTINE WISE POLIER[151]

Justine Wise Polier was the first woman ever appointed as judge in the state of New York. As the daughter of Rabbi Stephen S. Wise, steeped in the Jewish ethic of seeking justice and equity, Justice Polier brought her Jewish background and its inherent values to her commitment to serve as a judge in the family courts. She was a voice of conscience for her generation.

Though our lives may be less in the public eye, our challenge today is no different from Justice Polier's. We are charged with infusing our daily lives with the values we learn from Torah. Judaism is not about dividing our world into various areas to which we apply religious and ethical principles only when they are convenient or if they fit. No. Judaism is about applying the moral principles that stand at the core of our people and heritage to *all* situations, even when it is uncomfortable and full of difficulty. If we give up this spiritual task, we diminish our role in the world. Let us not shy away from raising a moral voice and weaving our ethical consciousness into all that we do.   LF

A Yearning Heart
5 AUGUST

When your heart yearns, distance is no obstacle.

RABBI NACHMAN OF BRESLOV[152]

Rabbi Nachman is one of my favorite teachers. His simple wisdom and spiritual insights speak directly to me. It is no surprise that Rabbi Nachman's teachings speak to so many, regardless of our religious orientation or background. Even his own followers could not bring themselves to be led by another after his death, so his chair remains empty in their midst. And they continue to learn from the many things that he taught.

This simple teaching says all there is to say about Jewish spirituality. No matter how far we have traveled from God, no matter where our lives have taken us in the past, when our heart yearns to return, the distance we have to travel presents no obstacle for us. KO

Conscience
6 AUGUST

If I say I will not speak any more in Your name, then there is in my heart a burning fire shut up in my bones and I weary myself to hold it. I cannot.
JEREMIAH 20:9

Law and conscience are not enemies. Judaism knows that you need law, that without law there is anarchy. There is no civilization without rules and regulations and structure. You cannot live without law, but you can live with law only if it is invigorated by the fresh air of conscience. For the Rabbis knew that, as Nachmanides put it, "You can be a scoundrel within the letter of the law." If you exclude conscience from your decisions, you turn *halakhah* into another form of idolatry.

I'm not speaking about the conscience of superheroes, of Moses or the prophets. I am speaking of your conscience and mine. How does this address me and you? Do you have a conscience? What does it have to do with your religious life? Where does it come from? Is it something with which you are born? Either you've got it or you haven't? Is there such a thing as a Jewish conscience? There is no word for *conscience* in the Bible, or even in the Talmud. But, for that matter, there is no word for *religion* in the Bible. But surely the Bible is a religious book and as surely conscience is the spirit that hovers over the depths of Jewish law and lore. It is difficult to define conscience.

Conscience stirs up ultimate questions about ourselves: Who are you? What moves you? What makes you? What makes you cry? What makes you feel? What makes you sacrifice? Conscience cultivates a sensibility, an awareness, a body of concern.

Conscience is not innate. I am not born with a conscience. I am born into a community of conscience. That is the soul and heart of my Jewishness which I have internalized. It is what I think is meant by a *yiddishe neshamah* (a "Jewish soul"). Not something racial or innate but cultivated.

This is your task. Fathers, mothers, grandparents, you may not know the law, or the prescribed ritual, but you know the heart. Teach your children character. Teach them to feel. Teach them to be outraged at injustice. Teach them that Jewish heroism is to nullify the evil decrees. Cultivate their conscience—give them a Jewish heart, give them Jewish dignity. When you cultivate Jewish conscience you give your child an inviolable sense of self and of Jewish community.

RABBI HAROLD M. SCHULWEIS[153]

The Power of Imagination
7 AUGUST

Imagination is more important than knowledge. Knowledge is limited. Imagination encircles the world.

ALBERT EINSTEIN[154]

We spend a lot of effort and energy becoming knowledgeable and honing our skills to find the information we need to make wise business decisions and personal choices. We hear it all the time: We live in a knowledge-based world, and those who have the skills to acquire knowledge will be those who succeed. This quote from Albert Einstein stops me short. Now I am made to rethink my assumptions about knowledge and instead consider the role of imagination in our lives.

Here we have the most renowned of all scientists plugging the power of imagination. Why? Perhaps because those of us who can dream, stretch our imagination, think about the impossible, are better able to transcend the limits of the world, to reach the power of the spiritual. The challenge is not to be afraid to use our knowledge and imagination together to envision radically new things, spiritually enriching. The next time you are engaged in using your knowledge, whether tonight or tomorrow, do not turn off your imagination! Allow yourself to think beyond the normal scope by taking imaginative risks.   LF

The Lesson of Checkers
8 AUGUST

These are the lessons of checkers. You can't make two moves at once; you can only move forward, not backward; and once you reach the last row, you can move anywhere you want.

REB NACHUM OF RIZHYN[155]

And we thought checkers was only a game. In a game is often revealed the secrets of life. So like the Hasidic rabbis of old, who saw Torah in the way a master tied a shoelace, we can look to the simple game of checkers for spiritual insight and direction.

One move at a time. It is often difficult to even make one move at a time. It takes some strategy if you want your move to be successful. We have to plan, but there are limits placed on our planning time. Then we have to move quickly, thinking through the move even as we act on it. That's why we do not take our hand off the checker piece until we are convinced that what we have done is what we wanted to do.

Of course, you can't make two moves at once. After each move, you have to stop and think. You have to reflect and then plan for the next move you want to take. So you move slowly, deliberately—on your way home. And you continue to move forward until you reach home. Once you have found your way home (in the last row), then you can move in either direction.

How amazing that we can learn some of life's lessons in a simple game of checkers. Maybe that is why so many people play it. If you can master the game of checkers, maybe you can master the game of life or at least come close to it.   KO

Making Room for Others

9 AUGUST

No fast-day service is a genuine service unless sinners of Israel are included among its worshipers.

TALMUD[156]

This is the time of year, about one month before the High Holidays, usually in August when the holidays are observed in September, that people are supposed to begin the process of intensive introspection. Perhaps this process is helpful in mitigating our predisposition toward an attitude of "holier than thou." Almost like clockwork, the comments about "twice-a-year Jews" begin to surface.

But like God, we rejoice when people, regardless of their motivation, join together in community worship. It sounds simple, but it's true: Regardless of one's reason, it is better to come than not to come.

The Rabbis of the Mishnah understood this point of view a long time ago. The Mishnah states it this way, "If a person in prayer says, 'Let good people praise You, O God,' that person who prays must be silenced." Ovadia Bartenura, a fifteenth-century Italian scholar, clarifies the statement for us. He explains that we silence that person because of the implication that "Let good people praise You, O God" is a way of saying that *only* righteous people should be praying in the congregation.

The Talmud, as stated above, helps us out. If we were all self-righteous and considered the community to be entirely composed of noble people, we then would be far too smug and self-satisfied for a truly penitential fast-day service on Yom Kippur. And there would be nothing for us to think about or do this prior month. Not only should we not exclude "sinners" from our communities of prayer, we are prohibited from doing so.

So as we prepare ourselves to prepare for the High Holidays, open up your heart and your community to all its "sinners." Perhaps we might be counted among them!

RABBI JAMES SCOTT GLAZIER

Delayed Gratification
10 AUGUST

The difficulty is that when you give to others, you do not receive instant gratification. The benefits come your way only later on. But the reward is true, for it is long-lasting and nothing will spoil it.

VILNA GAON

We live in a fast-paced world where we often want, if not demand, instant results and immediate gratification. Especially if we work in a high-pressured situation, we may feel that we do not have the luxury to sit back and let the results unfold without active intervention. Can we adopt a different perspective in our personal lives? Can we realize that the gifts we give to others, whether in the form of attention, friendship, care, or love, are lifelong investments? We can never be sure if, or when, we will receive any benefits. In fact, gratification may be a long time in coming. When we demand instant gratification from our relationships it is often a sign that they are not true friendships in the model of the I-Thou relationships Martin Buber speaks about, but rather, I-It relationships, where we objectify the other person. Let us strive for I-Thou relationships, for here what we extend comes back to us in ways that we could never imagine at the outset. Let us act on faith and extend ourselves time and time again to those we love.   LF

God in the Present
11 AUGUST

Only God can be in the absolute present tense; humans can only approach that state. Even when we are present, mindful, flush with our experience, there is still a synapse of milliseconds between the experience itself and the time it takes . . . to process it. So we are never really in our experience, just watching a movie of what happened . . . , but the closer we get to the present, the closer we get to God.

RABBI ALAN LEW[157]

Other cultures have said it in different ways. The Greek philosopher Heraclitus once remarked, "You can't step in the same river twice." Things are never the same. Life changes as it moves forward in the same way the waters rush forward in a stream. But Rabbi Lew is teaching us a new lesson here. Because we have to objectify the experience in order to reflect on it, we can never be fully in the present of the experience. Our senses usually get in the way.

This is the lesson that Moses learned at the burning bush, so teaches Rabbi Lew, particularly when God tells Moses that the divine name is "I am what I am." When the same text is interpreted as "I am what causes all to be," as some people prefer to translate this text, we miss the point. God invited Moses to gaze at the burning bush as it burned without being consumed in order to be fully in the presence of the experience of God. Perhaps God was successful in doing so. Maybe that is why Moses is later described with a light in his eyes that never dimmed. But even Moses was only able to approximate being fully present at the bush. He had a head start. He noticed the bush. Then he removed his shoes as an acknowledgment of God's presence. In other words, God was fully present there.

How often are we someplace where we are not fully present? Things rob us of our concentration. Our minds are busy reviewing the day, what we have done and what we have yet to do. We are distracted, unable to concentrate on our ongoing dialogue with the Divine. The routine of prayer is one method we can draw on to help overcome this, designed as it is to help us learn to be fully present throughout the day.

So let's do what Rabbi Lew advises us to do: get closer to the present so that we can get closer to God.   KO

Random Acts of Kindness

12 AUGUST

The highest wisdom is kindness.

JEWISH FOLK SAYING

It was a bright summer Saturday afternoon. My family was enjoying some time in a local park with family friends. An ice cream truck came *ding-a-ling*ing along, stopping right in front of the area where all the kids were playing. But it was Saturday—Shabbat—and neither of us parents carried money on the Sabbath. The boys approached, wide-eyed and expectant. We reminded them both that it was Shabbat. Their response: "What if we explain to the driver of the ice cream truck that it is Shabbat, that we can't pay him today but we will gladly pay him tomorrow?" and off they went to the truck.

My husband hoisted up our seven-year-old to that window way up and he began to explain, "Excuse me, are you Jewish?" he asked the driver, who appeared to be all of eighteen. "No," came the abrupt reply. Now realizing the serious nature of his mission, our son continued, "Well, we are Jewish and today is our special day, Shabbat. It comes once a week, on Saturday. And to make this day special, we don't use money—although we *are* allowed to have ice cream. I was wondering whether we could get one cone today and come back tomorrow to pay for it."

No response. Only two cones: one for our son and one for his friend. Utter joy. Someone from the world of the grown-ups had validated them as people and trusted them.

Perhaps we all have the opportunity to be that ice cream truck driver at one time during our lives. Faced with the opportunity to perform one act of kindness, we have to seize the opportunity: a phone call; a card; a thoughtful word; a shoulder to lean on; a meal; a night of babysitting; a little thing that someone needs us to remember; a soft voice; a loving stroke on the cheek; taking the time to stop, bend down, and listen; or even giving someone an ice cream cone.

Jewish tradition teaches that before the Messiah comes, Elijah will herald that special day. But in order to see if we are really ready for a better world, Elijah will come disguised. The day following our ice cream, we returned to the park to pay for it, as we had promised. But the driver was not there. Nor on Monday or Tuesday or Wednesday. The ice cream truck never came back. "What do you think happened?" I asked our son. He turned to me and said, "It's obvious. The ice cream man was Elijah. We just didn't realize it."

Tomorrow, may we do something so that someone else might say, "One simple act of kindness changes the world."

RABBI ELYSE GOLDSTEIN

Respect for Community

13 AUGUST

Let respect for the community always be with you.

TALMUD[158]

What does it mean to have respect for community in today's world? Many of us seek the support and presence of community, and yet we also seek to maintain our autonomy and individuality. The pull toward these two axes—community and individuality—exists in all of us. Sometimes we feel the tug of community more strongly and we are willing to cede parts of our individual desires and needs in order to be part of something larger. And then there are times when we stand by our individual needs and are unwilling to cede anything for any larger communal structure. At those times when we step back from community, we must do so with respect for all that the community provides, so that when we are away "doing our own thing," we are still respectful of the communal structures that remain in place for others and for ourselves when we should choose to return. For, sure enough, time will pass and we will once again seek out the embrace of community in one way or another. Thankfully, the communal structures persist and are there for us when we seek ways to educate our children and renew our spirit. Let us remember that the community is only as strong as those who labor to keep its services and structures in place and its purpose focused and invigorated. May we find ways to pay them tribute and to contribute ourselves.   LF

The Soft Sounds of the Almighty

14 AUGUST

There was a great and mighty wind, splitting mountains and shattering rocks by the power of God; but God was not in the wind. After the wind—an earthquake; but God was not in the earthquake. After the earthquake—fire; but God was not in the fire. And after the fire—kol demamah dakkah— the sound of delicate silence.

I KINGS 19:11B–12

In this sensitive translation of the biblical text by Rabbi Daniel Gordis, we see an alternative description of God, one that we do not generally see in the rest of the Bible. One expects God to emerge in the midst of the power of nature, since God is the source of all nature. That is the way divine communication is often framed elsewhere. But here it is not the case. God dwells in the silence.

God is in the calm that comes after the storm, offering support and strength to help us through what we just survived. As we face tragedy, whether the result of human intervention or divine providence, we turn to God and ask, "Why?" Like Job who suffered in the Bible, we want to know why this happened and why God did not intervene to stop it. At the very least, we want to know what we are supposed to learn from the suffering we are being forced to endure. Here the Bible wants to teach us another lesson, which is incredibly profound in its simplicity. When we ask these questions of God and get no apparent answer, God is in the silence of response. This awareness gives us strength enough to survive and carry on, knowing that God's presence dwells among us.

KO

The Perfect Garden

15 AUGUST

May their souls be bound up with the souls of the living.

LITURGY[159]

The first thing we did when we arrived was to rent a car. It was summertime so we splurged on a convertible. Then we drove to the cemetery. Many in my family are buried in that cemetery.

I read on nearly each stone the traditional abbreviations from the memorial prayer that links souls together in bonds that death itself cannot rescind, "May their souls be bound up with the souls of the living."

I stood between my mother and father, a few feet away from my grandmother and grandfather. I took out a story to read, something that I recalled from my childhood, something that I had been carrying around in my knapsack—and I began to read.

My daughter, for whom I write my stories, wandered over to me and sat directly on the grave marker of my mother, with her hands wrapped around my legs as I read. She had heard the story before, but this time I was reading it to the souls of my parents and grandparents. I could feel their presence in the air around me, swirling like smoke, up above our heads.

When I finished reading the story, I realized why I had come to this place. Now I am the next, as I am the before, to the one at my feet with her arms wrapped around my legs who will one day do for me what I am doing for them. One day, my soul will wait for such a healing, and one of my children will come and do these acts of repair for me.

For a moment, just a split second, I saw and understood it all. I rose to the top of Ezekiel's chariot. It was covered with the dew of light. I saw us all together, the souls of the living with the souls of those who were no longer living, bound up with one another in a way that nothing—not the enemy, not time, not the adversary—could interrupt. There was nothing, in this world or the next, that could corrupt this perfect garden or my memory of it.   RABBI JAMES STONE GOODMAN

Making Someone Part of You
16 AUGUST

The beginning of love is knowledge. Really knowing someone can transform him or her in your eyes from someone who is external to you into becoming a part of you.
RABBI YERUCHAM LEVOVITZ

We all meet many people as we go through life. Some we get to know well, and we warmly welcome them into our hearts and into our inner circle of friends. Others we may know only superficially, as our paths may cross infrequently. Think about the process of getting to know someone. Do we take the time to get to know the others person's passion and concerns? Do we relate to the person as a human being with a complex inner life? So often the first question we ask is, "What do you do?" What would it be like to ask, "What's important to you?" or "What do you love in life?" Meeting another person has the potential to transform us when we allow ourselves to be open to their full being. When we do so with a full heart, we make a connection that is eternal.   LF

Concentration

17 AUGUST

When a distracting thought comes to you in prayer, hold fast to God and break through to redeem the sacred spark that dwells within that thought.

HASIDIC TEACHING[160]

While it is difficult to admit, I often find it hard to concentrate in prayer—even after all these years of working hard at it. Each morning, thoughts of the day ahead flit through my mind as I try to pray. In the afternoon, I have to find a few minutes to separate myself from the frenzied world in which I find myself in order to pray. And in the evening, I am tired and I want to review the day just past, so that I don't forget what I have yet to do, so that I can learn from what transpired, and so that I can prepare for the day ahead.

I used to try to push out each thought as it wandered into my prayer. I would make sure that if I prayed alone, I did so in a place that offered few distractions. Often I will sing *niggunim* (wordless chants) to myself to help make the transition into prayer, focusing on a verse from the midst of my prayer as a *kavannah* (sacred mantra). During the morning, particularly during the *Amidah* (the core prayer of the service that is said while standing), I wrap myself in my *tallit,* covering my head with it so that I might focus only on the words of prayer. All of these techniques and many others help, but I still found it difficult to concentrate on praying until I read the words above of a Hasidic teacher.

He advised me to embrace the distractions, to bring them into my prayers so that I might discover the holy sparks that lie embedded inside them, so that I might be able to release them. And as I bring them closer to me rather than pushing them far away, the sparks ignite and they set my soul aflame.   KO

Sustaining Family Ties

18 AUGUST

Jacob saw [his brother] Esau coming. . . . Esau ran to greet him. He embraced him and, falling on his neck, kissed him; and they wept.

GENESIS 33:1, 4

For twenty-five years, my parents spoke of moving: to an apartment in New York City, to Pittsburgh to be near my aunt, to Philadelphia to be near my sister. I never took their talk seriously, and even though they'd go around with real estate agents in each town, in my bones I knew their looking at houses was but a hobby. That's why, when they started talking about moving to New Jersey to be near me, and spent each Sunday looking at houses, I just nodded distractedly.

Then they sold their house and bought one just seven minutes away from where I live. So that they could continue to look at houses, my dad began to study for a real estate agent's license.

I am not one of those people who like to live near their parents and be all involved in each other's lives. I have always lived a bridge, a tunnel, or another state away.

I never imagined that if my parents lived nearby, they could help out with the kids. My mother adores her grandchildren, but kids had always made her nervous, and after a few excited minutes, she would end up with a cold washrag on her forehead.

As I watched their moving van pull up, I confess I prayed, "Oh, my God, help us live through this."

Coincidentally, just when my parents arrived, I had started working in New York City. I had yet to figure out who would do all the driving around for the kids that I had always done.

My first week of work, my mom offered to drive my girls to and from ballet. I hesitated, not wanting to burden her, but she insisted. The next week she drove to ballet, picked one kid up at Hebrew day school, and took another to the Israel Experience seminar at the J.C.C. Soon after, she was also doing the bar/bat mitzvah class carpool, ballet, and Maccabee track practice. By the time daylight saving time was over and it got darker earlier, my dad, the better night-time driver, joined my mother's livery service. Come Shabbat, my parents preferred the same synagogue as my daughters, and so they would often come back together, collaborating on the postmortem on the sermon, the bar mitzvah, the kiddush.

At first I felt guilty about my parents' doing all the driving. While they are, thank God, healthy and don't need me to take care of them, I was uncomfortable to think that since they have moved here, they have, essentially, been "taking care" of us—even bringing over cauldrons of chicken soup when we are sick. But when I would do the driving myself, I noticed that my mother sounded genuinely disappointed to hear that this week she was "off the hook." She said it gave her something to do, something to structure her day, and something to look forward to. But most of all, she said, the shared car time had become precious to her because of the closeness to her grandchildren it created. She no longer need-ed to depend on me to report to her on how the girls were doing. She needed no photographs, no phone calls. She was fully present in their lives. She knew the details that constitut-ed my daughters' lives.

My mother says that the years that she has lived here—near us—have been the best years of her life. Each week, when we sit at the table on Shabbat night, when I hear my dad asking about the cute boy in the bar/bat mitzvah class, when my mother wants to know if a book she had found can be helpful in a book report, I can only agree—these years of strengthened family ties have been a blessing. While it may be hard to sustain such family intensity, the attempt to commit to one's family may be the best way to create the whole human being. VANESSA L. OCHS[161]

Balancing Feeling and Reason
19 AUGUST

A person cannot live by reason alone nor by feeling alone.
There must always be a synthesis of reason and feeling.
If a person should immerse oneself in feeling alone he will
fall into the depths of folly which bring about every
weakness and sin. Only an equitable balance between the
two will bring one's full deliverance.

RABBI ABRAHAM ISAAC KOOK[162]

Many of us may see this advice as belonging in the realm of psychology, not religion. We have read about the need for both intellectual and emotional balance, and the words of Rabbi Kook, the first chief rabbi of Israel, seem to resonate with what we now take as a common truth. However, the difference is that Rabbi Kook teaches this from a spiritual perspective. He doesn't speak about attaining this balance as a self-help theory. Rather, he teaches it as a path to deliverance, as a way to attain personal redemption. These are religious terms that we use when we talk about ways of overcoming our sense of exile and connecting with God, or alternatively, when we speak about a vision for a future filled with compassion and vision. If we look inward, we will be able to discern if we have a preference for reason or for feeling. Unfortunately, balancing these two doesn't seem to come naturally. Thus, Rabbi Kook teaches that striving for this balance is a spiritual goal. What would it take for us to balance these qualities so that we find moments of redemption in our lives? LF

Discovering One's Work in the World

20 AUGUST

*The Torah has seventy facets, but there are four hundred
ways to do God's work. After all, what value would
there be to God if, as if it were possible, there
was only one way to worship God?*

REBBE ELIMELECH OF LIZHENSK

I like to make the distinction between my job and my work
and I encourage others to do the same. When we are lucky,
job and work complement and support each other.
Sometimes they are one and the same. At times they are at
odds with one another, fiercely competing for dominance in
one's life.

With the proper training and education, a job is relatively
easy to secure and maintain. It is a bigger challenge to discern
what one's work is in the world. We have to be willing to ask
some difficult questions: "What work does God want me to
do in this world? What talents has God given me that it is
incumbent on me to apply in this work? Where should I be
doing this work and with whom?"

Sometimes, the answers to these questions come easily. We
wake up one morning and know exactly what to do. At other
times it is not so clear. We have to think. We have to study.
We have to pray. Then we have to think some more.   KO

Remembering Forgiveness

21 AUGUST

As soon as one repents, one is forgiven.

TALMUD[163]

The process of *teshuvah* requires us to return to and reflect
upon wrongs that have been done. Forgiveness does not come

240 · RESTFUL REFLECTIONS

out of denying or forgetting an event. One must arrive at forgiveness by remembering. This resonates in me as a helpful understanding of memory and forgiveness. Sometimes we remember too well. We have such a difficult time allowing ourselves to make mistakes that when we do wrong, we are our harshest judges. We will not allow ourselves to forget our wrongs, so we carry them with us. We memorize our failings, and when we recognize them in others, we are quick to condemn them.

As Jews we are mandated to go through a process of return, repentance, and forgiveness each year. Holding on too tightly to some memories makes *teshuvah* impossible. There are other memories that we may decide to continue to hold on to because the gravity of the sins committed against us demand of us not to let go of them, at least not yet. We may find that in order to truly move forward, we must achieve some level of forgiveness, forgiveness of deeds we may have never imagined ourselves capable of forgiving. There are certain elements of wrongdoing committed against us that we must blot out in order to be freed. Sometimes letting go of too much will cause us to slip back and repeat the same destructive behavior. Other times it is holding on too tightly to these memories that causes us to internalize wrongdoings and to act them out on others or on ourselves.

Teshuvah is a difficult process. The time allotted to this process in the Jewish calendar is forty days a year—the month of Elul (usually August-September) and the days before Yom Kippur. While we can achieve some resolution and renewal during these days, we may find that we need more time, that we are still considering the question late into the fall, after the holidays, as well. Not all forgiveness can be contained in any one month and ten days. Therefore, each year we return again and continue in the yearlong (and lifelong) process of *teshuvah*. AYELET COHEN[164]

The Footprints of Our Past

22 AUGUST

*Ritual, like precedent, is a footprint left by the encounter of
just and holy people with God, who is holiness and justice.
Footprints like these deserve to be followed, as they may
lead again to the source of holiness and justice.*

SHALOM SPIEGEL[165]

We are all intrigued by footprints, for they suggest the elusive presence of a person. Each of us, I suspect, has tried to
place our own foot into footprints left on a sandy beach or a
muddied path to see if, even for a moment, we could step
into another person's shoes. There are all kinds of footprints
that we come across in our lives. Not all are actual impressions made by another person; as suggested above, rituals,
too, can be thought about in a similar way. They are footprints from another time, from the past, that we bring ourselves to "try on" to see how they fit. Sometimes they may
feel too big when we first place ourselves into them. Yet,
when rituals work, we find that we can be moved by their
power, and through them we can be transported to another
dimension. Indeed, perhaps they have persevered through
time because they lead those who follow them down a path
of holiness. When we come across these traces of the past—
be they rituals or other kinds of religious observances—let us
not unthinkingly wipe them out or cover them over, but
rather, let our curiosity be aroused so that we might step into
them, try them out, and discover their source and the meaning they can have for our lives.   LF

Find Our Way

23 AUGUST

Each tractate of the Talmud begins with page two rather than page one to remind us that no matter how much we study and learn, we have not yet come to the first page!

ADAPTED FROM RABBI LEVI YITZCHAK OF BERDITCHEV

Dr. Jacob Neusner once quipped that the Talmud starts with page two instead of page one to emphasize that in the study of Talmud, as soon as we start, we are already behind. Some of us who started studying Talmud later in life rather than earlier certainly feel that way! But the Rabbis knew what they were doing when they compiled the Talmud. It may seem unmanageable to some, but their own unique sense of order emerges from its pages. Sure, the Rabbis wanted pagination to be made simple. So they started numbering with the cover page (inside and out). But they also wanted the Talmud to teach its students—who were often busily engaged in the intellectual challenges of the text—a few spiritual lessons: We need to be guided through the pages of Talmud. Even advanced students are always behind. And there is always more to be learned.   KO

Admitting That We Sin

24 AUGUST

For sins committed against another person, one is never pardoned unless that person compensates his or her neighbor and makes an apology. . . . That person must apologize and ask for forgiveness.

MOSES MAIMONIDES[166]

Because of the fall holidays, many of us feel burdened by all the things we have done wrong during the past twelve months. Even the little things that we might have forgotten weigh heavily on our souls this time of year. And when we review the entire twelve months at the end of each day, it is no wonder that we have trouble sleeping.

It is easy to go through our lives without acknowledging when we hurt another human being through our actions or through our thoughtless inaction. Because we think we understand why it is that we act the way we do, we look for ways to justify our behavior. Then we explain away our behaviors. Sometimes we place the blame on others. Oftentimes we simply write it off the way we might write off a business loss. It is just the cost of doing business, just the cost of interacting with humans in this fast-paced, frenetic world. We may even blame our behavior on some abuse (recent or distant) that was perpetrated against us. That seems to give us license for what we have done. After all, we couldn't help it! But we know that it is not true, and this time of year, we face all of those myths that we have told ourselves, myths that we have been unwilling to confront all year long.

When another person suffers as a result of either our action or our inaction, then it is our responsibility to find that person, look at him or her eye to eye and ask for forgiveness. We have to do whatever is necessary to make amends for what we have done and vow not to repeat the behavior again. This is *teshuvah,* turning our lives around.

Doing *teshuvah* is difficult because it demands that we acknowledge, then accept, our weaknesses and admit them to another person with regret. When we do this either publicly or privately, we may feel that we are "losing face." After all, people of our status in the community should not be doing such things. But through the admission of our misdeeds we gain respect as a result of the courage and honesty with which we have confronted our actions and begun to understand their implications for others. If we take the time to examine our behavior at the end of each day and ask for forgiveness without delay, we will find that we can sleep a lot easier. Pleasant dreams.   MARCIA COHN SPIEGEL

The Rule of Right Not Might
25 AUGUST

Jewish religion absolutely refuses to make peace with the status quo which it considers godless because, despite the outward form of law and respectability, it is based upon the rule of might and not of right.

RABBI MORDECAI KAPLAN[167]

A well-known saying is: *Might makes right*. Think of the power yielded by the largest conglomerates and the most powerful nations. Too often power overwhelms and wields its influence, but it is not always right nor just. Conversely, the Hebrew prophet Zechariah teaches, *Not by might and not by power, but by My spirit alone*, reminding us that our spiritual connection with God is what will ultimately triumph. It is easy to see the imbalance and misuse of power when we look around the world; yet, how often do we reflect on how we use our own power? Do we use it wisely? Do we use it to promote justice and righteousness? It is all too easy to misuse the power and influence we each possess. As Jews, let us remember that we stand on the side of *tzedek*—righteousness—though it may not be in line with the rule of the mighty or the majority.   LF

Standing in the Center

26 AUGUST

The center of the world is exactly where you stand.

MISHNAH[168]

For a tradition that encourages a certain measure of self-effacing humility and, at the very least, suggests that Jerusalem is at the center of the world, it is surprising to read such a statement, which appears to affirm self-centeredness and egocentricity. And yet, Jewish tradition has always been sensitive to the reality of the way people live their lives, even as it has suggested an ideal posture for living. People focus on their own needs. It is how we survive. Often, even after we have survived life-threatening trauma and changed our priorities for a while, we return to where we once were. It takes a great deal of effort to keep what is really important from being eclipsed by the unimportant stuff that clutters our lives.

We try not to be self-centered. We try to focus our attention on issues that extend beyond ourselves, beyond the narrow reaches of our everyday world. There are many things that we know are not important in the long run, but they just get to us and drive us crazy. So when things lie heavy upon us, it is difficult to focus on what is really important. It seems that every step away leads us back to the same place.

Nevertheless, if we keep moving forward, then the center of the world constantly changes. The solution: Take a step forward, even if it is a small one.   KO

Seeking Each Other in a Cloud

27 AUGUST

When Moses finished the construction of the Tent of Meeting, the Presence of God filled the Tabernacle.

EXODUS 40:34

One of the great mysteries of life is how two people are able to fall in love and build a home together. How difficult it is to know oneself—how many moods, feelings, thoughts, and experiences go into making every single person. We are often surprised by the force of our own reactions, even though we have lived with ourselves for our entire lives. Compound that depth of unknown history and unpredictable emotions by putting two people together. Two human beings—worlds unto themselves—are able to nurture each other in a relationship. What becomes astounding is not that there are many separations and divorces but that there are so few.

If each person is a little universe, then how can such universes coexist? We are so full of ourselves that there is little room left for anyone else, let alone for someone so complex and demanding as another human being. It is only by consenting to reveal our own hidden natures, by inviting someone else to share in our inner lives, that relationship becomes a possibility. Opening ourselves to each other's openness is the great miracle of life—where seemingly incompatible universes can meet, explore, and grow. The path of relationship is unanticipated, unlikely, and difficult. But without it we are nothing. Only by making ourselves available to each other—and to God—by sharing our joys and our sorrows, by learning and praying together, can we be fully human.

RABBI BRADLEY SHAVIT ARTSON

Interdependence

28 AUGUST

*The fact that a human being will always need the
assistance of others teaches us that we were not
created to exist just for ourselves.*

SIMCHA ZISSEL ZIV

We are well aware that newborn infants are born dependent. In fact, it is in part their dependency and innocence that touches our hearts and makes us melt when we see a baby. As we each pass through infancy to childhood, from childhood to adolescence, and from adolescence to adulthood, we lose much of our innocence and grow into independent beings. Hopefully, we gain the necessary skills to live independent lives. Yet we are never totally independent. We are interdependent. For as human beings, we need to live among the community of others and to be held by the bonds of relationship, responsibility, and reciprocity that are part of living with others. We might think we can go it alone, but once we reach a rocky patch in our life's path, we realize just how much we need others. If we understand this in the depths of our soul, then we can strive for interdependence in our relationships. We come to realize that we are created not just to independently fulfill our own needs and desires but also to be present for others and help them in their journeys.   LF

Getting Ready for the Harvest

29 AUGUST

*If one does not plow in the summer,
what will be eaten in the winter?*

MIDRASH[169]

In the late days of August, our minds are often focused on the fleeting days of summer and the special schedule that accompanies it. Early closings. Casual Fridays. Gardening. Weekends at the shore—if you are close to one. European or island vacations—if you can afford them! Some of us just take a few days off to sleep late and lounge around the house. During the summer we reap the benefits of all our hard work in the winter. Only a few more days until Labor Day and then the fall—and the schedule that accompanies it—begins, even if fall technically does not start until weeks later.

But there are many summer projects that we just did not get to! We had the best of intentions, but the lazy days of summer drew us in. Maybe we don't take enough advantage of such leisure time. Just as Shabbat provides us some respite each week, maybe summer is the Shabbat of the year and we should let go of the many things that occupy us during the year. But there is one question that continues to nag at us. It is the sentiment expressed by the midrash: If we do not sow seed in the summer, there can be no fall harvest. And winter is rough enough without there not being enough to eat. Fortunately, summer is not yet over; there is still time to plant for tomorrow.   KO

Turning

30 AUGUST

Great is repentance. It prolongs life.
TALMUD[170]

It is a small step from the languid days of summer to the crisp days of fall. We turn, almost imperceptibly, from the last corn and tomatoes of the season to the first sips of apple cider. Every year this time seems to slip away and we are carried along with it into a new season. We are finally used to summer and suddenly our kids are getting ready to go back to school, the football exhibition season has started in earnest, and the leaves are beginning to get their "pre-turning" look about them. It all seems to happen without any awareness on our part and certainly without our participation in the process.

Yet, for those of us who live in Jewish time, the month of Elul, which falls around this time of year, asks us to be conscious of the passing of time. Elul calls to us to prepare for the upcoming season of High Holidays. It asks us to take note of each day and not to just let it pass. Elul asks us to plan for our repentance and our eventual atonement. And just how do we do this?

The recipe for atonement is very simple. It has not changed in two thousand years. Take a liberal dose of prayer, add full-hearted remorse, the charitable giving of money for *tzedakah*, and loving acts of kindness to others. Sounds easy and straightforward, doesn't it? Yet we know how difficult it is to actually accomplish.

Every year we face the same end-of-summer challenge. August says: Wait, enjoy, all our worries will pass us by anyway. Elul says: Don't let the chance to turn pass you by. You may not have this opportunity again. Act now, and next month, our atonement will be earned. Something to think about when you go to bed this evening. It will make you sleep better, just knowing what you have to do. And then in the morning, find the family and friends that you have hurt; seek them out and make peace with them.

RABBI JAMES A. GIBSON

The Demands of Leadership
31 AUGUST

To inspire means to demand. . . .
A leader inspires and demands.
RABBI HERBERT A. FRIEDMAN[171]

Who will inspire us in the century? We recall the last century's words from President John F. Kennedy, "Ask not what your country can do for you but what you can do for your country," and those of the Reverend Martin Luther King, "I have a dream that one day this nation will live out the true meaning of its creed: *We hold these truths to be self-evident that all men are created equal.*" Inspiration can span the centuries, as we know from our search for meaningful teachings from Jewish sources. One such saying comes from *Pirke Avot*. It says, "It is not incumbent upon us to finish the work but we are not free to desist from it." Think of those people in your life whom you consider to be leaders. How do they lead? How do they inspire? How do they demand? True leaders know how to make demands on us that we aspire to fulfill. Let us be courageous in choosing wise, inspirational leaders. And, in the times when we ourselves are leaders, let us not be afraid to demand as we reach to inspire.   LF

SEPTEMBER

A New Year of Blessing

1 SEPTEMBER

As the old year and its maledictions end,
the new year and blessings begin.

TALMUD[172]

Why is it that we generally feel so good about the New Year—so much so that we are thrilled that the calendar allows for so many of them? In the fall, we celebrate the Jewish New Year, also called Rosh Hashanah. At about the same time, the school year begins—for those of us who use the academic calendar to guide our lives or have children who do so. In any case, the work year—even though neither the fiscal year nor the tax year comes in the fall—begins anew at the same time. It is the end of the summer vacation and we go back to work. And in the middle of winter, we celebrate the new year of the trees, a simple system for taxation that assigns collective birthdays of sorts for trees on one particular date regardless of what day in the previous year they were actually planted.

This is our way of measuring time, but it is also our way of renewing hope for the future. Even as we celebrate the old, we resonate with newness in a variety of ways. The new year means that we have passed over the hurdles of the past year. We give ourselves a clean break. The new year means that we have the potential to transcend some of the mistakes we have made in the past even though we may be still working to repair them.   KO

Striving for the Universal

2 SEPTEMBER

God was charitable toward the world by not endowing all talents in one place nor with one person nor with one nation, nor with one country, nor with one generation, nor with one world. But the talents are diffused. . . . The disposition to universality always fills the hearts of the refined spirits of the human race.

RABBI ABRAHAM ISAAC KOOK[173]

Rabbi Abraham Isaac Kook was the first Ashkenazi chief rabbi in Israel. He reflected in his writings and his life a deep understanding that to be a religious, spiritual person one has to have respect for others. Rav Kook had the unique ability to use the particularism of Judaism as a spiritual lens to understand all people. He understood that each person or group of people has its own particular strength and vision and that each is needed for a complete world.

So let us ask ourselves, "How do we expand the boundaries of our own particularity?" As we look around, are we mindful of the talents of our colleagues, friends, and family members? Can we celebrate the diversity within and among us? When we respect the plurality of skills and talents along with the differing approaches and opinions that exist in our world today, then we can draw upon these many differing blessings and find strength and vitality in our lives.   LF

Transforming Darkness

3 SEPTEMBER

God turns my darkness into light.
II SAMUEL 22:29

God waits for us in the dark pathways of our hearts. God calls to us from our shadow, pleading with us not to give up, not to give in to fear, not to forget that the dawn is coming. God's tenderness and love await us. God asks nothing but that we join on the path with God, allowing the Holy One to light our way.

Yet, it is hard to find the light that the psalmist writes about. We fear that the beacon has gone out. It will take all our strength, all our courage to find it again.

This is what *teshuvah*, repentance, must be: a return to the light. To the light that dwells outside and to the light that is found inside. Shekhinah, Holy One, when I call on Your light in my soul, I come home. We come home to the light that helps us be unafraid. Come home to the light that shines in the face of every person, even those you fear the most. Come home to the light of the Divine that illumines our path. Come home to the light that gives us the courage to see the blessing even in the darkness. To the light of God which shines still in our souls. Come home to the light with which we bless each other.

May the face of the Holy One be turned toward us and fill us with light. RABBI LAVEY DERBY

Keep the Gates Open
4 SEPTEMBER

*Open for us a gate even at the time of the locking of the
gates, for the day is waning. The day is fading, the sun is
beginning to set. Let us enter Your gates.*

LITURGY[174]

For many people, including myself, this marks the most
powerful moment in the fall holiday period. We have been in
the synagogue all day—having started the night before. We
have been fasting. We are spent physically and spiritually. But
the gates of repentance remain open. God is willing—even at
this late hour—to hear our confession, to receive our prayers,
to help us to reach out to God even as the Holy One reaches
out to us. While most synagogues leave the holy ark open
during this time period—and therefore the congregation
remains standing—some congregations, borrowing from a
Sephardic custom, encourage their members to approach the
ark individually or as a family to offer a final, private prayer.

All year long, says the tradition, we have to search for God.
During the period of the High Holidays, God comes searching
for us—and leaves the gate to the house open so that we can
return home, even if we do not have the key.   KO

Judgment versus Righteousness
5 SEPTEMBER

*The Holy One annuls strict decrees
because of the decree of righteousness.*

TALMUD[175]

Judaism metaphorically speaks about God's moving from the
"chair of judgment" to the "chair of compassion" during the
days that bridge Rosh Hashanah and Yom Kippur. Tra-

ditionally we fear there is divine punishment when we transgress and act wrongly. What moves God, though, to let up on us, to turn away from a strict decree of judgment? Here it is suggested that when we manifest righteous behavior, God is moved and thus moves to sit on the "chair of compassion." If you are a parent, think about what moves you to soften when a child errs. You may be ready to punish him or her and then your child does something that reminds you of his or her innate goodness, humanity, and ability to pursue righteousness. When we, as parents, glimpse these qualities in our children, we are moved to be more compassionate. So, too, is God moved, for God's true desire for us is that we pursue righteousness in all we do. Let us remember that righteousness trumps judgment.   LF

Special Time

6 SEPTEMBER

Judaism is a religion of life against death.
RABBI IRVING GREENBERG[176]

Just the other day, I took a moment to look up, and behold, it was Rosh Hashanah again. Time flies by. There is no stopping it, no way to make it pause in its ceaseless forward movement toward that hidden place called "later." Time is implacable in its flight. And that is exactly why this New Year season, this holy time, is so precious.

We don't take time to think about time. We ignore it as if there were an unlimited supply of the stuff, as if for us it were endless. But it is not endless. It is our most precious commodity. It is the floor on which our life dance is performed. It is the arena in which we play out our years. Each year is significant; each decade, all the more so.

And so, we casually look up, and behold, it is the beginning of a new year. And how very fortunate we as a people truly are. For we are the only people on the face of this planet whose religion encourages us to celebrate time as we do. For most people, time is marked with party and gaiety, loud and raucous. It is as much a denial of time as a celebration. It is, I think, human nature to deny time, to mark it with acts of bravado. As if to say, what's to worry about. I'm still here, older but strong and flourishing. I am impervious to the effects of time. My clock ticks slowly. I persevere.

But such is not the Jewish way to view time. We are taught to mark its passage differently. We are taught to make the special times of our life sacred—to invest them with God's spirit. To bring that which transcends us into our life's passages. What a powerful message that can be to those who really hear it. We are taught to value time as a precious treasure and to celebrate it in such a way as to elevate our lives.

Time waits for no one. Treasure every moment you have. Use the time to introspect and reflect on just who you have become and on the who you want to be and on the journey you are willing to take to get there.

RABBI RAYMOND A. ZWERIN

In Dialogue with the Divine
7 SEPTEMBER

As you stand before God in prayer, you should feel that you stand alone—in all the world only you and God exist. Then there can be no distractions: nothing can disturb such prayer.

HASIDIC TEACHING[177]

According to the teaching of this Hasidic rebbe, once you have fully entered into a relationship with the Divine—one that is initially established and then maintained through prayer—no one or nothing can be imposed on that relationship or that prayer to interfere with it. Prayer is the most

direct form of communication that we have available, perhaps more efficient than study or ritual. Many things will
emerge to distract you in your prayer—family, job, leisure—
but nothing will be successful. Nothing can upset the harmony that is established through earnest and heartfelt prayer.
When you have reached such a state of prayerfulness, you
feel that nothing exists in the world besides you and God, the
Divine Source of all being. That's how you know that you are
really praying.

This does not seem possible until you have reached that
level of relationship. It may take years of daily prayer before
you are able to realize it. It takes discipline and hard work. It
does not happen overnight, as we would like to believe. That
would make living a religious life a lot easier and more per-
suasive, but it just doesn't work that way. Nevertheless, once
you reach that level of standing alone before God, your
prayer will be forever changed—and so will your relationship
with God.   KO

The Core of Religious Life

8 SEPTEMBER

*I was never able to pray in the usual manner by rote, and
even now neither can nor want to. But the dialogue man
holds with his Creator, and about which the prophet
preaches, is what I, too, have found. I see the sincere,
inner link, even if it comes through struggle
within myself and through some doubt.*

HANNAH SENESH[178]

Dialogue is the core of religious life. We may not often think
of it this way, but our questioning and doubts that we pose to
God form the basis of an ongoing dialogue. Martin Buber, a
famous Jewish German philosopher, called this an I-Thou

relationship. This relationship was marked by sustained open and honest give-and-take wherein neither side objectifies the other person. This is also true when we attempt to sustain a dialogue with God. However, there are many people who claim that prayers and the liturgical prayers that we find in traditional prayer books do not speak to them. Especially if we are not familiar with Hebrew, the English translations may seem formal and stilted, for example. However, do not let this type of "barrier" distance you from seeking a relationship with God. Search for ways around it; search for the words that emanate from your soul in establishing a dialogue with God. What does your soul yearn to express? We can also grow through our doubts, for they are an essential part of the spiritual path. No one seeks without bumping up against doubts. Rather than permitting the superficial barriers that we perceive to stand between us and God, let us seek an inner link that can nourish us and allow us to turn toward, and serve, the Holy One, *HaKadosh Barukh Hu*.   LF

Returning for Repentance

9 SEPTEMBER

Take words with you and return to God.

HOSEA 14:3A

Although the prophet Hosea was speaking specifically about the fall of the northern kingdom, it is his existential message of hope for both return and reconciliation that transcends history. Surely it's the reason that the Rabbis have assigned this verse and others to be read on the Sabbath that takes place between Rosh Hashanah and Yom Kippur, called *Shabbat Shuvah,* the Sabbath of Return.

In a play on the Hebrew of this verse, we can reinterpret this verse to read "Return O Israel, as a witness for Adonai your God"; that is, God is witness to all you do. In the simple read of the text, Hosea reminds us to repent because of the One who sees all our deeds and knows all our thoughts. While this may make some people uncomfortable, one Hasidic teacher, the Sefat Emet, following a midrashic interpretation of the text, finds comfort in this idea. One reading of the Sefat Emet suggests that we understand it this way: "Even if your intentions are thwarted and your thoughts of remorse are not translated into action, God will still testify [witness] to the internal repentance, the internal *teshuvah*, that takes place." In other words, return, for even if you are not successful, God will still be witness to the genuine effort that you make.

In the more playful translation of the verse, we understand the goal of *teshuvah* as becoming God's witnesses in the world—witnesses who testify through our actions. In doing *teshuvah*, we testify to the possibility of repentance, the necessity of goodness, our responsibility to continue hoping. Return, O Israel, and by virtue of your efforts at self-reflection and spiritual renewal, become a witness whose actions testify to the reality of God in the universe.   RABBI JONATHAN KRAUS

Choosing the Way
10 SEPTEMBER

God wants to be worshiped in all ways but it is up to the individual to choose his or her own way. This choice must be done with all his or her might.

BAAL SHEM TOV

If this is a key to worshiping God, then it does not give us much direction—or so it seems. The Baal Shem Tov, the founder of Hasidism, led the quiet revolution against the intellectualization of Judaism. He and his followers felt that Judaism had become joyless, that it had lost its mystery. Thus, he taught that we could approach God and worship God in a variety of ways. The way of the intellect that was fixed by the historical rabbinic community was insufficient. So he introduced the Jewish community to the world of fervent dance and song. He taught through story and was considered a worker of miracles. But what was most important about his work was not the specific path that he took or the specific path of his followers or even the paths that he urged others to take of their own choosing. Instead, what was most significant was that whatever path was chosen, we set out on it with all our might. So he and his Hasidim danced and sang and ate and prayed and studied with an unparalleled intensity.

We are to give to God "all we've got!" Anything less is insufficient and insignificant. KO

Peace and Goodness
11 SEPTEMBER

Establish peace [shalom], goodness and blessing, grace, and compassion on us and on all Israel.

LITURGY[179]

Rabbi Shlomo Carlebach was a musician, storyteller, and rebbe to all. Here is his teaching on the words *shalom* and *goodness* from the prayer above. The word *shalom*, peace, has three letters: *shin, lamed,* and *mem.* The first way to bring peace is to bring the two sides together, like the middle branch of the letter *shin. Lamed,* the second letter, is the tallest. It goes from the highest to the lowest. If you want to bring peace you have to be very high, to extend yourself, to stick out your neck. The final *mem* is a closed letter with no openings. Shalom has to be complete. It can have no breaches.

You can't say, "I am peaceful, but I need a little opening to use to escape through in an emergency."

Goodness means having good eyes. Some people look at you without saying anything, but with their eyes they cut you off and make you feel diminished and small. Other people look at you and not only do they make you as tall as you are, they make you feel taller, bigger. That's very special. According to the Hasidim, we strive to have "good eyes." For when we look at someone with "good eyes" we enable them to be more than they are. Let us strive for shalom (peace) and *tovah* (goodness) in all we do.   LF

Answers to Our Prayers
12 September
O God, answer me.
LITURGY[180]

We found an old synagogue that had been forgotten in the center of our city. For *Selichot,* the Saturday night before Rosh Hashanah, when penitential prayers are offered at midnight, we received permission to pray there. Nothing had been changed since it ceased functioning as a synagogue in 1944. We opened it up and sang our holy song to God in that space. I felt the breath, the souls, the hands, the eyes there, too. I felt them, the ancestors. I sensed their warm breath over my shoulder when I opened the siddur.

It was a small story in the life of our people and our community, but suddenly as we stood there praying, the small story became a larger story. Maybe there is no such thing as a small story. Perhaps all of our stories, including the stories of our individual lives that we reflect on each evening as they grow and accumulate, are all part of larger stories.

Still, the true prayer of the heart was difficult even in this special space that connected us to our past in ways that I had never experienced. I felt as if the true work of the prayer place is to bridge our worlds, to bring together out there, in here, up there, and down here. The hardest work of the synagogue is to bring the worlds together, for their separation is only an illusion.

Then there is also the spiritual tension between me and the space, between my experience of God and my experience of my self. The Baal Shem Tov taught it best: There is no room for God in a person who is too full of self. Here is what I think is the main thing: less self, more other, less self, more Other. Menachem Mendl of Kotzk said it a little differently. He said that the "I" is a thief. It snatches away the partial and mistakes it for the whole.

I asked the guy praying next to me that midnight what his theology was. "I don't have a theology," he said and invited me to join in his prayers. And I invite you, as well.

RABBI JAMES STONE GOODMAN

The Fall Holidays of Memory
13 SEPTEMBER

Only take heed, and be very careful to guard the memory of the day you stood before God in Horeb all the days of your life, and teach about it to your children and your grandchildren. Do not forget the things which your eyes saw and do not remove the memory from your heart.

DEUTERONOMY 4:9–10

I always joke about whose idea was it to have so many holidays in the fall, one after another, especially when there are other times during the year when there are few holidays or days of specific significance. Would it not have made more sense to spread them out a little more evenly?

Starting with Rosh Hashanah, which is named, among other things, *Yom Hazikaron,* the day of memory, there are many things that our tradition wants us to remember. This theme of memory is carried throughout the fall holidays. So what is it that the sages wanted us to remember? Is it the creation of the world? That certainly is what most of our teachers suggest. There are those who suggest, however, that it is the memory of Sinai that provides the context for Rosh Hashanah, rather than the memory of the creation of the world. Therefore, this idea of Sinai permeates the holidays that follow and provides a foundation for all of them. Without a covenant established between God and the Jewish people, of what import is Yom Kippur or Sukkot? It is the covenant that provides life for the holidays and for us—and offers us much to remember.   KO

Turning Evil into Good

14 SEPTEMBER

"Turn from evil and do good" (Psalm 34:15).
The meaning is to turn evil into good, because evil is the raw material of good.

BAAL SHEM TOV[181]

When we look around our world it is hard not to see that evil exists. Whether it is in the ethnic cleansing we witnessed in Kosovo or unexplainable murders taking place in high schools or hate crimes that take place all too often, we are stunned that evil's hold is so powerful. Unfortunately, in this century we have not eradicated hate. A basic philosophical question is, "Do we believe that evil can be transformed into good?" In other words, is human nature changeable or is it immutable? While Judaism recognizes evil, it teaches that individuals can, indeed, change for the good. Rosh Hashanah is a time when we reflect on how we can effect change within ourselves. While we are not evil, we do most likely have habits, behaviors, and attitudes that we have a hard time breaking even though we are fully aware that they are destructive to ourselves and harmful to others. Let us use this time of preparation before the High Holidays to transform these aspects of our character for the good. Let us not give up hope that change is possible even if we should find ourselves in the most difficult of situations.   LF

The Fall Classic
15 SEPTEMBER
*There is no righteous person on earth
who does only good and never sins.*
ECCLESIASTES 7:20

Rosh Hashanah and Yom Kippur are the World Series of the Jewish calendar. Attendance figures during the year may vary. Many people are only vaguely concerned with the fortunes of the home team during most of the season. But if the home team makes it, everyone becomes a fan. During the pennant race and into the World Series we are one. Every seat in the house is sold. Civic pride rises while the economy flourishes during those glory days. Sometimes, during a successful run, the citizens are even willing to build a new stadium for their team at their own expense.

What is it that we all hope for? Victory! Life is, after all, about competition. Winning is what it's all about. We all want to be winners. (Who wants to be a loser?) But one difference between sports and religion is that in religion, which is to say, in life, to be a winner does not require a loser. This is not to suggest that winning in life is noncompetitive. On the contrary, it is more competitive than any sport.

Like any game, the "game of life" has rules. If you want to win, you must play by the rules. The most important rule: you must not be a spectator. Rather, you must be a participant.

Rosh Hashanah, then Yom Kippur, marks the time that we retreat from the (battle) field to figure out where we stand. Our lives are at stake—the texture and quality of our lives, our integrity, our identities. The question is not what others think we should be, but the kind of person each of us wants to be. Not how well others know us, but how well we know ourselves. It's not easy. We have to stop strutting, pretending, inventing ourselves anew for each situation. We have to sit quietly and take our own measure. That's what Rosh Hashanah and Yom Kippur and this entire month are all about: figuring out the score. And if we are not winning (there are no ties in this game of life), we figure out how to do those things that give us a better chance of winning, of becoming the victor in life. RABBI JOEL H. ZAIMAN

The Purpose of Creation

16 SEPTEMBER

If you have learned much Torah, do not congratulate yourself. It is for this that you were created.

TALMUD[182]

The purpose of the creation of humans is hotly debated by the sages of antiquity. As might be expected, the Rabbis were concerned about the dissonance between the reality of human behavior and the potential for human perfection as described by Jewish tradition. They finally decided that it would have been better (and a lot easier on the world) had humans not been created. But since they were created, then each individual had the obligation to work to perfect himself or herself—and the world.

ie Rabbis are providing us with the blueprint for
.ection. For them and for us, Torah is more than a
scroll. It is more than religious literature. It is even
more than a spiritual history of our people. Instead, Torah is
a dynamic manual of discipline that guides our daily behavior. And it is this source for daily behavior—guiding our
interaction with others—that will bring the world to perfection and us along with it.   KO

Creating an Equitable World
17 SEPTEMBER

*Service to humanity must not be seen in the throwing of the
crumbs to the poor. . . . We must work out a world order
which shall rest upon equal distribution of labor and rewards.*

SHOLEM ASCH[183]

Often we translate the Hebrew word *tzedakah* as charity.
But this is not a precise translation because *tzedakah* is so
much more. *Tzedakah* is derived from the word *tzedek*,
which means justice. At the core of the Jewish enterprise is
the continual search for justice. *Tzedakah* encompasses the
Jewish vision that the inherent injustices in the world can be
made right by our efforts. While some of us may be generous
in giving from our financial resources, we also have the
responsibility to lend our voice and influence to policy matters that need long-term solutions. It is easy to write a check
and then close our eyes to the injustices that persist. One of
the greatest challenges that the Bible gives us is to pursue justice and not to expect it to come knocking on our door. For if
we have ever been the victim of injustice, we know in our
guts that it takes persistence, courage, and the strength of
community to right a societal wrong. Let us continue to
actively pursue justice so we can proudly add our names to

those who have blazed new paths by addressing societal injustices to create a better community for us all.   LF

The Silence of the Inner Self
18 SEPTEMBER

Like a hind crying for water, my soul cries for You, O God.
My soul thirsts for God, the living God, when I come to
appear before God.

PSALM 42:2–3

To fast for a day is not what makes Yom Kippur difficult for us. Fasting gets easier with age. The real challenge of Yom Kippur is to do without the distractions to which we are addicted. Ours is a society that abhors silence. We jog with earphones, fly with movies, and even entertain company with the television droning in the background.

In contrast, Yom Kippur asks us to take refuge in the silence of our inner selves. As the cacophony of distractions wanes, we begin to feel the yearnings of our repressed souls. We are more than our appetites and belongings, our ambitions and achievements. We also bear within us a touch of transcendence that has the power to sustain and ennoble us.

The supreme purpose of Judaism is to cultivate the inner life. Our souls also need attention. Rabbi Abraham Joshua Heschel said that "a person possessing nobility is one whose hidden wealth surpasses his outward wealth, whose hidden treasures exceed his obvious treasures, whose inner depth surpasses by far that which he reveals. Refinement is found only where inwardness is greater than outward appearance. The hidden is greater than the obvious, depth greater than breadth. Nobility is the redeemed quality that rises within the soul when it exchanges the transient for the permanent, the useful for the valuable."[184]

The intensity of Heschel's piety is surely in order for us on Yom Kippur when we reach for eternity, not via the roar of a spaceship but by the reverberations of our souls. It is the speck of divinity that resides at the core of our being and strives to be restored to its ultimate source, the Source of All Being. The linkage is indelible and inextricable. The universal quest for God is rooted in that spiritual patrimony.

And the purity of our soul derives from its origin, a conviction that we affirm each morning at the beginning of our prayers. The soul embarks on its earthly journey by being separated from God and then endowed with individuality. Thereafter God inspirits it into one of us at birth, giving rise to a singular expression in human life. The process is repeated daily. At night the soul returns to its divine soul mate, to be mercifully restored to us again in the morning, and hence the occasion for this thanksgiving prayer. Death, which is traditionally defined by the cessation of breathing, marks the final departure of our soul in its earthbound form. But the rupture is not permanent. In the life to come, as our souls are reabsorbed by God's all-encompassing Being, they are reattached to a semblance of our bodies for eternity.

The power of this conception of human life is that it makes us part of something infinitely greater than ourselves. For a fleeting moment, we become the vessel of a spark of pure spirit. To save our soul is the prerequisite for saving the life of another human being. If we were oblivious to the affinity between the human and the divine in each of us, we might not lift a finger to improve the welfare of our neighbors, near or far. May this insight inspire us to reach for loftier standards of piety and ethical behavior in the days to come.

RABBI ISMAR SCHORSCH

Returning

19 September

Return again to the land of your soul.
Return to who you are.
Return to what you are.
Return to where you are
Born and reborn again.

Rabbi Shlomo Carlebach[185]

In the fall, it seems that many of us find our way back to the synagogue. As an acknowledgment of this pattern, most synagogues require people either to purchase tickets or to make sure that their membership dues are paid in full by this time. It is an unfortunate aspect of synagogue life that has evolved over time. Some Jewish communal leaders call the folks who use the synagogue this way "twice-a-year Jews," referring to their brief synagogue appearances on Rosh Hashanah and Yom Kippur. Perhaps the visit is motivated by family—or maybe even guilt. But this is an unfair description, one that overlooks the motivation that is captured in this wonderful song by Rabbi Carlebach. Maybe it is the rhythm of the Jewish calendar that draws people in each year. It is as if the individual is saying, "I will give the synagogue—and Judaism—another chance. Maybe I will connect with it this year."

In a few lines, Rabbi Carlebach summarizes the driving force behind what really brings us to the synagogue. We want to return. It is a natural "instinct." Our challenge is to sustain the feeling—and not leave it to rabbis and cantors and educators to do it for us. That is where the words to this melody are particularly instructive. If we are able to return to who we are, to what we are and where we once were, then we can be reborn and begin the year and our lives anew.

May your visit to the synagogue this year be a visit to the land of your soul! KO

What Is Your Purpose in Life?

20 SEPTEMBER

Wherever we find life, it is charged with purpose. We can see this even in the very lowest forms of life. For example, when an amoeba is hungry, it reaches out for food, forms itself into new shapes, and surrounds what it wants to eat. It acts with a purpose to satisfy its hunger. This is the wonder that we cannot understand.

EMIL FACKENHEIM[186]

Life is certainly charged with purpose. That idea is basic to our tradition. But knowing that may not make it any easier for us to answer the question, "What is my purpose in life?" Usually this question arises when we are faced with moments of transition such as birth, illness, marriage, new job, or death. This question may arise when we feel some sort of dissatisfaction with how we spend our days, as we search for some meaning and purpose to remotivate our waking hours. We are also more inclined to think about this during this time of year as Rosh Hashanah approaches and we reflect on the past year and the year ahead.

Think about someone you know who exudes vitality and a love of life. Usually these individuals have an overriding sense of purpose that infuses all their actions, from the smallest to the largest. It is all too easy in today's world to lose our purpose, but it is our challenge to find that purpose and to then try to keep it front and center in our lives. As Jews we can embrace the values of *tikkun olam,* mending the world; *tzedakah,* creating a just world; and *rachamim,* being compassionate. Here are purposes that can stand at the center of our lives; here are answers to that question, answers that we can truly live with.   LF

God in Victory and God in Defeat

21 September

*Only through your own cleansing, through self-purging,
can you appear clean before God.*

RABBI MENACHEM MENDL OF KOTZK[187]

They are linked together but they are not the same. Rosh
Hashanah is not Yom Kippur and Yom Kippur is not Rosh
Hashanah. They each speak with different voices, express different attitudes. As I have grown older, I have come to understand through Yom Kippur revelations a different part of
myself and of the tradition. I come to Yom Kippur services
not as I do to the Rosh Hashanah services. I enter Kol Nidre
not as a success, not as victor nor as conqueror. I enter with
the sting of defeat, my own and those who know despair,
with the memory of those who have had their wills broken.

In contrast to the assertiveness of the Rosh Hashanah self,
the Yom Kippur self comes closest to what Hasidism called
bittul hayesh—the nullification of the self. *Bittul hayesh*
offers a paradoxical wisdom. Lose yourself in order to find
yourself, forget yourself in order to remember yourself. The
nullification of the self is a form of liberation. It means to rid
myself of the debris that buries my real self. It means to
remove the rubble of power, property, prestige, and pettiness,
the rocks of competitiveness, the dust of greed, the arrogance
of the small self that suffocates my real self.

Rosh Hashanah and Yom Kippur are complementary. They
are needed to correct the polar extremes of independence and
dependence, of will and submission. Their end is the last
prayer of the *Neilah* service, with the long blast of the shofar.
The sound of the shofar is blown through us, through our own
breath. The breath in us is God given. Listen to the breath of
life within us. That breath is our strength, our comfort, our

consolation, our help. The breath is innate, it is inborn. That breath enables us to fill our lungs with hope.

Where shall we look to strengthen our will? Above or below, God's will or ours? Rosh Hashanah joined to Yom Kippur informs us. The choice is not between doing God's will and thereby extinguishing our own, or not doing God's will and thereby blowing our own horn. Humility and self-regard are not opposites. God's will and our own capacity must become one.

Let us hold on to both Rosh Hashanah and Yom Kippur wisdom: how to conquer and how to lose, how to seize initiative and how to wait. RABBI HAROLD M. SCHULWEIS[188]

Harvest Season

22 SEPTEMBER

The sum of the matter, when all is said and done:
Revere God and observe God's instructions!
This applies to all humanity.
ECCLESIASTES 12:13

Once the ancient Israelites ceased wandering, after they journeyed through the desert, particularly after they settled the land of Israel, our ancestors became an agricultural people. They worked the land and it bore fruit for them. The echoes of this notion are still found in various parts of the liturgy. Thus it is not surprising that so many Jewish holidays have an agricultural theme that is woven through its celebration even if the holidays are also linked with some other aspect of Jewish history. So in the Jewish holiday calendar, Sukkot becomes the fall harvest festival even while it is also identified with other aspects of Judaism such as the desert experience that bridged Egyptian slavery and freedom in the land of Israel. Perhaps this is why it became such an excellent model for Thanksgiving for the American pilgrims. The values of our biblical forebears resonated with those who settled North America. They had taken the journey toward religious freedom and they fully understood, as did the ancient Israelites, how their survival and ultimate destiny were tied to the land of promise on which they lived.

But the Rabbis understand that the physical harvest was only part of life. The harvest of the land mirrored the spiritual harvest of the soul. It is one of the reasons the Rabbis instruct us to read and study the book of Ecclesiastes during this period of time. Ecclesiastes, or *Kohelet,* as the book is named in Hebrew for its primary character, contains the reflections of one individual (who tradition suggests is King Solomon) as he looks back on his life and evaluates it. To some extent, the book is the product of what social gerontologists refer to as life review. Throughout his life, Kohelet had written down things that he had learned, lessons that guided him as he navigated his way through life: thoughts, sayings, musings. As he grew older, he took a second look at these axioms. We, by evaluating them publicly in the context of Sukkot, are able to reap the benefits of his wisdom. The harvest of his life becomes ours as well.   KO

Renewing the Tradition
23 SEPTEMBER

For a few weeks and a few months I copied what I was given to copy. And during my copying I fixed the language, slightly here and there, just as one who had received broken vessels from his father's inheritance and fixed them. But the content of text I did not change.

S. Y. AGNON[189]

As Jews we are the recipients of a great spiritual inheritance that has been passed down from one generation to the next.

Upon receiving this inheritance, each generation has had to copy it in a fashion that makes sense out of it for themselves and their children. In this process, we copy the words and insights of our sages and our grandparents into idioms and images that speak to us more personally. It is a "fixing" in the most profound sense because otherwise this precious inheritance might be seen as unusable, as "broken vessels." Of course, not everyone engages in this process. But it is this very process through which our religious and cultural traditions are renewed and reinterpreted for every age. Shai Agnon, the poet laureate of Israel, speaks here of his painstaking work of copying old Hebrew manuscripts word for word. His work can also speak to us today as we, too, seek ways to maintain and preserve the traditions of our past while tweaking them slightly here and there.   LF

Next World Privileges
24 SEPTEMBER

For the pious person, it is a privilege to die.
RABBI ABRAHAM JOSHUA HESCHEL[190]

Some people don't understand the answers to the problem of Abraham binding his son, which the Torah calls the *akedah*. I don't understand the question. Did you think the Torah was a Boy Scout manual? A goody-goody book? A politically and theologically correct celebration of human life? Where have you been during the other Torah readings about incest, murder, plagues, violence, and punishment from God and humans?

We all risk our lives and our children's lives and our communities' lives all the time. I sent my son to Israel the very week the Six Day War ended. He learned, just in time, the Hebrew word for "land mine." He lived with a family that had survived, and, fortunately, he survived. But I had no hesitation in sending him into danger, as I had no hesitation in volunteering myself for chaplaincy in the Korean theater of war. Would I always do what God commanded just as I had done what my country asked? I hope so.

Life is precious, but it is not the most precious thing of all or we would not dare to remain Jews. Judaism is risky business. Circumcision is only the first trauma we bequeath to our sons. In Israel they prepare them to die like Trumpeldor for their country, and many have and many will, until peace comes, and some even after that.

God is much more important than life. Judaism is very good for us some of the time. It must be good for God all the time. The *akedah* is only the most upfront demand among many: God is entitled to our death. Life is temporary; only God is permanent. Life is good; God is The Good. Life is worth living, but mostly because it gives us the opportunity to serve God with all our heart and soul and life.

For us Americans, it is hard to put God at the center. We all feel that *we* belong at the center of everything, but we do not. All of our children will die. Only God will never die. Only the sacred is immortal. Abraham was right: to obey is much better than merely to live. To obey is the best of all.

May this New Year bring us closer to the consciousness that while our life is but a moment of eternity, it has meaning in the mind and heart of God, if in the end, only there. Let us climb Mount Moriah courageously, as did Abraham and Isaac, whatever will befall us on its summit.

RABBI ARNOLD JACOB WOLF

Mundane Beauty

25 SEPTEMBER

The beauty in the sublime and the mundane is found in the perspective that there is no real difference between them.

RABBI KARYN D. KEDAR[191]

Those who are on a spiritual journey, whom some people refer to in this generation as "spiritual seekers," are in a constant search for peak experiences of the spirit, particularly in worship and ritual. Many have turned their backs on material success and want to soar to the mountaintop. We want to experience the divine presence each time we pray or study a sacred text or perform a ritual. The level of expectation is high, and rather than approach the religious experience as an empty vessel, we challenge it as if to say, "I dare you. Lift me up." This is a sure way of preventing access to the holy. So we often walk away disappointed and disillusioned, making the challenge to be raised up by the next experience more difficult. But the religious enterprise is not marked by peak encounters. Rather, it is better described as a deliberate journey through the desert. And if we have a chance encounter with the Divine, then the trip is all the more worthwhile.

In the desert, things often look the same. According to tradition, what was noteworthy about Moses' encounter at the burning bush was that he paid attention to it. Apparently it was not unusual for tumbleweeds to catch on fire and be quickly consumed in the desert sun. What was unique about Moses' "burning bush" experience was not just that the bush burned unconsumed. Rather, what was spiritually noteworthy was that had Moses not paid attention to it, he would have missed the opportunity to encounter God. Thus, we learn that seekers of the spirit have to pay attention to the mundane— for it is often in the mundane that one can find religious truth. And this will help us reach the heavens. KO

Not Building on the Misfortune of Others
26 SEPTEMBER

*This is how I began to work my own way back to religion.
I investigated what religion is all about, and I came to the
conclusion that the essence of religion is this: you must not
build your own fortune on another person's misfortune.*

ISAAC BASHEVIS SINGER[192]

Depending on whom you talk to, you will hear of many
approaches to synthesize Judaism in order to come up with a
summary statement, or a way to state its essence. Here the
famous author Isaac Bashevis Singer suggests that at its core,
Judaism is about not taking advantage of others or using others' misfortune as the basis of success. Unfortunately, many
people do become wealthy owing to the hardship and disas-
ters others experience. We don't have to go far to find stories
of people being taken advantage of by con artists; not to
mention how big business makes millions of dollars off the
sweat labor of children in foreign countries. It is all too easy
to take advantage of those who have less than we and turn
suffering into profit. This is never the path Judaism espouses.
Judaism teaches that we are to see the misfortune of others
and find compassionate and effective ways to relieve that suffering. The Jewish way is to open our hearts, extend our
hands, and alleviate misfortune wherever we find it.   LF

The Most Important Lesson
27 SEPTEMBER

*The one lamb you shall offer in the morning, and the
second lamb you shall offer in the afternoon.*

NUMBERS 28:4

If you had to choose the most important sentence in the
Torah, what would it be? Would you pick a verse about God

or about a particular person? Would it be a mitzvah, or holy deed, that resonates to your religious beliefs, or an observation about life?

A midrashic commentary records a disagreement among three rabbis regarding which sentence in the Torah is the most important. According to the first opinion, the Torah's key verse is *Shema* Yisrael—"Hear, O Israel . . ." (Deuteronomy 6:4). This famous biblical statement declares our monotheistic belief in God. From "Shema Yisrael," all else follows.

The second opinion refers to the sentence "Love thy neighbor as thyself" (Leviticus 19:18). Through loving and respecting other people, the argument goes, one will not only grow to appreciate God's greatest creation, a human being, but also God. Clearly this is an all-encompassing commandment.

The third opinion chooses a sentence from our Torah portion that details the daily Temple sacrifice known as the *Korban Tamid* (literally, "continual offering"): "The one lamb you shall offer in the morning, and the second lamb you shall offer in the afternoon" (Numbers 28:4). According to this rabbi's understanding, the most important element in the whole Torah can be found right here.

While one may not agree with the first two opinions, it isn't difficult to understand why they were chosen. However, the third opinion leaves us intellectually confounded. What could possibly be so important about an animal sacrifice that supersedes all other biblical verses?

According to the Maharal of Prague, the answer can be summarized in one word: consistency. The day-in, day-out, week-in and week-out regular and reliable act of religious commitment is the key ingredient to spiritual success. The *Korban Tamid* isn't just about an animal sacrifice, the Maharal wrote, it's also about the value of consistent behavior. How important is this? Ask a parent raising a child, an athlete in training, or a businessman interested in developing loyalty among clients. Consistency is what enables him or her to anticipate with sureness; it's a vital ingredient upon which trust is developed.

As you sleep tonight, reflect on the quality of consistency in your life. How consistent are you in your practice? Remember the lesson of the *Korban Tamid,* for it suggests what it takes to achieve long-term success and is perhaps the most important lesson of all.   JEFFREY KORBMAN

Becoming Prayer
28 SEPTEMBER
I am prayer.
PSALM 109:4

Being prayerful has become an approach to life in Judaism, one that previously went unrecognized, was deemphasized or perhaps even overlooked. In the past we spoke little about prayer in Jewish tradition; we spoke about liturgy and worship services but seldom about prayer. But as we have been becoming more aware in recent times, prayer is more than a collection of words inclined to the Almighty. It is more than a series of formulas joined together to fit within the pages of a prayer book and the rubrics of a particular service. Prayer is an attitude, an approach to living that has the potential to permeate every aspect of daily living.

To assume this posture, we have to let go of the sense of entitlement to which we have become accustomed in this generation. We have to express our thanks to God and to others for the little things that we experience in life—and for the struggles, no matter how difficult it may be to do so.

The psalmist said it best. By expressing her emotions so powerfully in the words of the psalms, she was able to say, "I am prayer." You can become the same.   KO

Priorities

29 SEPTEMBER

One must not eat before feeding one's animals.

TALMUD[193]

Here is a piece of wisdom about caring for others that we can take to heart—namely, that at times we are to put even animals ahead of ourselves. It also speaks to the value of delaying gratification, a skill that we each need to learn. Certainly, we all prefer immediate gratification. But learning to step back from a situation and delay the fulfillment of our needs is a necessary life skill. While many of us today do not have farm animals that we care for, we can still reflect on ways we can take a step away from our immediate needs and care for someone else less fortunate than ourselves *first,* before tending to our own interests, cares, and desires. We do this most naturally when we care for our children and others who may be dependent on us. How else can we delay gratification and tend to the needs of others? Let us take this spiritual ethic and expand its application into other areas of our lives. LF

A September Song

30 SEPTEMBER

Who lives in joy does the will of the Creator.

BAAL SHEM TOV

Sukkot is a September (sometimes October) song, like the end of daylight saving time and the beginning of school. Sukkot is about the world equinox and the onset of autumn. It is also about the fragility and beauty of fall, when the days grow short as we reach September and when the prospect of winter is all around us.

Sukkot takes us from our comfortable homes into a "temporary hut" for the week of rejoicing. It presents us with the four species of *lulav* and *etrog* we wave, the four kinds of people we welcome. It reminds us again of our duty to the poor and of our duty to study one more year the perennial Torah of our holy tradition.

The origins of our holiday are obscure. All origins are obscure and elusive. But we are told that our ancestors once lived in huts in the wilderness and that the farmer lived in a hut during the late harvest season (shine on, harvest moon). Who knows? In any case, may we all be united this Sukkot and Simchat Torah in a bond of closer friendship and fragile peace. May we truly deserve our own rejoicing.

RABBI ARNOLD JACOB WOLF

OCTOBER

Minimizing Our Possessions
1 OCTOBER

It is a good thing when a person minimizes his possessions and gives them to tzedakah.

COMMENTARY ON THE TORAH[194]

In a world where consumerism and the acquisition of possessions seem endless, it is heartening to read that minimizing the things we own is a Jewish value. We can easily become blinded and think that acquiring more homes, cars, jewelry, and electronic gadgets is a life goal. Yet it is clearly a Jewish value to limit our drive to consume and to redirect our money to *tzedakah*. Surely, giving may not give us the immediate uplift that purchasing something new does, especially if we use shopping to lift our mood. Yet in the long run, our donations can give us a deeper sense of connection to our community and the world at large. It is one important way we actualize the values that have guided our people for thousands of years. While we each enjoy acquiring new things, we can reflect whether we need each new thing we buy or whether, in its stead, we can give more to *tzedakah*.   LF

Timeliness

2 OCTOBER

God will answer you at your time of trouble.

PSALM 20:2

It doesn't matter what time of day you need divine guidance, God is always ready to help. The psalmist, as quoted above, understands the nature of the covenantal relationship between us and the Holy One of Blessing. This relationship takes time. It may seem to evolve in erratic and unequal stages, but the relationship is based on regular communication through prayer, study, and ritual: the three primary ingredients that the Rabbis have been talking about for a long time. Through these paths, God is poised to answer us when we are in need. Nevertheless, God can only *answer* our prayers if we call out. This relationship requires action on our part: We complain when our prayers go unanswered, but they sometimes go unanswered because they are never really made.

Since we blithely assume that God knows all the intimate details of our lives, we may feel that we need not ask for divine help. Yet it is presumptuous of us to think that God will aid us whenever we need assistance even if we don't ask for it. Remember, God has also given us free will and won't get in our way when we choose to exercise it. It's true that God knows more about us than we know about ourselves and is able to pierce the protective walls that we have built around ourselves, those walls that often prevent us from reaching the depths of our own inner selves. But it is up to us to realize when we need divine help, to reach deeply within ourselves so that we can reach far beyond. When we choose to face any of life's troubling times "on our own," we can only gain the strength to face them in the context of a relationship with the Divine. Thus, we never truly go it alone.　　　　KO

Opening the Gates

3 OCTOBER

*Open for us the gates, even as they are closing,
for the day is waning.*

LITURGY[195]

In the final hours of Yom Kippur, we plead with God to help us do what we have been trying to do all week long: to open "the gates." For some of us, these may be the gates of a family relationship that have been closed: brothers who don't speak to each other; parents who don't talk to their children. For others, they may be the gates of a problem in our work that we cannot seem to solve. For still others, it may be that our ears and our eyes have been closed to the miracles that are with us daily, the miracles that live in our houses or that surround us when we step outside.

We ask God to help us open the gates because we acknowledge that the day is waning. On Yom Kippur, "the day" refers to the Day of Atonement, that awesome and wonderful gift of a day to think about the larger picture of our lives and the direction we want it to take. But on another level, "the day" that is "waning" is our life, which is made up of lots of different kinds of days. We ask God to help us open the gates because time is passing and our days are finite; our lives, however long or short, are limited, and we know that we cannot wait. We must change what needs to be changed *today*.

The knowledge that our days are waning can be discouraging. And to actually change, to open a gate, requires strength and courage. The two together might make for an overwhelming challenge were it not for the context of this prayer. Our prayer is addressed to God, to the One who gives strength and comfort to those whose sorrow we can only imagine, to the One who helps people overcome seemingly impossible situations. The God who helps people do the impossible wants to help us do the possible: to make the necessary changes in our lives. God wants us to do *teshuvah*, repentance, to try harder and do better, for ourselves and for the world in which we live.

As we reach out to God this day, may we feel God's presence helping us on our way.   RABBI ELANA KANTER

Difficult Changes

4 OCTOBER

The most difficult thing of all is to repair those who are unjust.

MIDRASH[196]

What is it about being unjust that is so difficult to repair? Is it that we leave it to God to do the fixing and feel no responsibility to participate in the repair? Judaism teaches that the door to *teshuvah*, repentance, is always open. Yet, perhaps some characteristics are more stubborn than others. It may be one thing to stop our negative activities that have become second-nature routine, like gossiping, or even to take the positive step of treating others with more kindness and compassion, but it is much more difficult to right the unjust behavior of an unjust individual. For injustice is larger than ourselves. It affects the society around us, since being unjust requires others to receive the injustice. It may surprise us to learn that it begins with ourselves. Be honest and ask yourself the tough questions: Have I behaved unjustly today? Who did my injustice affect—and how does that affect me? If we start to believe that we can "get away" with unjust practices, whether personally or professionally, then it may truly be "the most difficult thing" to turn ourselves around. Nevertheless, while the task may be arduous, as Jews we never say it is impossible. To change the world, we begin with ourselves. And we will begin with a fresh start tomorrow, rested and energized. The ability to transform oneself is always at hand if one is desirous of it. And in the transformation toward justice, the image of God is revealed ever so clearly in the depths of our souls. LF

Sweetening the Remaining Bitterness

5 OCTOBER

Sugar in the mouth won't help if you are bitter in the heart.
YIDDISH FOLK SAYING

The Hebrew month that stands between the fall holidays (Rosh Hashanah, Yom Kippur, Sukkot, Shemini Atzeret, and Simchat Torah) and the winter holiday (Hanukkah) generally falls around October-November in the secular calendar. Its name is Cheshvan, but the Rabbis have added the word *mar* (bitter) as a prefix to it to make it Marcheshvan. Thus it is known by both names. It is bitter, they say, because there are no holidays in it. And we particularly feel this omission after having just completed a full month of holidays. After such an intense period of time and the juggling of responsibilities the holidays entail, the ancient Rabbis are perhaps the only ones who feel embittered as a result of the lack of holidays! Maybe the bitterness is what remains in our soul after the process of repentance and renewal during the High Holiday season; it's nearly impossible to rid ourselves entirely of the misdeeds of the past year and we might feel burdened by them. Or maybe the bitterness comes from a fear that Jewish tradition does not seem to be providing us with the opportunity to work on the remaining "stuff" during this month. It is possible that the tradition wants to give us a measure of respite, recognizing the hard work of repentance that we have just concluded. But we do have another opportunity. As the Hasidim teach: we can finish our *teshuvah*-repentance work next month during Hanukkah.

So don't be bitter once the fall holidays have passed. We can continue our work of repentance tomorrow, and the next day and the next. And we'll have the opportunity next month as well. So rest easy. KO

Dwelling in a Different Place

6 OCTOBER

So that future generations will know that
I made the Israelites dwell in sukkot
when I brought them out of the land of Egypt.
LEVITICUS 23:43

I admit it. I hate camping. The thought of sleeping on the hard ground among bugs makes my skin crawl. And so, as you can imagine, Sukkot was never my favorite holiday. Sleeping outside in the equivalent of a poorly designed tent that has no floor and hardly any roof, among the spiders and raccoons? Hardly.

To make matters worse, I am completely incompetent when it comes to anything mechanical. I don't know which end of the screwdriver to hold. All of my early attempts at constructing my own sukkah met with disaster. From then on, I preferred to smell an *etrog* and shake a *lulav* within the comfort of my own home or in the synagogue rather than to actually build a sukkah and then sleep in one. So I found myself asking the question: How can I find meaning in Sukkot without building a sukkah?

Thanks to our sages, I found my answer. A dispute arose regarding the nature of the *sukkot* described in the text from Leviticus cited above. Rabbi Akiva believed them to be genuine booths that our ancestors built for shelter. But Rabbi Eliezer disagreed. He taught that the *sukkot* weren't actual booths constructed by human hands. Rather, they were the miraculous clouds of glory that accompanied and protected the Israelites in the wilderness. These clouds were a majestic manifestation of God's sheltering presence, guiding and sustaining our ancestors, providing them with the strength to persevere.

So here is the question: When we find ourselves in our personal wilderness, consumed by dark and frightening circumstances, unable to see a way out, where will we find those clouds of glory that reveal God's presence? Perhaps we can find them in the loving embrace of family and friends or in the serenity and clarity of prayer, or in the wisdom of sacred study. If we are able to reach outward to one another and, like our ancestors in the desert, gaze upward to the heavens, we might just see those clouds and know that God is close.

RABBI MICHAEL WHITE[197]

Acting Jewish

7 OCTOBER

What I am describing here is . . . a rigorous and demanding Judaism that asks us to "act Jewish" in the world. . . . It demands that we repair the world, little by little, day after day, by actively pursuing justice and peace and battling against cruelty and inequity.

LETTY COTTIN POGREBIN[198]

At the end of the day, as you think about your interactions with others, one question may rise to the surface: What does it mean to "act Jewish?" Like so many aspects of life, it depends upon whom you ask. Some people understand Judaism through prayer, while others understand it through holiday celebrations, and yet others understand it through a deep connection with Israel. Another path to expressing one's Jewish commitment has been through active engagement in making the world a better place. In Hebrew this value is often summed up with the phrase *tikkun olam*. One common translation is "to mend the world." At its core it relates the idea that we are partners with God in making our imperfect world a little bit better by looking for the holy spark that resides in everyone and everything we touch, and then elevating it back to its source; namely, God. Thus it becomes a spiritual practice that is expressed beyond the self. It bubbles over into the lives of others. How do you do this in your world? How do you make your commitment to Judaism and its values, your commitment to being a partner with God, visible in the life you are leading?   LF

Purity

8 OCTOBER

The soul that You have placed within me is pure.

LITURGY[199]

Every morning as I say these words, I get stuck on them. It's early in the morning and unless it is Shabbat or a lazy Sunday, I am usually in a rush. During my first experiences in public speaking, I would write the word "slow down" on top of each page as a reminder of my tendency to rush through things—always in a hurry. Perhaps this is also one of the reasons that I like hectic-pace big cities like New York. But when it comes to worship and study, I muster all my inner resources: I try hard to take time for my morning prayers, try to prevent the day ahead and everything that awaits me from interfering. During morning prayers, I feel the tension—from devoting time to prayer and knowing what work lies ahead— bubbling up in my soul. So when I get stuck on this prayer and its words, I am not entirely surprised. I usually think that it is the desire to move forward and get to work that causes near-paralysis. Then I realize it is not the cause at all. Instead, a short line of liturgical text grabs at my inner being so intensely that I can't move forward and I am reminded why I take time out to pray and what I carry into the day or night ahead.

I know the many challenges that await me in the day ahead. This prayer helps me to prepare for them.

Sometimes I reflect on these words before I go to sleep at night. It may have been a tough day and I feel mentally fatigued and spiritually drained. So I call to mind these words of the morning prayers and of our tradition, knowing that whatever debris I may have accumulated during this day's encounter with the world, the soul that God placed in me remains pure. KO

Blessed in All Things

9 OCTOBER

Abraham was now old, advanced in years, and Adonai blessed Abraham in all things (ba-kol).

GENESIS 24:1

To describe Abraham as blessed *in all things* is a reflection of his spiritual greatness. It is his faith in God that carries him throughout his life and brings to him, near the end of that life, a life blessed with everything.

Can each of us achieve that same sense of blessing? It is a very difficult spiritual state to attain. Instead, we strive for the spiritual state encapsulated in the word *emet*—truth. In Psalm 145:18, the text says, "God is near to all who call upon God in truth/*emet*." What does it mean to call upon God in *emet*, thus enabling us to come closer to God?

The word *emet* is made up of three Hebrew letters: *alef, mem,* and *tav.* If you take away the *alef,* which as the first letter of the first word of the Ten Commandments, *anokhi*, stands for God, you are left with the word *met*, meaning "death." If you take away the last letter, *tav*, which stands for Torah, you are left with the word *im*, meaning "if." Without one you are left without God. Without the other you are left with a world that is conditional, without rules or set definitions. *Emet* then, as truth, encompasses everything.

When we come to pray to God, we need to come with the truth about ourselves. Yet the truth about us is not just found in the extremes; it is the extremes plus everything in between. And the everything in between is represented by the other letter of *emet*, the letter *mem*.

To make this explanation of the word *emet* work just right, then the letter *mem* should be the middle letter of the Hebrew alphabet. *Mem* then could say that truth is found when we come to the exact middle point of ourselves. However, *mem* is not the middle letter. Thus, *mem* tells us that we have to *strive* for balance and the clarity that comes with it, but most of us will not achieve it. At best we will reach the letter *mem*, which is *close* to the middle of the alphabet.

The Hebrew alphabet actually has two middle letters: *khof* and *lamed*, the two letters that make up the word *kol*, "everything." Abraham at the end of his life has achieved the blessing of *ba-kol*, of everything. The blessing of *ba-kol* means that Abraham has achieved a clarity of vision to see all of life as a blessing from God. Thus, he has "everything." For us, who may never achieve that level, we strive for a coming close to God within truth, a truth that validates who we are in both our failures and our successes. We seek nothing less than to be blessed with *ba-kol*—and like Abraham in this seeking, we, too, "shall be a blessing . . . and all the families of the earth shall bless themselves by you."

RABBI MICHAEL STRASSFELD

The Braid of Ritual and Social Values

10 OCTOBER

God rejects those who do good, trusting in their own righteousness to save them, looking to their own works to purchase redemption; but God equally rejects those who supinely sit, contented in God's word, and think nothing depends upon themselves. As works without faith are unacceptable, so equally is faith without works.

GRACE AGUILAR[200]

At its best, Judaism is a religion that does not distinguish between ritual observances such as observing Shabbat and moral obligations such as refraining from stealing or speaking ill of others. The fabric of the Jewish social values braids together the *mitzvot* of faith and the *mitzvot* of action. Pull out one thread and the fabric unravels. We lead ourselves down the wrong path when we think that our faith alone will save us and so, too, if we think that our good deeds alone will be our path to redemption. Let us strive to bring together these two aspects of Jewish life into harmony and balance.

As you drift off to sleep this evening, worried about what you may have forgotten to do today, consider what rituals you may have observed *and* what ethical actions you may have performed. Strive for balance between the two. It is there that you will find God and, in so doing, discover the Divine in yourself and in others.   LF

Exercising Control

11 OCTOBER

We may eat of the fruit of any tree in the garden.
But regarding the fruit of the tree which is in the
center of the garden God has said, "You should
not eat it or touch it or you will die."

GENESIS 3:2–3

Most people read the Adam and Eve story the same way. God creates Adam. As a result of God's compassion for Adam's loneliness, God then creates Eve out of Adam. They live in paradise until Adam is tricked into eating a fruit—and then they all get expelled from paradise. As a result, the serpent has to crawl on its belly. Women must contend with the pains of childbirth. And we all have to work the land so that it may yield its produce and we may live.

Such a reading of the text explains many things in life. But why would the Torah go to the trouble of providing us with a mythic story to explain the obvious? Rabbi Irwin Kula likes to look at the text and give it a subversive reading, as he calls it. Rabbi Kula suggests that Eve knew fully what she was doing—and so did Adam. Like most of us in this day, she operated from a position of power. Even in the Garden, she had to exercise her will. Today this is the challenge with which we have to contend.

Many of us have influence and power over the lives of others. We sometimes exercise our control without thinking. But as we may have learned as recently as today, what we do with this influence and power is totally up to us. We may have been cavalier today, but tomorrow may we use them both wisely to improve the life of others and, in so doing, find the sparks of the Divine that are hidden in the world.   KO

From Bitterness to Sweet

12 OCTOBER

Out of the strong came forth sweetness.

JUDGES 14:14

Sometime usually in the middle of October, we begin the Hebrew month of Cheshvan. Traditionally this month is known as Marcheshvan, the *bitter* month of Cheshvan. The month is said to be bitter because no holy day takes place during it. The omission of holidays is particularly glaring after the Hebrew month of Tishrei, filled with Rosh Hashanah, Yom Kippur, and Sukkot—along with Shemini Atzeret and Simchat Torah. I suspect that Cheshvan is holiday-free for good reasons. Here they are:

Perhaps rabbis and synagogue staff need a bit of a rest.

The most sacred day of the year, Yom Kippur, is called the Sabbath of Sabbaths. While each Sabbath is our holiest of days, we have a tendency to be distracted from it by other holidays. Since Cheshvan is free of other holy days, we have an opportunity to reemphasize the Sabbath and put it back at the center of Judaism where it belongs.

The real test of the meaning of Judaism in our lives is not how we celebrate our holy days but how we integrate Judaism into the "normal" days of our lives. I have heard it said that the test of a great musician is not how he or she plays the notes but how he or she "plays" the rests between the notes. The holidays are the high, dramatic notes in the music of our Jewish lives. Cheshvan, nestled between the High Holy Days and Sukkot on one side and Hanukkah on the other, is like a rest between those notes. This month our Jewish living is not public and dramatic but routine. We pray. We study. We apply the teachings of Judaism to the ways in which we conduct our personal and our professional lives.

May this not be a time of bitterness for us. Instead, may we make Judaism meaningful and sweet on this day, and on every day.   RABBI BARRY H. BLOCK

Making Meaning of Our Lives
13 OCTOBER

As each situation in life represents a challenge to humans and presents a problem for them to solve, the question of the meaning of life may actually be reversed. Ultimately, humans should not ask what the meaning of life is, but rather they must recognize that it is they who are asked. In a word, each human is questioned by life; and one can only answer to life by answering for one's own life; to life one can only respond by being responsible.

VICTOR FRANKL[201]

As seeking men and women, we each want a life of meaning. We are all too familiar with the age-old philosophical question, "What is the meaning of life?" We may search for teachers to lead us to a satisfying answer. Often we think that the answer is "out there." However, we learn along the way that there is no one meaning in life and that people find meaning in multiple ways. Some find it through their work, others through artistic expression, and still others through community building and social action projects. The burden is on each of us to find ways to make our own life significant and consequential. Frankl, a Holocaust survivor and a psychotherapist, suggests that we turn the question around and ask ourselves not "What is the meaning of life?" but rather "What must we do to make our lives meaningful?" We must take an active stance, for this is not a passive search. We each know of too many lives that have been wasted. We each know too many people who are searching "out there" for meaning without looking inward.

As we drift off to sleep tonight, let us reflect on the relationships, commitments, and values that we cherish and that are the fullness and meaning of our lives.   LF

Ridding Ourselves of Nightly Terrors
14 OCTOBER

You shall not fear the terror of the night; nor the arrow that flies by day. Nor the pestilence that walks in gloom; nor the destroyer who lays waste at noon.

PSALM 91: 5–6

When we were young children, many of us kept a light on in our room. And in the synagogue, we keep a light burning brightly to remind us that we are not alone. While most of us have grown out of the need to keep a lamp on or keep the door to our room open, none of us have outgrown the need to be reminded that with God we are never alone, no matter how dark it may seem around us. Acknowledging the brightness of the divine light helps us to sleep more soundly.

Perhaps that is why the psalmist mentions terror in the night. It is not merely a poetic reiteration of a primitive fear. It is something that the psalmist understands that we are just beginning to learn.

When Moses feared facing Pharaoh on his mission to free the Jewish people from slavery, he was afraid of going it alone. So God told him, "I will be with you." That is all Moses needed to face the tasks that were ahead of him. It's all we need as well. When we go to sleep at night, we are flooded with thoughts from the day just completed—and we may be anxious about the day ahead. But we do not go it alone. We face each challenge knowing that God is with us.

When we go to sleep at night, we are instructed to recite the *Shema* prayer. It is an acknowledgment of God's presence and a reminder of it. Then we can rest easy, no matter what lies before us in the day ahead.   KO

The Consuming Power of Torah
15 October

Taste and see that God is good.
PSALM 34:9

One year, Simchat Torah, the fall festival that marks the end of the cycle of reading the Torah and its beginning again, fell on the first night that seemed like there was winter in the air. It was cold, rainy. A small group gathered at the synagogue. We unrolled the Torah on some long industrial tables so that everyone could look at it before we gathered up the scroll in our arms and danced around the room.

As we sat down with the Torah on unadorned tables between us, two rows, a quiet fell over everyone. We all sat there staring at the Torah, drawn toward it, the humidity in the air raising an earth smell, an animal scent rising from the sheepskin scroll laid out between us. The black fire on white fire, the smell of earth, rock, animal.

Someone made a Torah joke, "I want to eat it," quoting the Psalms text from above. I felt that if I were to sit there longer, maybe a week, maybe two, and stare into the scroll, the entire story would gobble *me* up, in a way only at that moment felt in my bones, in my blood. I had never felt that way before.

We continued to sit with the Torah open in front of us in silent reverie, awe-drawn, inching closer to the scroll, leaning in toward the sheepskin spread out on the table between us. The jokes stopped. It was an adult moment, captured only once in time and then repeated in different ways in different places throughout time. As if bound to the story in the scroll by invisible fibers of attachment, we all felt the release and deep cleansing exhalation of meditation, of lovemaking. We shed our separate skins and entered the story, drawn into it by its smell, taste, and touch. I wondered if we were going to enter the story, step into it. How long would we sit before the tale simply drew us in like the fire?

Perhaps we would pop into the story, walk around in it for a while, then pop out.   RABBI JAMES STONE GOODMAN

Students as Teachers
16 OCTOBER

*I have learned a lot from my teachers, and I have
learned more from my friends. But from my
students I have learned the most.*

TALMUD[202]

From whom have we learned today? And what were we taught? We learn in a variety of ways and from lots of different people. Some of us open a book, while others of us find an experience through which we get firsthand knowledge, and yet others of us look for teachers and mentors to guide us through life's challenges. While we may likely attend formal educational institutions at some point in our lives, we also learn more casually from our friends and colleagues. Here the Talmud suggests that we learn the most from those whom we think we are supposed to teach—our students. But students take many different forms that transcend what we think of as a classroom: the clerk at the supermarket who helps us with our groceries, even the stranger on the street who stops and asks for directions. Sometimes we find that, in the end, these individuals teach us as much as we teach them. And when we are really open to learning what they have to teach, we realize that God brought us together so that we might both learn. May we open ourselves to the many teachers who cross our path, who help us continue to learn even as we continue to grow. LF

From One World to the Next

17 October

Imagine that the first thing you will hear in the next world is everything you have ever said in this world.

Rabbi Lawrence Kushner

Often at the end of the day, we take stock of what took place during the preceding hours we have been awake. Sometimes this day's-end review of our lives takes the form of pillow talk with those whom we love. Together we appraise the events of our days as a way of sharing them, as well as to get another's perspective on them. We reexamine events, interactions, feelings. We relive them, trying to get a better focus on what took place. In a few minutes' time, we revisit an entire day.

But the words that filled these events, that shaped their occurrence, often go without any scrutiny. We have tossed them around during the day as if they had no abiding value beyond their use in our conversation. Rabbi Joseph Telushkin acknowledges that words have the power to hurt *and* the power to heal. What *we* do with words, how *we* use them, ultimately determines whether they contribute to hurting or healing. We forget that our words impact many people, more than just the ones who hear them. They also affect those people who have not heard our words directly until they are carried by others. These words we speak impact us as well, because they directly reflect our innermost selves. Words provide us with portals into our souls. KO

Moral Learning

18 OCTOBER

Morality is more important than learning.

TALMUD[203]

Virtues, personal moral habits, can be developed. Where might we look to find them? In the holiday prayer book, the *machzor,* in the liturgy for the holidays. As we stand to take out the Torah during the Days of Awe, we recite and chant the words *"Adonai, Adonai, El Rachum v'Chanum Erekh Apayim v'Rav Chesed v'Emet."* These are the qualities that we ascribe to God, virtues that we use to define the attributes of the Almighty. If our task is to emulate God, then we best do so by taking on these virtues.

Rachum v'Chanum—be just and merciful in all your dealings. *Erekh Apayim*—be slow to anger, count to ten before acting or speaking. Avoid road rage, no more flying off the handle, cool it, chill out. *Rav Chesed*—show compassion to everyone. We all have needs and we all have aches and pains, mental, physical, emotional; we are all fragile; let us remember to be more understanding of one another. *Emet*—speak the truth, don't lie. It will come back to haunt you. It will lead to distrust or misconduct or worse.

I would settle for those five virtues as a beginning. And then I would slowly add these others: *Sh'miat HaOzen*—be a good listener. *Sh'mirat HaGuf*—take care of your body. *Somach Noflim v'Rofeh Cholim*—lift up the fallen and be a healer, not one who wounds. *Anavah*—practice humility. For some of us that will take a bit of extra work. *Lo Levayesh*—do not embarrass anyone. *Hakhnasat Orkhim*—be welcoming and greet others with a pleasant demeanor.

There are dozens of Jewish virtues that are a part of our tradition. When followed, they can be ennobling and they can heal us and our community. When followed, they can decrease the evil we cause one another. The Ten Commandments teach us what we want to accomplish as a society. The practice of virtues shows us how to get there one day at a time, one decision after another, one act of kindness and generosity of spirit after another, one remarkable act of restraint after another. One act after another, day by day, hour by hour, moment by moment.

RABBI RAYMOND A. ZWERIN

Generous Friends

19 OCTOBER

A generous friend is a great find.

SOLOMON IBN GABIROL[204]

During our lifetime we acquire many kinds of friends. And during the day we have just concluded, we may have been blessed to spend time with some of them. In each of them we may encounter a bit of the divine. Kerry's wife, Sheryl, reminds us that they are angels, sent by God with a particular mission, sent by the Holy One of Blessing to teach us something, a bit of Torah that we might have otherwise overlooked.

We have friends that we know from childhood and other friends from college. We have friends from community involvement and friends from work. Some of these may be our pals, those whom we hang around with. Others may be great team players who help us get the work done. And yet others may be our colleagues and associates with whom we engage in office politics. Yet the one true find is a friend who loves us unconditionally. This is the person who goes out of his or her way to be there for us. This is the friend whom we can call upon in moments of crises and know that he or she will drop everything and come running. This is the friend who always makes time to listen to our concerns, our dreams, and even our complaints. Such friends are indeed a precious treasure. Among the many scores of people whom we call friends, may we find one or two truly generous ones over the course of our lives. When we do, let us cherish them. Knowing that they are on a divine mission helps us to hear them more clearly and sleep more soundly. LF

Our Interconnectedness
20 OCTOBER

The flag does not wave in the wind; the wind does not wave the flag. The flag and the wind are interwaving.
RABBI ZALMAN SCHACHTER-SHALOMI[205]

Individuals are not separate from one another or from the world. We are all connected. Poets have said it in different ways through human history. Although there are those who have tried to live alone, what Reb Zalman teaches is what we have all come to learn. Everything we do is somehow connected to someone and something else. While some may act as if they do, we do not, we cannot, operate alone in this world. Because of this, we have to be conscious of the impact of what we say and do on others. Even the simplest act may have far-reaching consequences.

In Jewish terms, we say that "All Israel is responsible for one another." It is one of the reasons that members of the Jewish community constantly look out for the welfare of their Jewish neighbors, near and far.

As you go to sleep this evening, and review the day just past, consider how your actions today impacted on others: things you did and things you said. Then make a promise to yourself that you will be more mindful of such impact tomorrow. KO

The Contemplation of Hope

21 OCTOBER

I hope always, I desire much, I expect little.

ZEV JABOTINSKY[206]

The world we live in often gives us little encouragement to touch the inner whisperings of our heart. Ironically, when our life has plunged us into darkness, it is in our heart, where we feel the greatest depth of our pain, by God's grace, that we discover the still small voice of hope that is crying out from deep within our heart. Once we are touched by the caress of that voice, we know that crisis doesn't lead to despair. It can instead lead to understanding the specialness of our life. It is by turning to face the darkness and the pain that we begin to understand our imperfections, accept them, and then make use of the tremendous and unique potential each of us possesses.

Touching on the wellspring of hope inevitably turns life into a wonder, and that wondrous realization becomes the door to unlocking the great mystery and sacredness of each of our lives. Cultivating the inner garden of hopes and dreams requires a bit of practice. After all, just as a garden needs tending, so too does the garden of the heart. Making a commitment to ourselves to sow seeds of hope in our own heart and in those of others builds a bond of trust and hope, not only within ourselves but for the world.

If we put forth a positive, hopeful countenance to the world, then the small world that we call our everyday life can become richer with meaning and filled with the positive presence of hope. RABBI YEHUDAH FINE

Being Consistent

22 OCTOBER

Don't forbid to others what you permit to yourself.

MIDRASH[207]

Double standards. They have a way of creeping into our lives even when we are on guard. Do you have one set of standards for yourself and another one for others? Maybe you even have multiple sets of standards that you apply to others depending on the situation at hand. Sometimes, having more than one set of standards could be considered compassionate. That's what Rabbi Barry Kogan teaches his students about the great philosopher Maimonides. He argued that while Maimonides might have been preoccupied with rationalism in the classroom and sought only the truth, when he cared for people, he spoke from his heart alone.

Yet, when the more usual situation arises—when we are more strict with others and forbid them what we permit ourselves—then we must take a close look at our character and our motivations. In some way we are not being truthful with ourselves if we permit ourselves to act in ways that we disapprove of in others. If this rings true for you, think why you do this. Are you hiding something? Protecting something? What underlies the double standards you apply? Are there ways you can begin to try to match your "insides" with your "outsides"? That way we will find that spiritual enrichment, through a daily encounter with the Divine, will have worked its way into our lives.   LF

Here and Now

23 OCTOBER

*When we accept each moment as a new opportunity
for fulfilling our purpose, we are always present,
always succeeding, always changing the world
for the better. And we are always "here."*

RABBI DAVID A. COOPER[208]

Here and now is the most important time in the history of the universe, because it is the only time that we have any measure of control and influence over. And each moment is fleeting and passes us by quickly. That is why it is important to teach others, particularly our children, the values that are most important to us and to express those values in what we do so that they can carry on our work when our lives are finished. What are those values on which you have founded your life? What are the principles for which you are prepared to do battle?

A major part of our journey in life is figuring out what indeed is our purpose, what God brought us to this earth to do and to accomplish. Some find the answer in their chosen vocation. Others find meaning in the avocational work they do. Still others find it in the link between the two.

To change the world for the better you need not be king or president or even prophet. Instead, all it takes is one human being doing good right here, right now.   KO

Living with God

24 OCTOBER

You who cleave to Adonai your God are alive,
every one of you this day.

DEUTERONOMY 4:4

It strikes me that this is the perfect time of year for this Torah reading: the community has passed through the endurance test of Yom Kippur, with its fasting and introspection. The final harvest is in, and the Jews, and the earth, pause before the approach of a winter's sleep.

The sukkah is a powerful symbol of God's protection and of our frailty. Indeed, the Kabbalists extend that biblical image and say that one who sits in the sukkah is sitting within the Shekhinah, God's immanent presence. The *Zohar* also notes that "the Torah and God are really one." If so, what better activity while dwelling within God's presence (space and time) than to attune the heart and mind to God made word. RABBI BRADLEY SHAVIT ARTSON[209]

Being Part of a People

25 OCTOBER

Today I frequently argue with God whose existence I
question, but I think that the Jewish people has a purpose, a
destiny, a reason for being. . . . I am no longer a mere
particle of genetic material spinning out of a single life span.
I have a past, present and future among my people.

ANNE ROIPHE[210]

Unlike the writer Anne Roiphe, who argues with the very God whose existence she claims to question, the theologian Rabbi Mordecai Kaplan did not question the existence of the Deity. Kaplan merely challenged the mainstream interpretation of the Divine and focused instead on the Jewish people. Martin Buber, on the other hand, saw God in the faces of the people he encountered, in the acts of goodness they performed. At the end of a long day, as we ponder what we have individually accomplished, we may also be motivated to think about what our people has accomplished, and what impact those accomplishments have on our lives and what role we play in them. After all, any people is the collective of each individual who consciously participates in it. And we are one of the few peoples who have existed for thousands of years. We have reestablished ourselves as vital communities in strange and foreign places. We have built a modern nation, the State of Israel, from swampland and sand dunes. Is there meaning in all this? We can each look back and see ourselves as part of a chain in the long line of tradition that stretches not only backward but also forward into the future.

"What does it mean to be part of a people?" This question is especially challenging given the multicultural world in which we live. Perhaps you can begin to give voice to answering this question by learning to study Torah or by reading about the lives of the sages (you may have more in common than you think!) or by thinking about whether there was some "Jewish" aspect to your day. When we can connect with the rich history of the Jewish people and see ourselves as a crucial link, then we can arise tomorrow and make a commitment to step on the shoulders of those who came before us and climb even higher. LF

Controlling Time

26 October

Praised are You, God, who distinguishes between sacred and secular time.

By the time I have to set my clock back for standard time (you know, fall backward; spring ahead), I am really ready for it. It is hard to go to work in the dark and return when it is dark once again. (Perhaps it would be easier for me to just change my work schedule!) So I welcome the opportunity to see the sun rise as I say my morning prayers before I rush off to my office. Inevitably, although I busily reset all of the clocks in my house (making sure that the VCR and television are changed, too), I always miss one. (It does not matter that the time change reminder is plastered on the front page of the newspaper, that TV news anchors announce it as part of the evening news, that even the rabbi at our local synagogue reminds us from the pulpit on Saturday morning and then again at *mincha* services on Saturday afternoon.) Then weeks later, as I worry that I am late for something or that my sense of time is all out of whack, I realize that I had just neglected to change one of the clocks in the house. Sometimes I think I do this subconsciously as a protest against the presumption involved in suggesting that humans can "control" time. Perhaps we can measure it, but we can never control it.

That is what I like about the fact that candlelighting times for Shabbat change each week. I always have to take cognizance of the time to get home on Friday. I cannot control it, nor can I be casual about it the way I might be about other things.

So just before the sun begins to set (eighteen minutes before, according to the convention of Jewish tradition), I take off my watch, then light candles with my family. Then

Shabbat begins and time becomes irrelevant·as I be͏
in it.

Light Up Our Hearts

27 OCTOBER

Happy is the Jew who learns Torah.
YIDDISH FOLK SAYING

How can I think about the holy day of Simchat Torah, pre-pare myself for its joy, even consider dancing with the Torah scroll, when I hear the steady hum of my mother's oxygen pump droning in the background? She is terribly ill, desper-ately ill. Hanging on my mother's bedroom wall is a text from the Torah: "Choose life so that both you and your descendants might live" (Deuteronomy 30:19). Again and again throughout my mom's illness, she and I have spoken about that text. No matter how bleak the future might seem, the Torah teaches us to "choose life." So we try.

And then it occurs to me that Simchat Torah celebrates a joy that is different from the happiness to which we typically aspire and about which we ordinarily think. It's not simply about having fun. When we finish reading our Torah and begin again, when we dance with her, when we delight in her, when we wrestle with her teachings, when we study her wis-dom with a caring community of learners, we open ourselves up to an eternal joy that can sustain and comfort us even in the midst of our deepest sadness, at the end of the most diffi-cult journey. The dancing and the singing on Simchat Torah point us to something deeper, a gratefulness for the meaning that Torah study can bring into our lives.

Torah can touch our hearts. It can help us grow in our relationships with God, as well as in our relationships with one another. The Sefat Emet, the great Hasidic master from the city of Gur, taught about heartfelt Torah learning. Why, he asked, do we recite blessings both before and after we study Torah? Wouldn't one blessing be enough? The first blessing, he taught, is for the Torah itself. The second blessing is for our prayer, that the words of Torah might "light up" our hearts. Just thanking God for Torah is not enough: We must pray that Torah touches us, changes us, and lights up our hearts—even the ones that are broken.

RABBI JOSH ZWEIBACK[212]

Our Shining Star

28 OCTOBER

Each and every person has a star in the heavens and according to their deeds does this star shine.

MIDRASH[213]

When we get an opportunity to escape the blinding streetlights of our neighborhoods and on a clear night look upward into the vast expanse of the heavens, we can be thrilled and, perhaps, overwhelmed by the numbers of stars in the sky. Some of us may know the stars and constellations by name and how to relate them to astronomical charts. Others of us may just enjoy how some stars shine with brilliance and others seem a little dimmer. Or perhaps we can delight in identifying the North Pole by finding the Big Dipper. I just stand in awe of them, knowing that they hold a certain mystical power over us. They hearken us to the majesty of another world beyond our reach, the realm of the Divine. Here in the midrash, we read that each of us has a personal star in the sky that shines in proportion to our deeds here on earth. How brilliant is your star? As you gaze at the skies and you drift off to sleep, consider what you will do tomorrow to make it emit even more light and brilliance. LF

A Shelter of Peace

29 October

Help us to lie down in peace and awaken us to life again.
Spread over us Your shelter of peace, guide us with Your
good counsel. . . . Remove the evil forces that surround us,
shelter us in the shadow of Your wings. . . .
Guard our coming and our going.

LITURGY[214]

According to Jewish tradition, we are obligated to pray three times a day: morning *(shacharit)*, afternoon *(mincha)*, and night *(maariv)*. The morning prayer service gets us ready for the day ahead by including a variety of psalms and morning blessings that reflect the activities of morning routine. Similarly, the evening service helps us to reflect upon the night and includes a special prayer called *hashkivenu* from which this text is taken. The *Zohar* says that "accusing angels," those that would do us harm, move about the dark hours before midnight. So the *hashkivenu* prayer asks that God watch over us, as we enter and exit each day, and wrap us in a shelter of peace (a sukkah). This idea of "peace" is better understood as the tranquillity we feel when we acknowledge God's protective care. No matter what we encounter, we are at ease, because God is with us. It is the same idea that is expressed throughout the psalms. In Psalm 23, the psalmist has captured what we all feel through the imagery of the shepherd, "God leads me beside tranquil waters and provides me with the opportunity to satisfy my thirst. . . . God is with me." This enhanced feeling of comfort is especially noteworthy at dusk, when the world is filled with shadows.

It is common for many people, particularly those whose prayer tradition is Ashkenazic, to pray the evening service immediately following afternoon prayers, providing the sun has already set. Thus, it is the dusk, the time that is filled with shadows, that provides the link between the two services and when God's shelter of peace is most welcome. When we are under the wings of the Shekhinah, we feel protected, surrounded by God's love. As the psalmist reminds us, "How excellent is Your love, God; for people find shelter under the shadow of Your wings."[215]

KO

Patience

30 OCTOBER
This is very *good.*
GENESIS 1:31B

I am not sure who the authors of home repair books intend to write for, but I know that when they allot time for a project, they're not thinking of me. Even for the simplest projects, I take the afternoon off and warn my kids not to come near. Ten thumbs and not a clue.

To think then about what was involved in creating the world is rather daunting, to say the least. God seemed to approach the task with a plan and a schedule. With divine focus, it looked like the job could be finished in a week, maybe even with some time to spare for a rest. It is, therefore, curious that on the second day of creation, the day when the waters were separated, God seems to "call it a day" before the job has been completed.

The Torah gives us a hint that the work is incomplete. It is the only day that the text does not call "good" after its creation. All the other days are "good" or even "very good," but the second day receives no star for its performance. To make the point, the Torah uses the "good" accolade twice in reference to the third day, when God gathers the lower waters together and creates the vegetation.

Sometimes we engage in projects, hobbies, even relationships, and we try to give them all that we've got. In the end we are drained, spent, exhausted. All we want is to see the "good" in what we've done. But sometimes we are unable to do so.

The Torah may be suggesting that although we would like immediate rewards for our labors, our toil may take a long time before we see any results. Ask any parent who raises a child, an investor who spends her time and money on an idea, or a farmer who plants his crops. And sometimes, the good is only a day away. Our test is for patience until tomorrow.

JEFFREY KORBMAN

The Perils of Taking Measure
31 OCTOBER

*With whatever measure you measure others,
you yourself are measured.*

TALMUD[216]

We live in a society that measures us at each twist and turn of our lives. At birth, babies are given an APGAR rating, to determine the relative strength of their basic systems; only a few years later they are tested in some areas to get into kindergarten programs; and during elementary school, statewide tests are routinely administered. Some people view the formidable IQ test as predicting, and even determining, one's educational and professional success. And in recent years, the EQ (emotional quotient) has been suggested as a new form of measurement—yet another standard by which to "measure up." As adults, we all too often live in the shadows of still other measures: how much we earn, how big our homes are, what our title may be, to name just a few. And we size up our neighbor's status too, comparing it with our own.

What if we don't measure up? Are we defeated? And if we do measure up, do we then elevate ourselves to a superior rank? Either way, do we set ourselves apart from others? Maybe this is one of the reasons that some people enjoy hiding behind Halloween masks! I suggest we have to try, hard as it may be, to push aside these widespread cultural norms and unearth the *neshamah*, the soul, that resides within every one of us. For our souls cannot be quantified or measured. In fact, the soul changes all the time, expanding when we grow spiritually and morally and contracting when we are self-centered or complacent. So let us "measure" our loved ones, our friends, and ourselves according to a new scale—one that treasures our *neshamot*, praying that when we wake in the morning, ours will be returned to us, refreshed and renewed.

LF

NOVEMBER

Redemptive Compassion

1 NOVEMBER

*I will take away the stony heart
and will give you a heart of flesh.*

EZEKIEL 36:26B

In an unusual moment of incredible compassion, near the beginning of the Book of Exodus and as a foreshadow of the redemption of the Jewish people, Pharaoh's daughter saves Moses. She wades into the Nile where Moses' mother had placed him in a floating basket. Some of us skip right over this scene because we are more interested in Moses' life than we are in the heroic act of this daughter of Pharaoh's. We miss the literary quality of the episode (particularly hidden in English), that the story "feels" similar to the story of Noah and his ark. Because of the intervention of the daughter of Pharaoh, the Jewish people is saved. Because of the intervention of this "righteous gentile," the Jewish people is eventually led out of slavery, receives the Torah, and enters the Promised Land. And the Bible never gives her name!

We heard nothing more of this kind of activity until the stories of the righteous gentiles of World War II began to surface. Rabbi Irwin Kula tells us that the Avenue of the Righteous that is dedicated to these people is located outside Yad Vashem in Israel (and not inside the museum) to remind us that we were saved by outsiders, by people who were not part of our community, and to separate those who helped from those who harmed. In the past it would have been easy to confuse them.

So before we avert our eyes from the strangers in our midst, or cast aspersions on them, remember that there are righteous gentiles who live among us, strangers whose redemptive compassion contributed to our further participation in the journey of Jewish destiny.   KO

Passing on Our Flame
2 NOVEMBER

Just as a person lights one candle from another and the original flame is not diminished, so too, we are never lessened when we pass our internal flame to another person.

MIDRASH[217]

One of the qualities of leadership—and all of us are leaders in one way or another—is to inspire with our passion, vision, and commitment. While leaders may become well known when they succeed in moving many people or creating a large following, true leaders are invigorated when they succeed in touching even just one person. They know that changes are made in this world one by one. When we are leaders, we put out a great deal of energy. We are not lazy or complacent people. Indeed, we know that our passion is strengthened and renewed when we share our vision and commitments with others. If we feel that sharing what we care most deeply about with others will diminish us, then we need to take a second look at ourselves. Yes, being a leader can be wearing at times, and it is an ongoing challenge to offer to others our hopes and aspirations in exciting, fresh ways. Even Moses grew tired of leading the People of Israel through the desert. He complained to God that the task was too burdensome.

Yet Moses rallied his energy. So can we. When we succeed in doing so, we spread the light and strengthen ourselves.   LF

The Miracle of Courage

3 NOVEMBER

The real exile of the people of Israel in Egypt
was that they learned to endure it.

HASIDIC TEACHING

Perhaps the real miracle of the crossing of the sea was not whether God's hand parted the waters or whether it was low tide but that the people of Israel found the courage to take the plunge into the sea, and in so doing, they birthed themselves and were birthed by God into a life of freedom.

...Now, once again, we must learn to be free.
We must banish the plague that has befallen the House
  of Israel.
As we sing our song of celebration this morning
recalling
our people's liberation so long ago,
help us, Source of Life, to liberate ourselves once more
from hatred, from zealotry,
from sinat chinam—wanton violence and fanaticism....

As a mother, Source of Life,
push us once more through the "narrow places,"
the mitzrayim of our own dangerous disunity.
As a father, Holy One,
hold our hand
as we walk the terrifying and life-affirming
path of peace.

(Adapted from a poem written in memory of Yitzhak Rabin)
LEILA GAL BERNER[218]

Peaceful Memories of Hope

4 NOVEMBER

God, grant us peace, Your most precious gift.

LITURGY[219]

Sometimes one word or a simple phrase is all that is needed. It expresses our innermost yearnings. No extra poetry or prose. No wordsmithing or clever constructions of language. We say what we mean, what we feel in our hearts. And that is sufficient for God to hear.

Moses taught us this lesson in the Torah when he asked that God heal his sister Miriam. He said, "Please God, heal her now." From that profoundly simple expression that still echoes through time, we have learned that it is important to keep our prayers short and simple.

This phrase is taken from a prayer that I say every morning. It asks for peace as the most important gift that God can give to the world. Everything else pales in comparison with it. But when I say these words on this day each year, they take on particular meaning. For it is on this day, November 4, 1995, that my words were cluttered by my tears. It was this day that marked the shooting of Israeli prime minister Yitzhak Rabin. One act and the world was changed. One act and the words of this prayer took on a different meaning in my life.

Some days get imprinted on our memories.

Some days get imprinted on our souls.

May it remind us of the work we have yet to do.   KO

The Prayers of God

5 November

God prays.

TALMUD[220]

Yes, the Talmud teaches us that God prays. This may be surprising, even shocking to us. Most of us probably think of prayer as a unique human activity, not one that we share with God. For after all, we beseech God for things that we desire and to help us with our problems, and we offer thanks and praise in our prayers. Why then would the Rabbis teach that God, too, prays? Certainly, God does not have a reason to beseech us. What could we do for God, after all? Let us rethink what prayer is. Can we think of prayer as a mode of communication between us and God and between God and us? This communication is not limited to bemoaning our plight. No. It is a vehicle through which we express to God our desires and yearnings, our gratitude and appreciation. It is also a way for God to express divine love, holy expectations, along with divine yearning. Just as we seek relationship with God, so, too, does God seek relationship with us. While we will never know the exact times God is engaged in prayer, let us assume it is ongoing and let us pray with heartfelt intention so that our prayers and the prayers of God will meet and become one.   LF

In Praise of the Quiet Ones

6 November

*Isaac sowed in that land and reaped a hundredfold
the same year. God blessed him.*

GENESIS 26:12

At first glance, Isaac seems to be the least prominent of the patriarchs. In the two most famous incidents of his life, he is more acted upon than actor: the "binding of Isaac" and the blessing of his son Jacob. Other than those incidents, we know very little of his life, in distinction to the many stories about Abraham and Jacob. Compare him for a moment with Abraham—Abraham, who leaves his whole family behind to go to Canaan; Abraham, who twice would rather pass off his wife as a sister to save his own skin; Abraham, who is ready to sacrifice his own son Isaac; Abraham, who is ready to send Hagar and Ishmael off into the desert!

Isaac is the only patriarch who doesn't act bad. Isaac is the quiet one, not big on public roles, unlike his father. In response to that powerful and public figure, Isaac acts *be-tzimtzum*—with the aspect of contraction and limitations. He is the stable one of the patriarchs. The only one with *one* wife. The only one whose name is not changed by God. The only one who stays faithful to the promise of the land, who never leaves the land of Israel.

Not as dramatic as his father or his sons, he models a life of faith, of well diggings, and of peace. His great achievement is cited above: He sowed the land and reaped a hundredfold the same year. A quietly impressive person who had faith, despite a famine in the land and a barren marriage, that God's promises for the future would work out. Unlike Abraham and Jacob, his overt actions did not split his children apart; perhaps that is why Jacob and Esau could finally be reconciled.

We can only catch glimpses of this tent dweller—only at those moments when the tent flap is raised. He sits inside his tent, not outside, as did Abraham waiting for strangers. And yet, I wish we knew him better, this *Yitzchak*—Isaac—whose name means the one of laughter. RABBI MICHAEL STRASSFELD

Making Order Out of Chaos

7 November

May we all be blessed to find comfort in being less than perfect, and to find peace in the eternal chaos of life.

RABBI DAVID A. COOPER[221]

When God created the world, God brought order to it. The world was a chaotic mess until God's spirit hovered over it and brought meaning to it through this order. Eventually humans were created and consequently depend on that order that was part of the creative process of the Divine. Our daily prayers reflect an acknowledgment and awareness of the orderliness of the world, particularly in nature. Night follows day. One season folds into another.

But the world is not perfect and neither are we. This is difficult for many of us to accept, particularly those of us who are used to solving any problem that comes our way, fixing whatever is broken. Some will argue that this posture emerges from a history of powerlessness in Jewish history and is no longer relevant to our lives. But it is just the opposite. When the Jewish people had little power in the world, particularly over their own destiny, the teaching meant less than it does today, now that we have significant control over our lives and the destiny of the Jewish people.

We now humbly admit that we are imperfect in the face of all that we have accomplished and because of all that we have accomplished. So we continue to work together to bring perfection to the world and to ourselves, knowing full well that it is a nearly impossible task, that someone is going to have to finish the work for us. But that will not prevent us from starting the work and taking it as far as we can go!   KO

Learning from Our Troubles

8 NOVEMBER

I have learned a lot from my teachers, and more from my books. But from my troubles, I have learned the most.

MIDRASH[222]

Learning is a more complex process than we usually realize. We seek out teachers and mentors who will guide us. And when we find ourselves in a formal educational setting, we spend plenty of time poring over books. We do research, write essays, and take tests. Hopefully, along the way we also learn to ask questions. Yet, some learning just cannot be gained through formal education. We may have a master's degree or even a doctorate but still be stymied when it comes to learning from the challenges we face in life. Some of life's best lessons come when we find ourselves in challenging situations. We resist these times, for they are often full of pain and anxiety and, at times, despair. Yet, when we gain some perspective, we often realize that we have, indeed, learned something of great value. Tonight think about how you might learn the most. Take the time now to put down your books and learn from the richness of your life's experiences.   LF

Connected to the Past

9 NOVEMBER

The past is to be there and not forgotten, but it is to be retired to the background and is not to invest us with pride before the fresh task to which each new day calls [us].

RABBI SAMSON RAPHAEL HIRSCH

When it comes down to it, there are two kinds of people. There are those who finish the job as soon as possible no matter what. They clean and put away all the dishes each evening, regardless of the time it takes or the lateness of the hour. They unpack all their luggage as soon as they return from a trip. And they never leave the office without completing all the tasks that are to be completed that day. Then there are the rest of us.

It is not that we are all lazy. It's just that we feel that we do not need to finish everything. Sometimes "it" can wait.

In the Torah it is surprising to read that the priests are told (actually commanded) to emulate the behavior of the latter group. As part of their responsibilities to the sacrificial system, the priests were told to clean up and dispose of the ashes that were not used for ritual. However, they were not supposed to clean everything up immediately. Instead, they were told to wait until the following morning.

Why wait until the next morning? Wouldn't our parents have told us when we were younger to "finish the job"? Waiting until the next morning hardly sends the right message from community leaders.

That is where Rabbi Hirsch's message comes in. By waiting until the next morning, we teach continuity. Each morning, when a person rose to worship and went to the Temple to deliver a sacrifice, the priest had to first get rid of the ashes that remained from the previous night's burning. The priest taught that although a person rises each new day for worship, that person's prayers are connected to the previous day.

Waiting until the next morning to take out the ashes suggests that our religious expression is intricately tied to those of our ancestors. But our responsibility to religious continuity suggests that we must find deeply personal meaning behind our religious behavior. Finding such meaning, the kind that resonates in the depths of our souls, helps to assure that those who come after us will do the same. JEFFREY KORBMAN

Holy Sparks in Everything

10 NOVEMBER

*There is no sphere of existence, including organic and
inorganic nature, that is not full of holy sparks
which are mixed up in* kelippot *(husks) and need to be
separated from them and lifted up.*

RABBI ISAAC LURIA[223]

This teaching is part of Rabbi Luria's mystical understanding
of creation. It is a complicated idea that has made it into the
mainstream through its simplification. Basically, Rabbi Luria
taught that the world was created through a series of spheres,
known as the *sefirot,* that contained God's divine energy. But
the lower sphere nearest the material world could not contain
God's energy and shattered (kind of like pouring hot water
into a glass), sending shards into that world, our world.
These shards became embedded in the material world. We
now have the obligation of finding these holy sparks and
releasing them. In doing so, they bring holiness to the world
and to the ones who release them. As we lift them up, as
Rabbi Luria suggests, we will get lifted up, too.

We are supposed to find the husks *(kelippot)* that hold the
divine sparks and release them. To do so, we must remove
the husks so that we can find the holiness that lies buried
within.

Love is the most potent "husk remover" available to us.
When love does not work, there is only one thing to do: love
them more. Rabbi Rami Shapiro helps us to understand this
idea by shaping the words in the prayer book this way: "We
are loved by an unending love. We are embraced by arms that
find us even when we are hidden from ourselves."   KO

Thinking about How We Communicate

11 NOVEMBER

When you begin, start with a good word. And when you conclude, end on a good word.

MIDRASH[224]

One might think that this is good advice for a politician or for those who give public talks and presentations. And indeed it is. Each of us, however, can take this insight to heart even if we do not have a public life. We all find ourselves in situations where we try to persuade others to get involved, whether it is to get them to join in a project, a community event, or a business deal. The art of persuasion is something of a gift. Yet we also need to use some common sense when we speak with others. When we begin our "pitch," do we begin on a positive note? Do we enumerate the advantages of coming aboard, or do we begin by saying, "I know your time is limited, but I thought you could just . . ." Of course, a positive opening would be much more effective. What if we were to say, "You could really contribute here because . . ." Similarly, we need to think about how we conclude a discussion, too. This advice comes in particularly handy when we find ourselves in the situation of giving someone criticism. Such conversations are never easy and we may find we speak too quickly just to get it over with. Yet we should always try to think of a positive way to begin and end such discussions. If we do so we may succeed in paving a way to a new understanding rather than dismissing someone with painful words—and raise ourselves and another to a higher spiritual plane. LF

Nearness to God

12 NOVEMBER

God is with you while you are with God.

I CHRONICLES 15:2

People who have truly stood in the presence of God are awed by their own insignificance. The insight gained gives them the ability to return to their more mundane existence with a sense of confidence, but with the knowledge that the true source of their leadership and creativity comes from beyond themselves. Moses' encounters with God make him feel both unworthy and commanded. From the moment he turns aside to view the burning bush, he confronts his perceived limitations and the insistent word of God. By the time Moses gets to Mount Sinai, his relationship to God and to his task have been forged and tested many times.

Moses is a difficult but not impossible role model. His career begins with the willingness to confront injustice and to risk his high position to serve a higher standard. His journey from the fleshpots of Egypt to the pastoral calm of Jethro's tent in Midian and back to Egypt is instructive. His instinct to flee is natural and could have led to permanent avoidance. One brave or foolish act could have ruined his legacy and he would never have been remembered. The shepherd's life could have been sufficient, but his willingness to turn aside (or his inability not to turn aside) to investigate the burning bush launches the journey to Sinai.

Our first task, if we are to emulate Moses, is to pay attention, because I believe each of us has a burning-bush moment. All too often we miss it because we are unwilling to turn aside. Our second task is to remember that it is God who has summoned us. Our third task is to remember that Moses was a very humble man, more so than any person on earth. Each of us is a Moses who, in awe and humility, may climb the mountain and transform the world. And when we have trouble sleeping, worrying about what we did or might have done today, we have to remember what Moses' life taught us.   RABBI PETER S. KNOBEL[225]

Suffering Love

13 NOVEMBER

When God delights in a soul, God inflicts suffering on the body so that the soul may gain freedom.
ZOHAR I, 140B

Of all the lessons that I have learned from Judaism and from life, this is among the most difficult for me to understand and accept. I know that just because it is part of Jewish tradition does not mean that I have to accept it on blind faith. Rather, because it is a Jewish teaching, I am obligated to struggle with it. Nevertheless, even if I choose to reject this notion, I do feel an obligation to try to understand it. Perhaps we can try to do so together.

While there is no separation of body and soul in Judaism, the *Zohar*, Judaism's primary source text on mysticism, acknowledges that the material world (of the body) is less pure than is the spiritual world (of the soul). Therefore the soul yearns to be free of the body. The body literally and figuratively weighs the soul down. The only real way that the soul can be freed from the body is through death (to be reunited, according to similar tradition, at the final judgment, which is to take place at the end of days). Suffering—that leads to death—frees the soul so that it can return to its Source.

Some people will argue that this is the text's way of trying to provide a theological understanding of something that is pastoral to bring comfort to the one who is suffering or perhaps to his or her loved ones. But there are other passages in

Judaism that provide such comfort without such provocative theology. Thus it is the theology here that is more important to the mystics. Spirituality (which is about the relationship between the individual and God), they would argue, is not always warm and fuzzy. Sometimes it is filled with fear. Out of that fear may come reverence.

Rabbi David Wolpe has suggested that when we are ill, we often feel closest to God because we call on God more frequently and more intensively. Through our suffering, we are able to develop a relationship with God that might otherwise have been unavailable to us. So when we suffer, even when death may be imminent, this part of our tradition wants to teach us that it emerges from our relationship with God, and although it may be beyond our understanding, God wants to help us set the soul free, and we along with it.   KO

Knowing When to Speak and When to Act
14 NOVEMBER

There is a time to speak at length and a time to speak briefly.
MIDRASH[226]

When Moses and the People of Israel are standing on the bank of the Red Sea, the tribal leaders begin to squabble among themselves about who will jump in first, and Moses begins to beseech God at length. Having just fled Pharaoh's troops, no one seems equipped to know what to do. We should not be surprised at this confusion. Wouldn't we, too, be confused if we had just escaped slavery in the dead of night? Moses is also confused and neither knows what to say or do. This midrash teaches us that God responds to Moses by saying, "There is a time to speak at length and a time to speak shortly. Now is not the time to address me with many words. Act!" And so God instructs Moses to extend his rod to split the sea. Here action, not prayer, was needed.

We can take this midrash's advice to heart and apply it in many areas of our lives. How do you respond when you are faced with a confusing situation? Do you speak too much or do you limit your words? Do you act when action is called for? Do we weigh our words when we speak or do we speak too quickly? Our challenge is to evaluate the many situations we find ourselves in—to act when action is called for and to speak when speech is needed.   LF

Everything and Nothing
15 NOVEMBER

So God blessed them and God said to them, "Be fruitful and multiply. Fill the earth and subdue it."
GENESIS 1:28

The great clue word here is *subdue [v'kivshua]*. As the great medieval rabbinical commentator Rashi points out, the word is written using the Hebrew letter *vav*. The word *v'kivshua* is *chaser*—technically, "missing something"—missing something that will come in the deeper understanding that the world was not made for us. Or deeper yet, that the world was made for us and not made for us, a kind of Janus idea that refers to both the obvious and the opposite.

As the psalmist says, "What is a human being that You are mindful . . . for You have made us a little lower than the angels" (Psalm 8:5–6). "God, what is a human being, that You should take knowledge. . . . It is as if a person is a breath, our days are like a shadow that passes" (Psalm 144:3–4). It's not an either-or proposition but a both-and idea. Either notion alone is *chaser*, missing something: we are either great or we are nothing. That's the point: we are both great and nothing.

That is more complete wisdom, that we are both something and nothing. Godliness and stuff: "And the Eternal

God formed Adam out of the dust of the ground, and breathed into Adam's nostrils the soul of life, and Adam became a living soul" (Genesis 2:7).

Radically "and" we are, both Godliness *and* stuff. Everything *and* nothing.   RABBI JAMES STONE GOODMAN

Overcoming Hate with Love
16 NOVEMBER

Our job is not to set up a battleground to eradicate evil but to search out its spark of holiness. Our task is not to destroy but to build; not to hate but to find a place of yielding; not to polarize but to discover the points of commonality so that we can work together.

RABBI ZALMAN SCHACHTER-SHALOMI

In our encounters with others, particularly those who have not been good to us, there are two ways of approaching them. First—and this may be our knee-jerk self-protective reaction—we may want to counterattack. When someone causes us grief that we rationalize, then we should do the same in return to them. If they undermine us in our work, then we make sure that they fail. If they say something distasteful about us, then we respond in like measure. The other option is to do what might be considered to be the unexpected. Instead of lashing out in return, measure for measure or even worse, we can respond positively, with love, with compassion, and with understanding. This is what Reb Zalman wants to teach us. An evil response to evil is a victory for evil and not for good.

Our responsibility as covenantal partners with God is to search out holiness in this world, particularly where it is hidden. It is easy to find goodness among good people. It is easy to speak well of people who do good works in the community. It is easy to affirm the holy works of holy people in our midst. But real work of the spirit is not so easy. It takes a reserve of inner strength. But by joining with others, this personal strength is multiplied. And we are fortified in our work.

And it is the work of the Divine that we are doing—to build a more perfect world. KO

Noticing Blessings
17 November

A person is obligated to say one hundred blessings a day.
TALMUD[227]

One hundred blessings a day? For many of us this may seem like an impossible goal. What are the Rabbis trying to teach us when they suggest that we fill our days with so many blessings? My sense is that they want to teach us to develop a grateful attitude. For what is a blessing if not a moment when we pause and express our gratitude for the things that fill our lives? It is easy to walk around being caught up in our daily routine. No blessing here, just a harried schedule. Yet I suspect we each find plenty of things to criticize in the course of twenty-four hours. Our children dawdle, meetings are canceled, buses run late. Think of the most recent complaint that just ran through your mind. The challenge is not to let these things that irritate us gain the upper hand but rather to capture those things, no matter how small they may seem, for which we are thankful. These are the blessings we are to stop and take note of. Then, hopefully, by the day's end we can each rest our heads on our pillows and fall soundly asleep with the full knowledge that the day we just ended was full of blessings. LF

Going Forth to Do Good

18 NOVEMBER

Lekh lekha. *Go. Get out. Get going. Move forward. Get a life.*
GENESIS 12:1A[228]

In a midrash, Rabbi Berakiah compares Abraham to a "vial of myrrh closed with a tight-fitting lid and lying in a corner, so that its fragrance was not disseminated." It isn't hard to guess Rabbi Berakiah's estimation of a bottle of perfume that is so tightly sealed that no one can smell it at all. And it isn't hard to extrapolate his opinion of people who are well-off, well-educated, and full of opinions, yet who somehow never seem to find the time to apply their opinions in a practical way. Good advice on how to live, if sealed in a cozy corner, doesn't do the world any good. At the height of Abraham's discomfort and self-absorption, God shattered his complacency forever. With one forceful call God forced Abraham to abandon his posturing and lectures and to apply his wisdom to helping his fellow human beings. "Go forth from your native land, from your ancestral house, to the land that I will show you" (Genesis 12:1). Without even knowing where his involvement would lead, Abraham shifted his focus from editorializing to activism—working on behalf of morality, God, and other people. Rabbi Berakiah shrewdly notes that the sealed perfume, "once it was taken up, disseminated its fragrance." Similarly, the Holy Blessed One said to Abraham, "travel from place to place and your name will become great in the world." Perfume gains value by sharing its rich fragrance with all who can smell it.

A wise education, moral balance, and physical strength are worthwhile to the extent that they translate into action on behalf of building a better world. Rather than hoarding our viewpoints and our energy, we become rich to the extent that we share them with others. There is nothing so glorious, nothing so rewarding, and nothing so needed as reaching out to a needy stranger. In caring for an anonymous creature in the image of God we uncover a new reflection of God's precious love, and we illumine our own lives by the light of that beauty. And we make someone else's life a little more pleasant, too. RABBI BRADLEY SHAVIT ARTSON[229]

Waiting and Working for the Messiah
19 NOVEMBER

As long as we are anticipating the Messiah, our hopes and expectations might have the opposite effect.

TALMUD[230]

This surprising statement is recorded in the Talmud in the name of Rabbi Zera. One would expect that the text would instruct us to always be in a position of anticipating the arrival of the Messiah, especially since we have been waiting throughout Jewish history for his (or her) appearance in our midst. This notion is epitomized near the conclusion of the movie *Fiddler on the Roof*. After a pogrom, the Jewish community is forced to leave its hometown. As people are scurrying to get their belongings together, one of the townspeople of Anatevka asks the local rabbi, "We have waited four thousand years for the coming of the Messiah. Would this not be a good time for him to come?" There is no direct response to the question. Instead, the rabbi comments, "We will just have to wait for him someplace else." He understood that we have to go about our daily activities. That is the preparation that we make for the Messiah.

Elsewhere in the Talmud, we are taught that if we are in the middle of planting a tree and the arrival of the Messiah is announced, we must first finish the planting, then we can go welcome the Messiah into our midst. One would think that the Messiah and all that might come with the messianic era would take precedence. But the same wisdom of the rabbis is expressed once again here. We still have to be content with the everyday, the routine.

But this is insufficient for the rabbis. They are suggesting that if we focus on anticipating the Messiah's arrival, it may, in fact, delay or even prevent the arrival. Simply put, we may live a life of the spirit, but our feet must always be firmly planted on the ground.   KO

A Good Name
20 NOVEMBER

The way of everything is toward death, and one should rejoice if s/he leaves the world with a good name.

MIDRASH[231]

Death is not a topic upon which we usually dwell at great length. Judaism is a religion that embraces life, and many of us don't contemplate death as a matter of course. Yet death is an integral part of life. The teaching here is about what remains after we leave this world: We learn that it is a good name. Many people try to memorialize themselves through dedicating objects or buildings that remain after their passing. But when we are honest with ourselves, it is our actions, though they may not be made of concrete or bricks, that last the longest. Think about those individuals whom you would say left the world with a good name. What was the nature of their being and their work that qualifies them for this epitaph? Did they contribute to the community at large? Or did they perhaps go about doing good deeds in quiet, yet meaningful, ways? A good name is something that takes years to establish. We create a good name for ourselves through the stands and actions we take in the course of a lifetime. There is often not a self-consciousness about those individuals who have a good name. They go about their work simply because it creates meaning in their lives, not because they are consciously trying to create a reputation for themselves. We can do the same, tomorrow and every day remaining to us.   LF

Holiness That Leads to Wholeness
21 NOVEMBER
I will extend peace to her like a river.
ISAIAH 66:12

Torah is a map of the human quest for holiness (or rather "wholeness"); her characters and images are aspects of our own psyches. In the Joseph saga, Pharaoh is the ruling mind, the ego, and Joseph is the intuitive mind, the soul. Separated from each other, the one is haunted and the other wrongly imprisoned; united with each other, they hold the key to personal and planetary transformation.

Pharaoh had a dream. He stood by the river and saw seven healthy cows rising out of the river, only to be eaten by seven ill cows; seven ears of healthy grain swallowed up by seven lean ears. Pharaoh dreams of the impermanence of all things; he is haunted by the inevitability of old age, sickness, and death.

Pharaoh's whole world is death-denying. He is a god-king who will live forever. Ego posits this illusion in each of us. Ego, like Pharaoh, seeks to control the world, to ward off personal suffering and deny the reality of its own mortality.

Yet Pharaoh cannot control his dreams. As the text above suggests, the *Zohar*, Judaism's central mystical text, tells us that to dream of a river is to long for peace. In Hebrew, *peace* and *wholeness* share a common linguistic root. Peace comes only when we are whole. Being whole means embracing the flow of life from birth to death and accepting the ego's transience in the process. Only when the ego sees its own impermanence as part of the eternal flow of life can it relinquish its mad quest for control and enjoy the wondrous blessings of life.

RABBI RAMI SHAPIRO[232]

Regaining Joy

22 NOVEMBER

The strength of the forces of holiness and the destruction of the shells that imprison holy sparks depend upon joy.

RABBI NACHMAN OF BRESLOV[233]

I can't pass by this date on any calendar without thinking about the death of John F. Kennedy on this date in Dallas, Texas, in 1963. I imagine that most in my generation feel the same way. That moment and the events that followed significantly altered the course of events in the United States—and in the world. The euphoria that ushered in his presidency was lost for many years, overshadowed by inner city riots, campus unrest, and the Vietnam War. Even our childhood and adolescence took on a certain color of darkness. What might have been different had President Kennedy not been assassinated is something that we can never know. The regretful questions of "what if" once events have transpired usually bring us no real insight or information. They are better left unexplored.

I know exactly where I was when I learned of President Kennedy's death. I imagine that most people do—as if it were yesterday. However, what is more difficult to discern is who I was then. What events really shaped the path to get me here today, really contributed to my life's journey? Who helped to shape them for me, whether knowingly or unknowingly, whether to be supportive and helpful or to be malevolent and subversive? As I reflect on them, I am conscious of how what I do impacts the lives of others.

If Rabbi Nachman was right, and I believe that he was, then we have to make sure that even such catastrophic events do not impede our ability to find joy, for it is through joy that holiness can be discovered.   KO

Guardians of Wealth

23 NOVEMBER

The wealth we accumulate is considered to be a temporary deposit.

IBN EZRA[234]

We are a generation that has seen the accumulation of great wealth. We have created sophisticated ways of preserving our wealth for our children and perhaps even future generations. We take great pride in this material success. However, is this wealth truly ours alone? I know that many people would say, "Of course it is. I worked night and day for decades to make sure my family would never have to worry. If it's not mine, then whose is it?" A spiritual understanding may guide us in another direction. We can be grateful to God for giving us the insights and acumen to succeed and then choose to share our success with others. In *Pirke Avot* 5:10 we read about the following dispute: "[One who says] 'mine is mine and yours is yours' is the average person; some say that this the quality of the city of Sodom." How do you evaluate this claim? Is it just the mark of an average person or is it a mark of depravity and immorality? Remember that Sodom in the book of Genesis was a city destroyed for being filled with perversity and evil. The moral question here is, "Do we have rigid boundaries regarding our possessions or are we able to share them with others?" What would it mean for us to think of ourselves as simply guardians of our wealth and "things" and to know in our heart that they are ours only for a short time?   LF

Getting Closer with Each Step

24 NOVEMBER

Moses said, "I will turn away and see this great sight, why the bush is not consumed."

EXODUS 3:3

It is said that the Baal Shem Tov derived a lesson in *teshuvah* from the episode at the burning bush. In the text quoted above from Exodus, Moses said, "*Asurah-nah,* I will turn away." Why would Moses have an audience with God and then turn away?

Asurah is an unusual word. Rashi writes that it means "to go away from here and to come close there." This is what *teshuvah* is, said the Baal Shem Tov, "getting unstuck." It's about movement and transformation. It's not about arriving but about approaching. It's not about destinations but about journeys; not about arrivals at all but about roads; not about achieving but about being; not about performance but about effort; to move from here and come close to there. It's not even about sin; it's about change.

We celebrate the journey when we make *teshuvah.* And when we lose our way we are taught that the right path calls us back; when we lose our way the roads go into mourning. This is especially true of the hardcase scenario, of every difficult transformation. From one moment to the next the transformation that is possible for everyone might be concealed. This means you never give up on anyone—including yourself. This means that the possibilities for repair and reconciliation, transformation and reclamation, *teshuvah,* are always present. You never give up on anyone. Especially the hardcase stories. I consider myself such a story. If I could get it, anyone could get it. RABBI JAMES STONE GOODMAN[235]

Beyond Comprehension

25 November

God's understanding cannot be grasped.

ISAIAH 40:28

Here is the conundrum: We work to develop an intimate relationship with the Divine. The Hasidim say we can develop *devekut*, a word used to describe a relationship of intimacy with God that is so close that there is near abdication of the ego, a relationship that is as close as is possible without losing the self in the Divine. However, we also acknowledge that God is beyond our understanding, beyond human comprehension. Thus, however we might try to figure out the purpose of God's actions, and even discern God's role in them, we cannot do so. So we are caught in the middle, not sure what to do or how to act.

Isaiah captured the idea and then moved on with his work. He communicated this notion simply and straightforwardly, something that we really appreciate from a prophet whose poetic writings are sometimes difficult to decipher.

This idea might paralyze some people. Their argument would be that if God is beyond our understanding, then why should we bother trying to get close to the Divine at all. It would be like the rabbit in a dog race. The dogs run fiercely trying to catch up with the rabbit, but the rabbit is always just a little out of range of the racing dogs. And if, by some chance, the dogs close in on the rabbit, the rabbit (since it is not real) is just made to go faster, staying ahead of the dogs.

God has many attributes. Perhaps it might be said that God has an infinite number of attributes. It is one of the reasons Maimonides was disinclined to list them and suggested that an attempt to do so actually diminished God rather than praised the Holy One. This collection of attributes makes

God beyond our comprehension. Nevertheless, one of the attributes of God includes a desire for us to get close. It is part of the deal that was struck at Sinai and chronicled throughout many of the narratives in the Torah.

So we can pray to God. We can communicate with the Divine. We can develop an intimate relationship with the Holy One of Blessing. But we can never fully know God or understand God's actions in the world—even though we may challenge them.
KO

Disavowing Idols
26 NOVEMBER

Whoever acknowledges idolatry disavows the whole Torah, and whoever disavows idolatry acknowledges the whole Torah.

MIDRASH[236]

Judaism from its start has denounced idolatry. Who doesn't know the famous midrash about how Abraham smashes the idols in his father's shop before leaving for Canaan to follow God's call, "Go forth from your native land and from your ancestral home to the land that I will show you" (Genesis 12:1)? Even after Abraham embraced monotheism, his descendants and our ancestors, the Israelites, were always struggling to maintain loyalty to the idea of one God. For one thing, they were surrounded by pagan religions with idolatry at the core of their practice and faith. However, we are a people who are called upon to denounce the idols of the day. And yes, idolatry is alive and well. We may no longer have wooden or stone images in our home that we pray to but we do idolize people, things, money, and status. When we do so we often get confused about what we stand for and what is a true reflection of our values. Living by the Torah is about having our values front and center and returning to them when we are faced with the lure of contemporary idols. Of course, this path is not easy. However, let us stay the course and hold fast to Torah's eternal path. We, too, can be like Abraham and smash the idols that cause us to stumble and forget the true values we are called to live by.   LF

Seeing the Future
27 NOVEMBER

Every wise-hearted person among you shall come and make everything that God has commanded.

EXODUS 35:10

The word *chokhmah*, wisdom, is applied to the artisans who were charged in the Torah with putting together the *mishkan*, the portable sanctuary that accompanied the Israelites through the wilderness on their way to the Promised Land. The sense is that wisdom and artistic skills go hand in hand. But in general, wisdom is applied to intellectual capability, not art.

In the Talmud the Rabbis ask, "Who is the wise person? The one who sees what is yet to be."[237] I do not believe they were linking wisdom with fortunetelling but rather with seeing future consequences of present action. An artist generally sees the portrait or project as it will turn out if she or he uses certain colors or certain materials in certain ways.

It is said that each of us paints a portrait of life with the details of daily activity. The wise person is thus anyone who thinks not so much about the details of life as about the way those details come together to form a portrait of life, a work of art that we enhance each and every day by what we choose to do.   RABBI RICK SHERWIN[238]

Thanksgiving Gratitude
28 NOVEMBER

*Do not think that the words of prayer as you say them
go up to God. It is not the words themselves that ascend;
it is rather the burning desire of your heart that rises like
smoke toward heaven. If your prayer consists only of words
and letters and does not contain your heart's desire—
how can it rise up to God?*

HASIDIC TEACHING[239]

Lots of people get together for Thanksgiving in the United
States. When I lived in Israel, those of us from America even
found ourselves making Thanksgiving dinner there. It had
become so much a part of our culture that we could not let
go of it even in Israel.

There is usually plenty of turkey on Thanksgiving tables
(although I am a vegetarian) and plenty of pumpkin pie. But
what I often find missing are the *prayers* of thanksgiving that
should accompany the fall harvest. And these prayers,
according to the Hasidic master, should emerge from the
heart. If they come from the heart, then they will find their
way to heaven and carry us along with them.   KO

Thinking as Part of our Spiritual Path
29 NOVEMBER

*Renunciation of thinking is a declaration
of spiritual bankruptcy.*

ALBERT SCHWEITZER[240]

Sometimes spirituality and thinking are pitted one against
the other. If you are a thinking person, it is assumed you are
not "spiritual," and conversely, if you present yourself as
"spiritual," others may assume you are no longer a "thinking

person." This unfortunate view is very prevalent today. Judaism, though, teaches that the two are not at odds. As Albert Schweitzer put it above, the process of thinking is at the heart of our spiritual lives. Spirituality does not mean we become disembodied or take leave of either our bodily or our cognitive faculties. Indeed, by using our minds, we can explore our inner lives in multiple ways. If we discard our intellect and all that it opens to us, then we are in danger of becoming spiritually bankrupt, void of content and meaning. One way we can approach this aspect of the spiritual path is to make regular "deposits" through learning, exploring, and analyzing our tradition to make sure our inner "bank" has a full reserve. Let us embrace the power of our minds and work to meld spiritual and intellectual pursuits. Indeed, they not only can but must go hand in hand. Let us drift off to sleep tonight and awake refreshed, ready to engage both our minds and souls.   LF

A New Thanksgiving Ritual

30 NOVEMBER

Whoever extends the festival another day for eating and drinking, Scripture accounts to them as if they had built an altar and sacrificed an offering on it.

TALMUD[241]

Long ago, in the earliest days of my marriage, my husband worried about where we would go for Thanksgiving, to his family or to mine. I thought we should be with his family. I had many reasons. Most important, his family took Thanksgiving very seriously and there was a lot of family excitement beforehand about who was coming and where everyone would sleep. By contrast, my family, which celebrated multiple events together—Rosh Hashanah, Sukkot, Shavuot, various *Shabbatot*—had little claim on Thanks-

344 · RESTFUL REFLECTIONS

giving. Each year of my childhood, the day before Thanks-giving, my mother would ask my sister and me, "What is Thanksgiving to us, anyway? Did our family come over on the Mayflower? Where does it say in the Torah you have to eat a turkey on Thanksgiving?"

"Will your family be hurt?" my husband asked, and I assured him my people would not even notice we weren't with them for Thanksgiving, because they never celebrated Thanksgiving anyway.

After that first Thanksgiving with my in-laws was over, my uncle Ephraim—my mother's brother—was delegated, as family patriarch, to call me and set me straight. He told me that on Thanksgiving, my parents had sat alone in their house like people in mourning. There was darkness, no food, no joy. You would think he was describing the Babylonian exile or Tisha B'Av, not a house in the Five Towns of Long Island.

There was only one way I could imagine keeping peace between ourselves and our families, and since my mother had been inventive in creating Thanksgiving memories out of thin air, I was encouraged to be equally inventive: I created *Yom Sheni shel Thanksgiving*. I explained to my mother that just as the second days of Rosh Hashanah, Sukkot, Pesach, and Shavuot are just as important as the first, the second day of Thanksgiving—which always fell on a Shabbat—was also very important and very holy. From then on, we would go to my in-laws' house for *Yom Rishon shel Thanksgiving* (explaining that as Reform Jews, they celebrated only one day) and promised to go to my own family for the second day.

We can always extend the holiness, and the days of gratitude.

VANESSA L. OCHS[242]

DECEMBER

The Divine Image

1 DECEMBER

You shall love your neighbor as yourself.

LEVITICUS 19:18

God created humanity in the Divine image.

GENESIS 1:27

There is an extensive debate in the Talmud as to which of these two verses best summarizes the essential, core teaching of Judaism. Some might think that the first verse, *You shall love your neighbor as yourself,* is the best summary statement because it expresses the value that we are to extend ourselves to others. In fact, we are to love others as we love ourselves. Not an easy task at all, the Talmud decides, because, in the end, we can only love another to the extent that we love ourselves. And if we don't have a good sense of self, then there is nothing upon which to base our love for someone else.

The second verse, though, *God created humanity in the Divine image,* is understood to be a better expression of Judaism. Here we are taught that everyone has within himself or herself a divine image. This aspect of a person's being cannot be diminished or eliminated based on *our* own feelings of self-worth. It is a gift from God. It is eternal. As you drift off to sleep tonight, think about your reflection of the divine image. Then recall each person you remember meeting during the course of the day and strive to see the eternal divine image that resides within each one.   LF

Charitable Review
2 December

Charity has the power to widen the entrance to holiness.
When a person wants to embark upon a certain path of
devotion, he or she needs to make an opening in order to
enter this new path. This is why all beginnings are difficult.
But giving charity makes the entrance wider.
Rabbi Nachman of Breslov[243]

We are nearing the end of the tax year. In addition to everything else I have to do, I make sure that I pay attention to all of my *tzedakah* obligations. This is not about fulfilling pledges that I have made. Nor is it about conferring with my accountant in order to make sure that I have taken full advantage of all my charitable deductions. No, this is about fulfilling my obligation as a Jew.

Some people throw away the many requests for solicitations that they receive in the mail. I stack them on my desk so that they are always in front of me—mixed in with the bills that have to be paid. They do not take a backseat to my other obligations. And each time I sit at my desk to pay the bills, which is usually one night a week, I review the organizations that have asked for my support. Sure, it is impossible to financially support all of them. But the process of evaluating them is important.

So at the end of the year, I review all the organizations to which I have donated funds and those that I either chose not to donate to or skipped over. Each one gets a second chance.

I figure it this way: If God has given me another chance through Yom Kippur, then I can imitate the Divine and exercise my power to do so as well.   KO

The Miracle of Strength
3 DECEMBER
Praised is God . . . who only does wondrous things.
PSALM 72:18

Hanukkah is a double-edged sword. On the one hand, it is a fabulous war story, one of the most remarkable in human history. That is why Judah Maccabee is immortalized in a statue at West Point as the equal of Alexander the Great or Napoleon. The few defeated the many, a small guerrilla band stopped the Syrian forces under the mad King Antiochus, who called himself a god. Jews saved the day for monotheism by fighting for their own rights and for the rights of all.

The other story is the miracle of the oil. The talmudic Rabbis want to know nothing of a Hasmonean military victory, since the descendants of those generals proved to be not very savory kings and high priests. The Rabbis downplay militarism and ascribe the unexpected victory only to God, by Whom all victories are won and without Whom no conquerors are of consequence. God fought for us, thank God.

Some of us don't want to believe the war story. We don't like to think of our ancestors as warriors; even our brothers and sisters in Israel today seem to us strange, if also authentic military superheroes! We prefer images of kibbutzniks, scientists, statesmen and -women. We remember the Maccabees, if at all, vaguely and without personal identification. They weren't like us, were they?

More of us resist the legend of the oil. We don't believe in miracles, even in a scientific age of quarks, black holes, the uncertainty principle, and the infinite probabilities that our most courageous scientists tell us our world contains. Miracles are only impossible in a closed Newtonian system; if we construct the world we inhabit, why can't God construct, or create, a prearranged "miracle"? In any case, the miraculous was never a brute fact but always a way of interpreting history, nature, or our own lives.

I suggest that we take both of our Hanukkah stories seriously. History is often made by fighting men and women; still, our history is ultimately a God narrative. We ourselves have seen military coups fail and the powerful wicked defeated. We have seen our own kind of miracles. Hanukkah should not be too problematic. It is how we ourselves live, how we experience and understand, a little better, who we are.

RABBI ARNOLD JACOB WOLF

Rejoicing with Others
4 DECEMBER
One who rejoices in the accomplishments of his neighbor or colleague will wear ornaments of light.
TALMUD[244]

Do we rejoice when others succeed? Some of us may quickly respond affirmatively and say, "Yes, of course I do." Others of us may pause and realize that such a full-hearted sense of rejoicing at the accomplishments of colleagues and friends is not always so easy to come by. We may experience normal human emotions, including jealousy, competition, and even envy, which get in the way of each of us from time to time. If we are truly honest, we acknowledge that sometimes another's accomplishment may make us compare ourselves with them and we may become distressed if we perceive that we have come out with the short end of the stick. Perhaps this is why the Talmud praises those who genuinely feel joy when someone else succeeds and tells us that such people "wear ornaments of light." This is a beautiful metaphorical way of saying that God's light shines from their very beings because they are able to suspend jealous and envious feelings that can be such nagging obstacles. Their beings are somehow lighter and allow light to radiate from their very core. May we strive to overcome jealousy and envy so that we, too, can fully rejoice with others and "wear ornaments of light."   LF

Doing What Others Have Taught
5 DECEMBER

One who says Torah in the name of the one who said it hastens the redemption of the world.

TALMUD[245]

This statement is recorded in the Talmud as the teaching of Rabbi Eleazar who taught it in the name of Rabbi Chanina. While we may expect the Talmud to state that it is important or even praiseworthy to mention who taught you what you learned as you teach it to others, it seems strange to suggest that such an approach "hastens the redemption of the world." But like many of the ideas in the Talmud, while the particular behavior is important to the Rabbis, the posture that it engenders—which is carried into other walks of life— is even more important. Elsewhere the Rabbis remind us that the performance of one mitzvah leads to another.

So what does it take to mention who taught you what you have learned? First, one must reflect on where one learned the particular lesson. Sometimes we repeat things so often that we forget whether someone taught it to us or we learned it on our own. That is why it is important to reflect back, particularly at the end of the year, on the many things that we have learned and the many people—some who remain unnamed—who have taught us. In helping us to grow, in our remembering them and their impact on our lives, we are working together to bring forward the redemption of the world.

But I would like to suggest that there is one more ingredient. And it is this step that ensures the redemption of the world. Once we have figured out who has helped us to learn something, even if it was a simple action of a helpful clerk at the local supermarket, we have the obligation to return to that place and thank the person for what he or she has taught us and, in turn, share what we may have learned. Sounds silly? At first you might feel awkward or strange in doing so. But that is the key to changing entire patterns of behavior among people. If we show others what is possible through what we do, then perhaps they will do the same. One small act can, over a period of time, change an entire community. And *that* brings the redemption of the world more quickly.

KO

Unknown Heroes
6 DECEMBER
As your days, so shall your strength be.
DEUTERONOMY 33:25

We know all the heroes of the Hanukkah story except one: Who buried that tiny jar of pure, sanctified oil? And why?

As the Greeks entered Jerusalem bringing the worship of Zeus to the Temple, they brought a sophisticated and seductive culture. It was a universal culture—embraced by the entire Mediterranean world. Greek philosophy, arts, theater, sport, and religion soon filled Jerusalem and eclipsed Judaism. Greek culture was welcomed, celebrated, and promulgated by Jerusalem's leadership. Even the high priest, Menelaus, advocated that Jews give up their provincial old ways and take the new, universal Greek culture to heart.

But not everyone succumbed. There was one anonymous hero—perhaps a priest, a Levite, or an attendant of the Temple—who saw things more clearly. This one saw into the dark side of the Greek world—a culture of grandeur and power but no holiness. This one beheld a society built upon slavery, where human worth was measured by class and social position, a callous culture that treated its statues with more reverence than its people, the shallowness that worshiped the body's beauty before the qualities of the soul, the brutality and cruelty beneath the veneer of sophistication. There was one who knew that Jews would one day return to affirm the image of God within all human beings. Jews would one day return to seek the God of justice and compassion, to search for the light of Torah and its wisdom. And so he or she hid a tiny relic of purity and sanctity, a little jar of oil to rekindle the light of Jewish faith.

The one who hid the oil is my Hanukkah hero. This one is my spiritual ancestor. Because of that vision and faith, there are tiny bits of light, sparks of holiness, hidden all over the world—buried behind the walls of callousness and the altars of superficiality. There are traces of purity and wisdom waiting for us when we finally tire of the emptiness and futility of the predominant culture.

To believe in the return of light, when all the world is plunged into darkness, is the lesson of the Hanukkah holiday and the entire season over which its casts its glow. To make possible the rekindling of hope, of wisdom, of holiness, of God's light, when all around there is darkness, is the true battle of Hanukkah.   RABBI EDWARD FEINSTEIN

Learning to Love Slowly

7 DECEMBER

The one who hurries love hurries hatred.

MIDRASH[246]

We all seek love. Some of us are more cautious than others when it comes to pursuing it. Others of us may fall in love easily. We each know our own patterns when it comes to falling in love. Here we are warned not to hurry love. Why would this be sage advice? The wisdom offered here suggests that if we let love unfold in a slow way, then we give ourselves the needed time to get to know all aspects of our beloved. In this way we can process and learn to accept those characteristics that we find to be bothersome and difficult. When, on the other hand, we rush into love, we may be surprised when we bump into character traits in our beloved that irritate and bother us. Without giving love a chance to unfold, we may find it emotionally hard to accept and live with these irritating qualities; we might soon find ourselves hating the very person whom we say we love. Thus, as the saying goes, "Take it slowly." If we do, if we allow the necessary time to pass, strong roots can take hold so that we and our beloved can grow together for years to come.   LF

Righteousness

8 DECEMBER

The Holy One does not let the sun of a righteous person set until the sun of a righteous person rises.

MIDRASH[247]

This is a comment on the text from Ecclesiastes, "The sun rises and the sun sets" (Ecclesiastes 1:5), which has an explicit and implicit message to those who would benefit from the wisdom of the author, wisdom he gained as a result of the life that he led. It seems as if the author of this text wants to show us that the routine of the world is boring and not very progressive. Since the sun rises and sets each day, the world is unable to evolve. Our lives reflect this dullness. And the result of it all—which he will eventually also tell us, his readers—is that death is all that awaits us at the end of this routine life. Moreover, we can do nothing to change the way the world is.

But if the reader is prepared to dig deeply into the text—and into the self—Ecclesiastes reveals a very important truth. Because of the orderly routine of the world, we can depend on it. Each day, the sun sets. We go to sleep at night knowing that the sun will rise in the morning. And we take this all for granted. But this orderliness is the result of the work of the Creator. who continues to maintain the order of the world.

The author of the midrash appreciates this wisdom and adds another layer to it. This is the beauty of the midrash. This teacher suggests that just as the sun brings light to the world, so do righteous people. But there is an orderliness in righteousness on which we can similarly depend. For when the righteousness of one individual wanes, the righteousness of another rises to illumine the world.

Then comes the really important message of the book that is tied to this midrash. When we see a righteous person, we have the obligation to emulate his or her righteousness. That is how we do honor to that person and make sure that the light of that person continues to rise. We are thereby linked with God in granting eternal life to others. KO

God's Closeness

9 DECEMBER

The nearness of God is my good.

PSALM 73:28

God is invisible. Our attempts to see God are rejected, and we are commanded to refrain from making visual representations of God. Idolatry, which limits God with a specific visual image, is a grave sin. God is beyond representation, and ultimately God's essence is illusive. God's presence is manifest to us through speech. "Hear, O Israel." At Sinai and beyond we respond to the divine call with performance of *mitzvot,* turning speech into deed and keeping the echo of the word reverberating in our lives. God's speech, however, is not constantly heard, and it remains in the telling of the story and the doing of the sacred deeds. Ears are designed to hear and eyes are designed to see. The eye is not satisfied with speech. So how can we represent that which is forbidden to be represented? Fire and light have no set shape and become the vehicle to manifest God's presence alongside speech, without violating the prohibition against idolatry. The light is constantly changing. The menorah, whose shape is drawn from nature and fire upon the altar, reminds us that even when God is silent, God is present. If we respond to God's speech, it will illumine our path and sustain us in a world that is often cold and dark. The Torah is a lamp, and the mitzvah is a light. The light that shines through Torah (learning) and the light that shines through mitzvah (deed) are the lights that lead to God.

RABBI PETER S. KNOBEL[248]

Banishing the Darkness

10 December

Even in the darkest of times we have the right to expect
some illumination, and that such illumination may come
less from theories and concepts than from the uncertain,
flickering, and often weak light that some men and women,
in their lives and work, will kindle under almost
all circumstances and shed over the time-span
that was given them on earth.

HANNAH ARENDT[249]

Since we ended daylight saving time and turned our clocks back, we have felt the darkness of the winter season surround us. Just look outside at 4:00 P.M. and you'll see the night beginning to descend. Our days are shorter during this time of year. The rhythm of our lives changes to fit the shorter hours of natural light. In mid-December we reach the winter solstice, when daylight is at its shortest and darkness prevails. This seasonal shift comes at the time of Hanukkah. And on Hanukkah, as we all know, we light candles as we reflect on the heroic spirit of the Maccabees and celebrate the pursuit of religious freedom and political sovereignty they bequeathed to us. Yet there are many times that the darkness in our world is not due to a shift in the earth's orbit, nor is there always a holiday close at hand to dispel it. In these situations, no matter what the calendar month, we ourselves must become the lit candles to provide the illumination, the light to banish the darkness, and bring hope to one another and our world. So whether the time of year is dark or light, light your candle and carry it with you wherever you go.   LF

Our Trials

11 DECEMBER

You have tried us, O God
refining us as silver is refined.
We came through fire and water
and You brought us out to abundance.

PSALM 66:20, 12B–C[250]

We can resonate with the pain and yearning of the psalmist perhaps more than any other character in the entire Bible, even more than Job. The psalmist's life is much like ours. Ironically or, as I believe, purposely, the psalmist goes unnamed (although tradition links the Psalms with David), because psalms express the uttering of every person. They find words for emotions that most of us know but cannot describe. They offer us a means to express the deep-seated murmurings of our souls when we feel paralyzed and are unable to say anything.

In this selection of a psalm text, the psalmist speaks to God, but in doing so is speaking to all of us who have experienced life-threatening challenges. (And who among us has not?) We have been forced to undergo trials that we never expected. And we have been profoundly affected as a result. But just as silver has to undergo fire to find its strength and brilliant luster, we can potentially emerge stronger and more resolute.

But that is not enough for the psalmist. It is insufficient for him to tell us that he struggled and survived. Rather, he struggled, survived, and emerged feeling blessed and uplifted. He might even go so far as to say—as so many have told me—were it not for this (you fill in the blank) experience, I would never have gotten to this enchanted place in my life. Were it not for what I faced, I might never have come to understand how blessed I am.

I thank You, God, for the privilege of my suffering and the journey that I have taken as a result of it!   KO

Garb for the Soul

12 DECEMBER

This one at last is bones of my bones, flesh of my flesh.
GENESIS 2:23A

In the beginning, Adam and Eve were naked and innocent. Only after eating from the tree did they feel the need for clothes. Clothes can mark a person as special or help identify a person's role. Clothes can help make us feel good about ourselves and our bodies. Clothes can also help hide our bodies if we are not happy with them. Yet, most of all, clothes cover our nakedness.

One of the early-morning blessings in the prayer book praises God for clothing the naked. Originally this blessing was recited when getting dressed in the morning. Yet we are not thanking God for giving us clothes. Instead, we think about clothing the naked. Is this to remind us to be concerned for those in the world who do not have clothes? Certainly, yet it is after all a blessing that we are saying for ourselves.

We are all naked and embarrassed. We try to hide those parts of our character that we are ashamed of. Perhaps then the blessing is to encourage us to find ways to move beyond our "nakedness." We are to come to see our bodies and ourselves as gifts from God. We are to accept those gifts even as we struggle to improve on who we are and what we have become. If we can move beyond embarrassment, then our clothes can become an extension of who we are rather than covering up what we consider ourselves to be. As you put your clothing out this evening before going to bed for the night, instead of thinking of your clothing as a disguise, consider it as garb for the soul.

RABBI MICHAEL STRASSFELD

Publicizing the Miracle
13 DECEMBER

One must place the Hanukkah menorah by the door of one's house or on the outside. If one dwells on an upper floor, one places it by the window sill nearest the street.

TALMUD[251]

Tonight when you walk down the street, look up and see how many *menorot* you see in the windows. The practice of placing our *menorot* on the windowsills facing outward is called *Pirsumet HaNes,* which means "to publicize the miracle." It is our way of sharing with the world the miraculous survival of the Jewish people. Today we take light for granted. We flip a switch and the lights go on. The power of light is nothing we find especially compelling. But before the advent of electricity in our homes, light was limited and, thus, precious. People just didn't have a lot of light after sunset. Then, the practice of lighting candles or oil lamps for eight nights in a row, increasing the light each night, was quite a sight. Tonight when you light your Hanukkah candles, turn off all the other lights in your house and let yourself be moved by the flames of the candles. They are a statement of hope and faith during the darkest time of the year, a visible sign to ourselves and to others of our ability to overcome hardship and adversity. LF

Practical Wisdom
14 DECEMBER

There is nothing as practical as a great idea.

WILLIAM NOVAK

I have spent a great deal of time in a classroom—first as a student, then as a teacher. Nevertheless, I have always remained a student. I never liked the confines of the classroom or of academia, for I have always felt that real wisdom emerges in the context of the real world. The classroom is safe, it is cozy, but it is not real. It is great to plot out something on paper, but it is meaningless unless it takes real shape in the world. Our people dreamed of Jerusalem for centuries. They spoke of it during daily prayers. They contemplated it during the Passover seder, and it served as the climax of the entire Passover experience. But it took on reality only once we settled the land, only once Israel became a modern nation, only once Jerusalem was reunited during the Six Day War in 1967.

Great ideas provide us with goals. It is then our task to turn these dreams into reality. KO

Rest toward Renewal
15 DECEMBER
Make for yourself an ark.
GENESIS 6:14A

Noah is told, *"Aseh lekha tevah"*—make for yourself an ark. He devotes himself to the task of his life. Nothing distracts him—not his neighbors who make fun of him for building a large boat far from any body of water, not his own doubts. Noah is *"tamim hayah be-doratav"*—he is simple and pure in his generation. Despite all that was going on around him, he constructed a sense of self that was unshaken by scorn or by floods. Amidst all the upheaval of his life, he was a haven of calm and self-assurance. He was at peace with himself. His name, Noah, which means "rest," is an apt description of him.

How does he do it? *"Aseh lekha tevah"*—make for yourself a *"tevah."* *Tevah* can also mean "word." Noah understands that to come to a place of rest, he needs to find the "word," the teaching, the belief, the melody, or the relationship that allows him to return to his center. Having built his "word" over a long period, he is certain of his ability to always find his way back again. Feeling certain, he can open the window of his self and go out into the world. His going out is no longer in an aspect of confrontation or of fear. His going out is now in the aspect of shalom—the peace that comes from wholeness, from being *"tamim,"* both simple and complete.

Shabbat is our opportunity to find the place of *noah,* of rest, of *menucha,* amidst the storms of our lives. If we can achieve that—and then bring some of that place into the rest of our week—then we can send forth our own doves that offer peace to the world around us.

RABBI MICHAEL STRASSFELD

Listening to Our Hearts
16 DECEMBER
The heart perceives what the eye cannot perceive.
MIDRASH[252]

We often think of our eyes as the windows to the soul. And often they truly are. When we look into someone's eyes we can get a sense of their trustworthiness or lack thereof. We're uncomfortable speaking to someone who doesn't look us in the eyes. No wonder we tend to distrust those who we say have shifty eyes. Yet even the eyes can lead us astray. Why is this? Because we sometimes see selectively: We often see only what we want to see and turn away when we see things that upset or trouble us. Often it is our heart, the seat of our inner consciousness, that begins to cry out at these moments when we deny important messages. When our heart is troubled, it is best to pay attention. True, we can ignore these communiqués that come from our heart. Yet these messages are important ways to stay spiritually connected. If we ignore our heart's perceptions, we can easily become disconnected. Let us listen to our heart so that we can be sure of walking down the path of awareness and not the path of denial.   LF

Praising Others

17 DECEMBER

It is exceedingly good.
GENESIS 1:31

At the end of creation, God stood back from creation, so to speak, and after briefly reflecting on what had been created, mused and said, "*Hiney tov meod.* This is very good." While some might take this as a less than humble posture, others read this as a commentary on the potential for the world. If it started out "very good," then we can return it to that state. But I see another lesson in this divine action. God wants to show us that it is good to praise creation, particularly the creation of things by others. In doing so, you provide them with a chance to join you in completing creation—the implicit charge in creating humanity as described earlier in the Book of Genesis. Then we can all step back and say, "It is exceedingly good."   KO

Firing the Lamp

18 DECEMBER

You should instruct the Israelites to take pure oil, pressed, for lighting, to fire up the lamp continually.
EXODUS 27:20

The first mitzvah (sacred obligation) of the building of the *mishkan* (the Tabernacle), what I like to call concretization of the spirit, is to make sure that a light issues within it. Light is one of the images of choice for the spirit, and for the intellect, but this will have to be a place of fire as well as light. *Ner* (lamp) is also an acronym for *neshamah* (soul) and *ruach* (spirit), feminine and masculine, human and godly, left and right, intuitive and rational, me and you, spiritual and material, light and dark, reconciled in the spiritual purity of raising the lamp of *neshamah* and *ruach* continually, that is, daily.

The Torah further tells us, "Aaron and his sons shall arrange it from evening until morning" (Exodus 27:21). Renewed every day, the life of the spirit is a daily notion, a few twenty-four hours strung together in the life of the spirit, embodied in the lamp, fired up in the sanctuary.

How do you live such a life of the spirit? Stay in the day. If not this evening, then tomorrow.

RABBI JAMES STONE GOODMAN

Granting Respect

19 DECEMBER

*Respect is in the hands of those who grant respect,
not in the hands of the honored.*

JEWISH FOLK SAYING

The word *respect* in Hebrew stems from the word *kavod*. It shares its root with the word *kaved,* which can connote seriousness and that something is actually physically heavy. To give someone respect is a weighty matter. We give respect not only to individuals but also to time, as in the case of Shabbat. When we light the Shabbat candles weekly we do so *likhvod Shabbat*—for the honor of the Sabbath. *Kibud* is another word associated with this Hebrew root. Traditionally, when you are asked to have an *aliyah* in synagogue to say the blessings before and after the Torah reading, you are receiving a *kibud*. We extend *kibbudim* in other ways as well: when we ask people to accept awards, to speak publicly, or to be our guest at a special occasion. All of these aspects of giving respect are, when we think about it, in our hands. We are the ones who find within ourselves the ability to step back and gently move our ego out of the way to grant recognition to someone else. It is not always easy to do. For we, too, yearn for recognition and respect. Yet, when we learn to give it away with a generous spirit, we may just be surprised when it comes back to us in unexpected ways.   LF

Good Memories
20 DECEMBER
Remember me for good.
NEHEMIAH 13:31

Most of us realize that memory is a powerful part of who we are. As our experiences become part of our memory, they have an impact on our personalities. However, few of us think about how memory can help us move toward what we want to become. Here the key is contained in the words of the prophet Nehemiah. If we strive to do good and we accomplish it, then we are motivated to strive even further. And if we do good, then people will remember the goodness that we have done. And it is this that helps direct us toward the goal of becoming who we most want to be. But it is the spiritual benefit that we accrue and that we offer the community through our good works that motivates us to want to do more, knowing that each step toward goodness we take also brings us one step closer to God, the source of all goodness.   KO

The Darkest Light

21 DECEMBER

Light is sweet.
ECCLESIASTES 11:7

The first night of Hanukkah occurs on the darkest night of the year. Not the shortest but the darkest, for on that night, the moon is shrouded by a heavenly cloak of velvet. Following the ruling of Rabbi Hillel, we begin with one candle, adding one candle each subsequent night until the third of the Hebrew month of *Tevet,* when the lights of Hanukkah commingle with the light of the waxing moon, bringing light into our homes and our lives. What can we learn from these lights?

First, these lights remind us how in a dark period of our history, a period that pitted Jew against Jew, a small band of Maccabees rose up, spoke truth to power, reclaimed our sacred sites, and restored the notion that Judaism was a tradition worth following.

Second, these lights remind us of the legend that a small jar of oil lasted eight days. While the details of this miracle may be subject to scholarly debate, the notion that God can enter our lives during times of great uncertainty to perform necessary miracles offers us great comfort.

Third, these lights and the emerging light of a new moon teach us that no matter how much darkness may trouble the mind, no matter how it may feel at times that we grope in a forest with no apparent way out, light will always appear. We can look to the lights of Hanukkah to lead us. We can look to the lights of Hanukkah to be a torch, illuminating a path for us. We can each look to these lights as a guide to a life imbued with holiness and touched by God's presence, echoing the declaration of the psalmist: "By Your light do we see light."

RABBI DANIEL GROPPER[253]

Child, It Is Still Good

22 DECEMBER

Faith is an attitude, part gift, part victory hard won, that allows each of us to look into our children's eyes, full of trust and purity, expectation and a little fear, and say to them, "I am so glad that I was able to bring you into the world. Despite all the ugliness we know the world possesses, despite war and hatred, greed and poverty that spoil the planet and erode the spirit, despite even the inevitability of death itself, faith is what lets us say, Dear child, it is still good.

RABBI NINA BETH CARDIN[254]

How do we come to the decision to have a child? Is it a rational decision that we think through with our spouse or partner, or is it an emotional, some would say biological, imperative that supersedes rational thought? Some people think it is self-centered to bear children, and maintain that we do so simply to perpetuate our genes and lineage. They point to the dangers and problems in our world and ask how we can responsibly bring human life into this mess. Yet, a less cynical way to think about this is to realize that it is a profound statement of faith to bring a child into this world, for we do not know what the world will be like as his or her life unfolds. We look around with our eyes wide open and, despite the imperfect nature of our world, say, "Yes, life is still, despite the violence, wars, inequity, racism, and the list goes on, worth living and passing on to a child—or loving and growing with one. And together, we will make the world even better." Perhaps there can be no statement of faith greater than bearing a child. So when you look at children, your own or the special children in your life, remember that despite your doubts, they are your statements of faith. Hold them close to sustain your faith and hope.   LF

Partners in Doing Good

23 DECEMBER

*The one who causes others to do good things
is greater than the doer.*

TALMUD[255]

Most of us were taught to worry about our own actions and not about what others do. It is a lesson oft-repeated in childhood, one that most of us have recycled for our own children. That is the beauty of certain truths. They can easily be passed from one generation to another. But the Rabbis of the Talmud want to teach us some alternative Torah here. They want to challenge slightly this bit of parental advice. The Rabbis are not suggesting that we stop doing what we are doing. They want to encourage us to continue to follow the path established by the Torah and to continue to take on more obligations. But they also want us to understand that our obligation does not stop there with what we do, however extensive is our pattern of religious observance. Instead, as we do *mitzvot,* we have the obligation to carry others along with us, helping them to do *mitzvot* as well. In this manner we all become teachers. By teaching others, we share in the reward that they receive for the good work that they do. And the world is better off as a result.

We can also look at this statement from the Talmud another way. We are all partners in what we do. So when we "cause" others to do something, we actually are participating in the activity as well. KO

Finding a Place for Joy

24 DECEMBER

There is no rung of being on which we cannot find the holiness of God everywhere and at all times.

MARTIN BUBER[256]

For many in the Jewish community, this is a lonely day. While so many others are rushing around with last-minute shopping and focused on religious ideas from which we feel alienated, this is just another day for most of us. So we have to find a *makom*, a place for ourselves. A *makom* is a place, any place at all. The most intriguing use of the word evolved soon after the destruction of the Temple, when it was decreed that God's personal name was never to be used. The Rabbis developed many appellations for God, hence the ban on using the familiar four-letter name for God. One of the names they developed was *HaMakom*, The Place. What a strange choice. Unlike the Merciful One or the Creator, *HaMakom* seems completely unrelated to the qualities of the invisible, intangible God. Does not the idea of place suggest substance? No, respond the Rabbis. *HaMakom* does not mean that God is made of stuff that takes up space. Rather, God is the space in which everything else takes place. Anything that exists does so within *HaMakom*, which is God. As *HaMakom*, God is the ground in which all being has roots. RABBI DAVID NELSON[257]

The Call

25 DECEMBER

The sacred call is transformative. It is an invitation to our souls, a mysterious voice reverberating with a string on our hearts that can neither be ignored nor denied.

RABBI DAVID COOPER[258]

Have you ever received a call that is so powerful that you could not walk away? The language of receiving a "sacred call" is somewhat foreign to us modern Jews. Perhaps the prophets of yore received divine calls, but today we don't often hear Jews using the phrase "I was called." Yet, perhaps it is a concept for us to reembrace. For certainly there have been moments, perhaps just one moment, in our lives when we were so moved that we had no choice but to put aside all else we were doing and commit ourselves to a particular mission or passion. It is certainly not easy to know when the sacred call comes. Nor is it simple to figure out how to reorganize our lives to follow its path. If we can remain open to what calls and excites us, then perhaps we can be more likely to hear the call that is meant especially for us. And even if we cannot put all aside, we can, hopefully, find ways to dedicate some of our precious time answering the call. The call can come at any time, but the night hours are often when we are most receptive to messages that come to us from our subconscious. As we enter into sleep tonight, let us be ever aware of whether there is a sacred call for us to hear.   LF

Human Light

26 DECEMBER

The human soul is a candle of God, searching out all the belly's chambers.

PROVERBS 20:27

People celebrate the winter holiday of Hanukkah in various ways. Some light lights, as is prescribed by Jewish tradition. Others simply exchange presents, a practice that has emerged in North America that parallels the giving of gifts during the Christmas season among Christians. While some people claim that it is a response to Christmas, the extensive giving of gifts probably emerges more from American civil religion (and its emphasis on material well-being) than it does from religious

ideas inherent in Christmas. The entire festiva
ing light into our lives and the lives of the people a
is this light that Hanukkah shares with Christmas.

Light is the overwhelming theme of Hanukkah. And in
it permeates most religious holidays that occur at this time o.
year. It is very dark outside. The nights are longer than are
the days, so we kindle our lamps in order to dispel the darkness—inside and out, to the innermost depths of our being.
And according to tradition, we place these lights on the win-
dowsill so that others can see them. We want to publicize the
miracle and share our light with others.   KO

Hope Inspired

27 DECEMBER

God desires not sacrifices, but hope.

MIDRASH[JJ8]

Hope gives us the strength to develop a peaceful optimism
toward life. Hope gives us great courage to face seemingly
insurmountable obstacles. When facing the darkness, fear,
and pain, hope teaches us that we can begin to understand
and accept our imperfections and make use of the tremendous potential we possess. By seeing the world through the
lens of hope, we can truly begin to honor our uniqueness.
Through honoring our own uniqueness, we can then come to
appreciate and honor the precious uniqueness of others.

Perhaps the deepest insight we can acquire from letting
our heart run to hope is that we are truly never alone. With
that realization, we can unlock a wellspring of love and
enthusiasm for life. By turning to hope, we discover that
God has given us the ability to turn our life around, and
through that turning, we discover the light within.

RABBI YEHUDAH FINE

d the New Century

DECEMBER

ry with a new heart of wisdom we
ifferently . . . and to break with the
as overtaken us, e.g., either Jewish
or universalism; either ritual
; either secular or religious.
BI HAROLD M. SCHULWEIS[260]

It is so easy for us to fall into split thinking, in other words, to see things in stark contrast, in either-or scenarios that leave no room for the ambiguities that fill our lives. This split thinking might begin when we say that someone is good or bad, or when we claim to love or hate someone or something. These are adjectives that convey an all-or-nothing perspective. No one is all good or all bad. And the things we love also have aspects that we don't always like so much. As Jews we have also, unfortunately, fallen into dichotomous thinking when we claim that Judaism is just one thing. For instance, some may say Judaism is primarily about *halakhah,* Jewish law, while others claim it is best captured by its devotion to social action. Some say Judaism is about ritual practice and others focus on ethical conduct. In truth, Judaism is a broad system of practice, faith, and action that embraces ritual, ethics, social action, and legal thinking. We lose out when we cut ourselves off from our multifaceted tradition and attempt to collapse it into a one-dimensional system that belies its true depth. As we conclude this secular year and prepare ourselves to take another step into this new century, let us refrain from split thinking in our personal lives, to better embrace Judaism and all its varied spiritual components.   LF

The Path to Holiness and Beyond
29 December

*Study leads to precision, precision leads to watchfulness,
watchfulness leads to cleanliness, cleanliness leads to
restraint, restraint leads to purity, purity leads to saintliness,
saintliness leads to humility, humility leads to fear of sin,
fear of sin leads to holiness, holiness leads to the holy spirit
(of prophecy), and the holy spirit leads to life eternal.*

TALMUD[261]

The Talmud records this wisdom in the name of Rabbi Pinchas ben Yair. At the end of the secular year, as we consider what we have done over the past twelve months and what lies ahead of us in the year ahead, we may want to consider taking one step each month, as has been outlined by this talmudic teacher. Whether we choose to use ben Yair's teaching as a prism on the past or a recipe for the future, its implementation paves the path for Jewish enlightenment. It is the path of the *tzaddik*.

Since some of the ideas may be hard to understand readily, Rabbi David A. Cooper has restated them in the following way: "Learning leads to respect, respect leads to generosity, generosity leads to acts of lovingkindness, acts of lovingkindness lead to moderation in living, moderation in living leads to purity of thought, purity of thought leads to joy, joy leads to selflessness, selflessness leads to awe, awe leads to equanimity, equanimity leads to extraordinary mind-states, and extraordinary mind-states lead to life eternal (God consciousness).[262]

This prescription for living does not evolve overnight, nor even over the course of a year. It takes time, as do most things of importance. Some stages may require more time and effort to reach than others. And just because we move from one stage to another does not mean that we let go of the preceding stage, nor does it let go of us. We are constantly vigilant, striving to reach even higher, fully realizing that our ultimate goal of God consciousness may be obtained for only a fleeting moment. Like Moses, who saw the glory of the Holy One only after it had passed, we can feel uplifted because we have seen God and lived; we have known God and this brought life to us.   KO

Sensitivity with Words
30 DECEMBER

Moses spoke accordingly to the Israelites, but they did not hear Moses, being short of breath and immersed in hard work.

EXODUS 6:9

It is rather curious that the Israelites do not understand Moses' message when you consider that Moses was scripted by God. Just preceding this text, God reassures Moses, telling him precisely what to say, word for word. Moses simply follows God's instructions.

The commentators explain that the condition of Israel at the moment—"short of breath and immersed in hard work"—precluded Moses' ability to connect with the people. After all, how receptive to a message of hope might you be when you are overworked and disillusioned? But the Hebrew word used hints at another reason for the people's lack of receptivity. The text uses the Hebrew verb *"vayidaber"* for "he spoke" rather than the more common *"vayomer."* The chosen form has a more aggressive, somewhat harsher connotation. Moses did not just speak to the people. He spoke to them sternly, and they were just too tired to listen.

Moses said what God instructed him to say. He said it to the right audience. He said it immediately after being instructed to do so. He just may not have said it in the most effective way possible.

Often we may feel like Moses in this regard. We have something to say. We believe what we have to say is right. We're convinced that we're saying it to the right person. We're even confident that our timing is correct. But then we pay little attention to *how* we say what it is we want to say. And the message fails.

Often the manner is as important as is the message. Sure, we believe we're right. We also believe that what we're saying is helpful. But even the words of God that we repeat to others may not be heard. Remember: A warm word can open a closed heart.

JEFFREY KORBMAN

Learning for Tomorrow
31 DECEMBER

A foolish student will say, "Who can possibly learn the whole Torah?" A wise student will say, "I will learn two laws today, and two tomorrow, until I have mastered the entire Torah."

MIDRASH[263]

Whether we start our Jewish learning late in life or begin as children, it's easy to become overwhelmed by the volume of information and skills needed just for everyday Jewish living. That's why it is easy to resonate with the foolish one of the midrash. Our knee-jerk reaction before we try is often, "I could never learn all of that." We have all felt overwhelmed at one time or another in our lives and uttered these words in exasperation. Whether we're trying to master the intricacies of the Talmud, the ancestral narratives of the Bible, or the choreography of the liturgy, we can take to heart the insightful advice of the wise student: Learn new things little by little. Savor each new word and idea. Reflect on them before moving forward. Take ownership of your own learning and revel in its mystery and majesty so that you can reach heavenward as a result. Soulful knowledge does not come in large chunks. It is accumulated slowly and carefully.

Do you remember when you tried cramming for an exam in school, staying up most of the night trying to make up for lost hours of study during the previous weeks? The material was briefly stored for the test. Then, as soon as the examination was over, you quickly let go of it—you had other things to make room for.

Jewish learning is rich. Let it penetrate the soul one day at a time. Then you can find it when you go looking. As you drift off to sleep tonight, probably much later than usual this last day of the secular year, let your dreams guide you on how to integrate what you've learned today into your life tomorrow. Then you will really remember it.   LF

NOTES

1. Arthur Schnitzler, *Buch der Spruche and Bedenken,* 1927, cited in *A Treasury of Jewish Quotations,* ed. Joseph L. Baron (Northvale, N.J.: Jason Aronson, 1996), p. 277.
2. Babylonian Talmud, *Derekh Eretz* 1:24.
3. Theodor Herzl, *The Jewish State* (Mineola, N.Y.: Dover, 1989).
4. Adapted from a translation by Danny Siegel.
5. From the prelude to the evening service.
6. Opening phrase of the *Amidah.*
7. Adapted from Vanessa Ochs, "The Power of Song" from CLAL (National Jewish Center for Learning and Leadership) Spotlight Online, at www.clal.org/wklybriefs.html.
8. *Genesis Rabbah.*
9. Steven Carr Reuben, in *Voice of the Spirit,* ed. Janet Bain Fattal (Los Angeles: Sweet Louise Music, 1998).
10. Midrash to Psalm 104:3.
11. Adapted from *Genesis Rabbah* 67:3.
12. Dov Peretz Elkins, trans., *Melodies from My Father's House: Hasidic Wisdom in the Heart and Soul,* ed. Simcha Raz (Princeton, N.J.: Growth Associates, 1996), p. 57.
13. *Lamentations Rabbah* 2.9:13.
14. Rami Shapiro, *Minyan: Ten Principles for Living a Life of Integrity* (New York: Bell Tower, 1997), p. 194.
15. *Numbers Rabbah* 19:3.
16. *Pirke Avot* 3:17.
17. Adapted from Steven Heneson Moskowitz, *A Few Jewish Fax: A Weekly Torah Study* (New York: The 92nd St. Y Bronfman Center for Jewish Life, 1996).
18. Milton Steinberg, *Basic Judaism* (New York: Harcourt Brace, 1996).
19. Cited in Elkins, p. 46.

20. Ismar Schorsch, "From the Chancellor," *Masoret* 5 (Fall 1995): 1.

21. Babylonian Talmud, *Tamid* 32a.

22. Baal Haturim on Exodus 20:8.

23. From the prayer book of Rabbi Isaac Luria and the introduction to the *vihu rachum* prayer.

24. Babylonian Talmud, *Bava Kamma* 38a.

25. *Yalkut Bereshit* on Babylonian Talmud, *Shabbat* 104a.

26. *Pirke Avot* 1:4a–b, as translated by Rabbi Eugene B. Borowitz.

27. Naomi Levy, *To Begin Again: The Journey toward Comfort, Strength, and Faith in Difficult Times* (New York: Alfred A. Knopf, 1998), p. 157.

28. Babylonian Talmud, *Berakhot* 29b.

29. Babylonian Talmud, *Sanhedrin* 106b.

30. Abraham Isaac Kook, *Lights of Holiness,* as quoted in *This Is for Everyone,* ed. Douglas Goldhammer and Melinda Stengal (Burdett, N.Y.: Larson, 1999).

31. Shapiro, p. 195.

32. Babylonian Talmud, *Nedarim* 62a.

33. Menachem Mendel Schneerson, *Toward a More Meaningful Life* (New York: William Morrow, 1995) p. 215.

34. *Pirke D'Rav Kahana* 12.

35. Adapted from Abraham Joshua Heschel, *God in Search of Man: A Philosophy of Judaism* (Philadelphia: Jewish Publication Society, 1955), p. 286.

36. Babylonian Talmud, *Berakhot* 10a.

37. Leo Stein, *Journey into the Self* (New York: Crown, 1950).

38. Barbara Myerhoff, *Number Our Days* (New York: E. P. Dutton, 1978).

39. Ibid.

40. Adapted from *Eyleh Ha-devarim: These Are the Words: In Concert for One People* (New York: CLAL, National Jewish Center for Learning and Leadership, 1995), p. 24.

41. Elliot Yagod, "Chanukah and Purim: Two Models of Jewish History," in *Guide to Purim* (New York: CLAL, National Jewish Center for Learning and Leadership, 1978).

42. From the evening service.

43. Cited in Jack Riemer and Nathaniel Stampfer, eds., *So That Your Values Live On: Ethical Wills and How to Prepare Them* (Woodstock, Vt.: Jewish Lights, 1991), p. 82.

44. Translated by Danny Siegel.

45. Babylonian Talmud, *Sanhedrin* 105a.

46. Levy, p. 46.

47. Commentary to Job 5:21.

48. Moses Maimonides, *Guide for the Perplexed*.

49. Lawrence Kushner, *Invisible Lines of Connection: Sacred Stories of the Ordinary* (Woodstock, Vt.: Jewish Lights, 1996), p. 121.

50. Solomon Schechter, *Studies in Judaism* (Philadelphia: Jewish Publication Society, 1958).

51. By attribution, as cited in Alfred J. Kolatch, ed., *Great Jewish Quotations* (Middle Village, N.Y.: Jonathan David, 1996), p. 34.

52. Babylonian Talmud, *Moed Katan* 28b.

53. Moses Hayyim Luzzatto, *The Path of the Just* (New York: Philip Feldheim, 1993).

54. Adapted from *Learn Torah With . . . Parashat Ki Tissa* 5 (March 6, 1999).

55. *Die Deborah,* 5 November 1896.

56. Adapted from *Learn Torah With . . . Parashat Pekudei* 4 (March 21, 1998).

57. Abraham Joshua Heschel, *Man Is Not Alone: A Philosophy of Religion* (New York: Farrar, Straus, and Giroux, 1972), p. 19.

58. Harold M. Schulweis, *For Those Who Can't Believe* (New York: Harper-Perennial Library, 1994).

59. *Ben Sira* 24:31.

60. Folk saying as cited in Babylonian Talmud, *Bava Batra* 16b.

61. Elie Wiesel, "We Are All Witnesses," *Parabola* 10 (May 1985): 26–33.

62. Babylonian Talmud, *Derekh Eretz* 1:15, 7:13.

63. Attributed to Rabbi Joshua ben Hananiah, Babylonian Talmud, *Pesachim* 68b.

64. Adapted from *Learn Torah With . . . Parashat Nitzavim* 4 (September 19, 1998).

65. By attribution, as cited in Kolatch, p. 386.

66. Lawrence Kushner, *Invisible Lines of Connection: Sacred Stories of the Ordinary,* (Woodstock, Vt.: Jewish Lights, 1996), p. 114.

67. *Pirke Avot* 2:4.

68. Moses Maimonides, *Guide for the Perplexed* 1:31.

69. Quoted in Reuben Wallenrod, "Some Contemporary Hebrew Novelists: Barash, Kabak, Berkowitz, and Schoffman," *Reconstructionist* 20 (November 26, 1954): 18.

70. Harold Kushner, *Hadassah* 74 (June–July 1993): 13.

71. Adapted from an online *parasha* dialogue, part of the *Learn Torah With . . .* series produced by Torah Aurah Productions.

72. *Likutei Maharan* II:48.

73. Attributed to Hanina ben Iddi, Babylonian Talmud, *Taanit* 7a.

74. *Pesikta Zutarta, Beshalach* 17.

75. Levi Meier, *Ancient Secrets: Using the Stories of the Bible to Improve Our Everyday Lives* (Woodstock, Vt.: Jewish Lights, 1999), p. 209.

76. Adapted from Vanessa Ochs, "On the Wisdom of Tears" from CLAL (National Jewish Center for Learning and Leadership) Spotlight Online, www.clal.org/wklybriefs.html.

77. From the author's unpublished sermon on *sefirat ha-omer*.

78. *Eliyahu Rabbah* 17.

79. Mishnah, *Peah* 1:1.

80. Adapted from *Learn Torah With . . . Parashat Emor* 4 (May 16, 1998).

81. *Sefer Maalot HaMiddot.*

82. Babylonian Talmud, *Yevamot* 121a.

83. *Raisheit Chochmah.*

84. From the morning service.

85. Quoted in Debra Orenstein and Jane Rachel Litman, eds., *Lifecycles, Vol. 2: Jewish Women on Biblical Themes in Contemporary Life* (Woodstock, Vt.: Jewish Lights, 1997), p. 187.

86. As cited in David Wolpe, *In Speech and in Silence: The Jewish Quest for God* (New York: Henry Holt, 1992).

87. As cited in Abraham Joshua Heschel, *The Insecurity of Freedom: Essays on Human Existence* (New York: Farrar, Straus, and Giroux, 1966).

88. Rebekah Kohut, "A Spiritual Hero," in *More Yesterdays* (New York: Bloch, 1950).

89. Retold in Martin Buber, *Tales of the Hasidim* (New York: Schocken Books, 1975).

90. Ibid.

91. *Exodus Rabbah* 36:3.

92. From the morning service.

93. Meier, p. 229.

94. Ibid.

95. Tzipporah Heller, *More Precious Than Pearls* (New York: Phillip Feldheim, 1994).

96. Speech to the Alliance Israelite Universelle at the Berlin Congress in 1878, for the toleration of Jewry.

97. E. M. Broner, *A Weave of Women* (New York: Holt Rinehart, 1978).

98. Heschel, *The Insecurity of Freedom.*

99. Babylonian Talmud, *Taanit* 22a.

100. Adapted by the author from her column "Bargaining with God," *Moment* (August 1994): 20.

101. Debra Orenstein and Jane Rachel Litman, *Lifecycles, Vol. 2: Jewish Women on Biblical Themes in Contemporary Life* (Woodstock, Vt.: Jewish Lights, 1997), p. 23.

102. Elkins, p. 108.

103. *Genesis Rabbah* 44:1.

104. Babylonian Talmud, *Shabbat* 127a.

105. *Numbers Rabbah* 12:4.

106. *Genesis Rabbah* 71:3.

107. *Derekh Eretz Zuta* 9a.

108. The traditional formula for blessing, from the liturgy.

109. Adapted from *Eyleh Ha-devarim: These Are the Words: In Concert for One People* (New York: CLAL, National Jewish Center for Learning and Leadership, 1995), p. 25.

110. Heschel, *God in Search of Man,* p. 283.

111. From "Rosh Hashanah 5758: Drawing Down the Light: Judaism as a Spiritual Practice" in *The Jewish Women's Book of Wisdom,* ed. Ellen Jaffe-Gill (Secaucus, N.J.: Carol, 1999), p. 77.

112. Babylonian Talmud, *Sotah* 5b; *Sanhedrin* 43b.

113. Babylonian Talmud, *Sanhedrin* 88b.

114. Adapted from *Eyleh Ha-devarim: These Are the Words: In Concert for One People* (New York: CLAL, National Jewish Center for Learning and Leadership, 1995), p. 22.

115. Rabbi Nachman of Breslov, *The Empty Chair: Finding Hope and Joy— Timeless Wisdom from a Hasidic Master, Rebbe Nachman of Breslov,* adapted by Moshe Mykoff and the Breslov Research Institute (Woodstock, Vt.: Jewish Lights, 1994), p. 64.

116. Adapted from Martin Buber, *The Knowledge of Man: Selected Essays,* ed. Maurice Freedman (San Francisco: Harper Collins Humanity Books, 1985).

117. *Derekh Eretz Zuta.*

118. Adapted from *Eyleh Ha-devarim: These Are the Words: In Concert for One People* (New York: CLAL, National Jewish Center for Learning and Leadership, 1995), p. 68.

119. Arthur Green, "The Role of Jewish Mysticism in a Contemporary Theology of Judaism," *Shefa Quarterly Review* 1 (September 1978): 29.

120. Meier, p. 243.

121. Babylonian Talmud, *Gittin* 7a.

122. Adapted from Francine Klagsbrun, *Voices of Wisdom: Jewish Ideals and Ethics on Everyday Living* (New York: Jonathan David, 1986), p. 293.

123. As cited in Kolatch.

124. Adapted from "Gleanings," *Central Conference of American Rabbis Newsletter.*

125. *Sifre* on Deuteronomy 11:6.

126. Karyn D. Kedar, *God Whispers: Stories of the Soul, Lessons of the Heart* (Woodstock, Vt.: Jewish Lights, 1999), p. 97.

127. Adapted from Leo Baeck, *The Essence of Judaism* (New York: Schocken Books, 1978), p. 147.

128. Taken from "Report of the National Committee on Religious School Work," in *Proceedings of the First Convention of the National Council of Jewish Women* (Philadelphia: Jewish Publication Society, 1896).

129. Rabbi Nachman of Breslov, p. 113.

130. Babylonian Talmud, *Sukkah* 53a.

131. Rachel Naomi Remen, "Spirit: Resource for Healing," *Noetic Sciences Review* 8 (Autumn 1988): 4.

132. Cited in Jeffrey Salkin, *Searching for My Brothers: Jewish Men in a Gentile World* (New York: G. P. Putnam, 1999), p. 228.

133. Attributed to Moses Mendelssohn as his motto.

134. From Stuart Ain, "Peres: We Cut the Right Agreement," *Jewish Week,* 6 October 1995.

135. Alan Lew, with Sherril Jaffe, *One God Clapping: The Spiritual Path of a Zen Rabbi* (Woodstock, Vt.: Jewish Lights, 2001), p. 30.

136. *Mekhilta* to Exodus 20:13.

137. Bradley Shavit Artson, "Moral Misers: Let It Shine," in *Learn Torah With . . . 1995–1996 Torah Annual: A Collection of the Year's Best Torah,* ed. Stuart Kelman and Joel Lurie Grishaver (Los Angeles: Alef Design Group, 1999), p. 26.

138. Abraham Joshua Heschel, *The Earth Is the Lord's: The Inner World of the Jew in Eastern Europe* (Woodstock, Vt.: Jewish Lights, 1995), p. 109.

139. Adapted from *Eyleh Ha-devarim: These Are the Words: In Concert for One People* (New York: CLAL, National Jewish Center for Learning and Leadership, 1995), p. 43.

140. Rabbi Bookman claims that he has been repeating this teaching for so long that he no longer remembers whether he learned it from another teacher or not.

141. Adapted from *Eyleh Ha-devarim: These Are the Words: In Concert for One People* (New York: CLAL, National Jewish Center for Learning and Leadership, 1995), p. 19.

142. *Avot d'Rabbi Natan* 13:4.

143. Cited in David Hartman, *A Living Covenant: The Living Spirit in Traditional Judaism* (Woodstock, Vt.: Jewish Lights, 1997), p. 111.

144. Babylonian Talmud, *Sanhedrin* 37b.

145. Adapted from *Eyleh Ha-devarim: These Are the Words: In Concert for One People* (New York: CLAL, National Jewish Center for Learning and Leadership, 1995), p. 80.

146. *Berakhot* 4:4.

147. *Mekhilta* to Exodus 17:6.

148. Elie Wiesel, "The Meaning of Life," *LIFE* 11 (December 1988): 78.

149. Rachel Naomi Remen, "In the Service of Life," *Noetic Sciences Review* 37 (Spring 1996): 24.

150. Kedar, p. 115.

151. Justine Wise Polier, "Prophetic Judaism, Fossil or Living Legacy," Stephen S. Wise Memorial Lecture, Brandeis University, March 1, 1957.

152. Rabbi Nachman of Breslov, *The Gentle Weapon: Prayers for Everyday and Not-So-Everyday Moments,* adapted by Moshe Mykoff, S. C. Mizrahi, and the Breslov Research Institute (Woodstock, Vt.: Jewish Lights, 1998), p. 2.

153. Excerpted from Harold Schulweis, "Jewish Conscience," a Kol Nidre–Yom Kippur sermon, Valley Beth Shalom, Encino, Calif., 1993.

154. Cited in "What Life Means to Einstein," in *Glimpses of the Great,* ed. George Sylvester Viereck (New York: Macaulay Company, 1930).

155. Cited in Salkin, p. 160.

156. Babylonian Talmud, *Keritot* 6b.

157. Lew, pp. 260–61.

158. Babylonian Talmud, *Sotah* 40a.

159. From the *El Maleh Rachamim,* memorial prayer.

160. *Likkutim Yekarim,* as cited in *Your Word Is Fire: The Hasidic Masters on Contemplative Prayer,* ed. Arthur Green and Barry Holtz (Woodstock, Vt.: Jewish Lights, 1993), p. 93.

161. Adapted from Vanessa Ochs, *In the Name of Heaven* (New York: CLAL, Jewish Center for Learning and Leadership, 1997), pp. 68–69.

162. *Orot HaKodesh* I.

163. Babylonian Talmud, *Chagigah* 5a.

164. Adapted from Mayan: The Jewish Women's Project, online at www.mayan.org.

165. Adapted from Shalom Spiegel, "Amos vs. Amaziah," *Essays in Judaism,* series 3 (New York: Jewish Theological Seminary, 1957).

166. *Hilkhot Teshuvah* 2:9.

167. Mordecai Kaplan, *Judaism as a Civilization: Toward a Reconstruction of American-Jewish Life* (Philadelphia: Jewish Publication Society, 1994).

168. *Bekorot* 8.

169. Midrash to Proverbs 6.

170. Babylonian Talmud, *Yoma* 86b.

171. Cited in Riemer and Stampfer.

172. Babylonian Talmud, *Megillah* 31b.

173. *Orot HaKodesh* I.

174. From the *Neilah* late afternoon–early evening service for the near-conclusion of Yom Kippur.

175. Jerusalem Talmud, *Taanit* 3:10.

176. Irving Greenberg, *The Jewish Way: Living the Holidays* (New York: Simon and Schuster, 1988), p. 182.

177. Ben Porat Yosef, cited in *Your Word Is Fire: The Hasidic Masters on Contemplative Prayer,* ed. Arthur Green and Barry Holtz (Woodstock, Vt.: Jewish Lights, 1993), p. 95.

178. Hannah Senesh, *Her Life and Diary* (New York: Schocken Books, 1973).

179. From the morning *Amidah*.
180. From a *piyyut* for *Selichot*.
181. Elkins, p. 89.
182. Babylonian Talmud, *Pirke Avot* 2:8.
183. Sholem Asch, *What I Believe* (New York: Putnam Books, 1941).
184. Abraham Joshua Heschel, *Moral Grandeur and Spiritual Audacity,* ed. Susannah Heschel (New York: Farrar, Straus, and Giroux, 1997), p. 56.
185. From his song "Return Again."
186. Emil Fackenheim, *Path to Jewish Belief: A Systematic Introduction* (New York: Behrman House, 1965).
187. *Emet V'emunah*, p. 62.
188. Excerpted from Harold Schulweis, "Behind the Twelve Steps: The God in Victory and the God in Defeat," Yom Kippur sermon, Valley Beth Shalom, Encino, Calif., 1996.
189. S. Y. Agnon, *Korot Beiteinu*, ed. Emuna Yaron (Jerusalem, Israel: Schocken, 1979).
190. Adapted from Heschel's original statement.
191. Kedar, p. 52.
192. Quoted in Nili Wachtel, "I. B. Singer on Modern Times," *Jewish Spectator* (Spring 1975): 20.
193. Babylonian Talmud, *Ketubot* 40a.
194. *Pesikta Zutarta, Parashat Shoftim.*
195. From the concluding service for Yom Kippur.
196. *Mishlei Israel* 6036.
197. Adapted from Michael White, *Torat Hayyim—Living Torah* 3, Lawrence Raphael, ed. (New York: Union of American Hebrew Congregations, September 25, 1999).
198. Letty Cottin Pogrebin, "Confessions of a Contradictory Jew," *NCJW Journal* (Spring 1998): 23.
199. From *birkot hashachar,* the morning blessings.
200. Grace Aguilar, *The Spirit of Judaism* (Philadelphia: Jewish Publication Society, 1864).
201. Adapted from Victor Frankl, *Man's Search for Meaning* (Boston: Beacon Press, 1992), p. 113.
202. Babylonian Talmud, *Taanit* 7a.
203. Babylonian Talmud, *Semahot* 11.
204. *Mivchar HaPeninim,* 264.
205. Zalman Schachter-Shalomi, *Paradigm Shift* (Northvale, N.J.: Jason Aronson, 1993), p. 267.

206. M. Sonnabend Johannesburg, "A Memory of Jabotinsky," in *Jewish Affairs* (July 1950): 17.
207. *Exodus Rabbah* 25:12.
208. David A. Cooper, *God Is a Verb: Kabbalah and the Practice of Mystical Judaism* (New York: Riverhead Books, 1997), p. 78.
209. Adapted from a *parasha* dialogue, part of the *Learn Torah With . . .* fax project (and online discussion) of Torah Aurah Productions.
210. From The American Jewish Committee, "Why Be Jewish?," *New York Times,* 12 September 1993.
211. From the *havdalah* blessing, used to distinguish between Shabbat and the rest of the days of the week and between holiday time and regular time.
212. Adapted from *Torat Hayyim—Living Torah* 3 (Union of American Hebrew Congregations, October 2, 1999).
213. Midrash on Psalm 148:1.
214. From the *Hashkivenu* prayer, in the evening service.
215. Psalm 36:8.
216. Babylonian Talmud, *Sanhedrin* 100a.
217. *Numbers Rabbah* 13:19.
218. This was originally written on the occasion of the assassination of Prime Minister Yitzhak Rabin, which was November 4, 1995.
219. From the prayer *Sim Shalom,* the final blessing of the morning *Amidah,* as translated by the Reform movement in the classic *Union Prayer Book* series.
220. Babylonian Talmud, *Berakhot* 7a.
221. Cooper, p. 79.
222. *Mishlei Israel,* 3400.
223. Cited in Gershom Sholem, *Major Trends in Jewish Mysticism* (New York: Schocken Books, 1941), p. 280.
224. *Kohelet Rabbah* 5:3.
225. Adapted from a *parasha* dialogue, part of the *Learn Torah With . . .* fax project (and online discussion) of Torah Aurah Productions.
226. *Mekhilta* on *Parashat Beshalach* 14:15.
227. Babylonian Talmud, *Menachot* 45b.
228. Interpretive translation by Rabbi Kerry M. Olitzky.
229. Adapted from Joel Lurie Grishaver and Stuart Kelman, eds., *5756 Torah Annual* (Los Angeles: Alef Design Group, 1999), pp. 26–27.
230. Babylonian Talmud, *Sanhedrin* 97a.

231. *Ruth Rabbah* 2:7.

232. Adapted from Grishaver and Kelman, p. 87.

233. Cited in Avraham Greenbaum, trans., *Advice: Rabbi Nachman of Breslov* (Jerusalem: Breslov Research Institute, 1983), p. 250.

234. Commentary of Ibn Ezra on Proverbs 18:17.

235. Adapted from Grishaver and Kelman, pp. 113–15.

236. *Sifre* on Deuteronomy.

237. Babylonian Talmud, *Tamid* 32a.

238. Adapted from Grishaver and Kelman, pp. 186–87.

239. *Or Ha-Meir,* as cited in Green and Holtz, p. 51.

240. Albert Schweitzer, *Out of My Life and Thought: An Autobiography* (Baltimore: Johns Hopkins University Press, 1998), p. 21.

241. Babylonian Talmud, *Sukkah* 45b.

242. Adapted from "A New Thanksgiving Ritual" from CLAL (Jewish Center for Learning and Leadership) Spotlight Online (www.clal.org/wklybriefs28.html).

243. *Likutei Maharan* 2:4, 1–2.

244. Babylonian Talmud, *Shabbat* 139a.

245. Babylonian Talmud, *Megillah* 15a.

246. *Shevet Yehuda,* 155:120.

247. *Genesis Rabbah* 58:2.

248. Adapted from an online *parasha* dialogue, part of the *Learn Torah With . . .* series produced by Torah Aurah Productions.

249. Hannah Arendt, *Men in Dark Times* (New York: Harcourt, Brace and Javonvich, 1968).

250. Eli Ezry, trans., *Praying for Recovery: Psalms and Meditations* (Deerfield Beach, Fla.: Simcha Press, 2000).

251. Babylonian Talmud, *Shabbat* 21b.

252. *Mishlei Chachmim* 113.

253. From Daniel Gropper, *Temple Isaiah Bulletin* (Lexington, Mass., December 1999).

254. Ellen Jaffe-Gill, ed., *The Jewish Women's Book of Wisdom* (Secaucus, N.J.: Carol Publishing Group, 1999), p. 192.

255. Babylonian Talmud, *Bava Batra* 9a.

256. Quoted by Elcott, p. 44.

257. Adapted from Elcott, p. 52.

258. David Cooper, "Invitation to the Soul," *Parabola* 19 (Spring 1994): 11.

259. Midrash to Psalm 40:2.
260. Harold Schulweis, *"With What Shall We Enter the New Century?"* Jewish Council for Public Affairs 1999 Plenum.
261. Babylonian Talmud, *Avodah Zarah* 20b.
262. David Cooper, *God Is a Verb* (New York: Riverhead Books, 1997), pp. 184–85.
263. *Song of Songs Rabbah* 5:11.

GLOSSARY OF TERMS

Amidah: The eighteen benedictions that constitute the core units of the daily prayer service. The *Amidah* is recited three times a day by traditional Jews. *Amidah* is Hebrew for "standing" and refers to the fact that the prayer is said standing up.

Chesed: Acts of kindness.

Dayeinu: Hebrew for "enough." Associated with the popular Passover song for which the refrain is *Dayeinu!* When used in a spiritual way, *dayeinu* refers to our gratitude to God for God's abundance and blessing in this world.

Emet: Truth.

Galut: Exile.

HaKadosh Barukh Hu: "The Holy One," one of the many names for God found in both the prayer book and Jewish texts.

Halakhah: The extensive system of Jewish law. From the Hebrew "to walk," thus denoting the path down which a Jew should walk through life.

Hasidism: Eighteenth-century reform movement that transformed Eastern European Jewry. Founded by the Baal Shem Tov and spread by his disciples, Hasidism emphasized joyful worship and aspects of the Jewish mystical tradition.

Kavannah: Intention; refers to the inspired motivation behind prayer.

Keva: "Set"; refers to prayers which are fixed as part of the liturgy. Together with *kavannah,* reflects the notion that we must strive to pray with consistency and spiritual intention.

Maariv: The evening prayer service.

Megillah: Literally, "a scroll." Refers to the books of the Bible kept on single rolled scrolls; generally used to refer to the scroll of Esther, which is read during Purim.

Midrash: Refers to the nonlegal sections of the Talmud and the rabbinic books containing biblical interpretations; sometimes referred to as "legend."

Mincha: the afternoon prayer service.

Mishnah: Legal codification of Oral Law, compiled by Rabbi Judah the Prince in the early third century.

Mitzvah: Plural, *mitzvot.* Refers to the 613 commandments traditionally acknowledged to have been given by God. Colloquially used to refer to a good deed, especially when pronounced as *mitzveh.*

Musar: Ethical guidance and advice encouraging strict behavior regarding *halakhah,* Jewish Law. Beginning in the nineteenth century *musar* developed into a full-scale literature.

Nefesh Yiterah: Literally, "an additional soul"; refers to the notion that on Shabbat we acquire an additional soul.

Niggunim: Wordless melodies that are often associated with Hasidism.

Omer: See *Sefirat HaOmer.*

Rachamim: Compassion. Related to the Hebrew word for "womb," *rachamim* reflects the protective, nurturing quality of God's love for us.

Shacharit: Morning prayer service.

Shichecha: The law that forbids a farmer to return to his field and gather fallen sheaves that were forgotten, left behind.

Seder: Hebrew word for "order." Refers to the Passover meal, which celebrates the holiday and retells the Exodus through reading of the Haggadah.

Sefirat HaOmer: The counting of the *Omer* is the period of time between Passover and Shavuot. During this time, certain observances of mourning are maintained, such as refraining from cutting hair and from getting married. It is also a time when we spiritually prepare ourselves for the giving of the Torah, which takes place on Shavuot.

Shema: Often called the watchword of the Jewish faith, this prayer is the closest thing to a Jewish creed. It proclaims the unity of one God: "Hear O Israel, the Lord Our God, the Lord is One."

Sheker: Falsehood, lie.

Tallit: The prayer shawl.

Tikkun Olam: Mystical notion of repairing the world.

Torah lishmah: The study of Torah for its own sake.

Tzedakah: Righteous giving through charity; the word is derived from the root for "justice."

Tzedek: Justice.

Zakhor: The command to remember.

Zerrizut: Zeal, quickness.

Zikhrono l'vrakhah: (fem., *Zikhronah l'vrakhah*) Epitaph which means "May his (her) name be for a blessing."

OUR TEACHERS:
AUTHORS OF
QUOTED TEXTS

Texts are the touchstone of Jewish spirituality. The authors of individual texts become our teachers as we study their writings.

Abraham ben Samuel ha-Levi Hasdai: Early thirteenth-century translator and Hebrew poet in Barcelona.

Shai Agnon: (1888–1979) Twentieth-century Israeli novelist and Nobel Prize winner for literature.

Grace Aguilar: (1816–1847) English author of Portuguese Marrano descent who wrote novels addressed primarily to Jewish women.

Hannah Arendt: (1906–1975) Political and social philosopher who left Germany after Hitler rose to power. She covered the Eichmann trial and published a book, *Eichmann in Jerusalem: A Report on the Banality of Evil,* which stirred up great controversy.

Bradley Shavit Artson: A Conservative rabbi serving as the dean of the Ziegler School of Rabbinic Studies at the University of Judaism in Los Angeles. He is the author of *It's a Mitzvah! Step-by-Step to Jewish Living* and, most recently, of *Dreams of Blessings: The Bedside Torah.*

Sholem Asch: (1880–1957) Outstanding Yiddish novelist and dramatist whose plays and novels depicted Jewish life worldwide.

Baal Haturim: (ca. 1270–1340) Also known as Jacob ben Asher. Halakhic authority whose major work was called *Arba'ah Turim,* from which he acquired the pseudonym Baal Haturim.

Baal Shem Tov: (1700–1760) Literally, "master of the good name," also called the *Besht.* The name Baal Shem Tov was used by the founder of Hasidism, Israel Ben Eliezer, a charismatic leader who became known through the oral tradition of his students who handed down tales of his travels and good works.

Leo Baeck: (1873–1956) A liberal theologian, he won recognition after the publication of his book *Essence of Judaism.* The only modern Jewish theologian who endured and survived Nazi death camps, he contended that evil was the misuse of human freedom.

Dov Baer of Mezeritch: (1704–1772) Also called the Maggid of Mezeritch. Successor of the Baal Shem Tov. Primarily a Talmudist who, after being healed by the Baal Shem Tov, became his disciple and sought out the role of itinerant preacher.

Terry A. Bookman: Known for his popular "Introduction to God" classes and "God: The Lab" workshops, as well as his speaking, writing, and online spiritual forum, is senior rabbi at Temple Beth Am in Miami, Florida. He is also the author of *The Busy Soul* and *God 101.*

E. M. Broner: Contemporary writer; author of two National Endowment of the Arts awards for literature; prominent Jewish feminist who has written new rituals to incorporate into contemporary Jewish life.

Martin Buber: (1878–1965) A religious existentialist influenced by Hasidic thought, most remembered for his dialogic I-Thou approach to relationships with God and between people.

Nina Beth Cardin: Contemporary rabbi, writer, and editor. She also lectures on a variety of Jewish issues, with special emphasis on women's contemporary spiritual matters. She is the author of *Tears of Sorrow, Seeds of Hope: A Jewish Spiritual Companion for Infertility and Pregnancy Loss* (Jewish Lights).

Shlomo Carlebach: (1926–1994) Rebbe, teacher, musician, and composer who touched the hearts of many Jews through his outreaching efforts to bring them back to Judaism.

David A. Cooper: A rabbi and teacher of Jewish meditation. He is the author of *The Handbook of Jewish Meditation Practices* (Jewish Lights), *God Is a Verb*, and other books on spirituality.

Albert Einstein: (1879–1955) Physicist and Nobel prize winner. Formulator of the Theory of Relativity.

Elimelekh of Lizensk: (1717–1787) Founder of the Polish and Hungarian branches of Hasidim.

Abraham ibn Ezra: (1092–1167) Famous Spanish Jewish grammarian (Barcelona) and Biblical exegete. His Bible commentaries were based on linguistic and factual examinations of the text.

Herbert A. Friedman: Founding president of the Wexner Heritage Foundation, former president of United Jewish Appeal, and the creative innovator of many of its programs. Author of *Roots of the Future.*

Solomon ibn Gabriol: (ca. 1020–1057) Poet and philosopher who lived in Spain. His writings reflect mystical tendencies and scientific knowledge, especially of astronomy. His major philosophical work is *Mekor Chaim.*

Jonah Gerondi: Spanish rabbi, author, and moralist who was often called "the father of the virtues of piety, humility, and asceticism."

Judith Glass: An independent consultant on organizational and gender issues.

Arthur Green: The Lown Professor of Jewish Thought at Brandeis University and the former president of the Reconstructionist Rabbinical College. He is a student of Jewish theology and mysticism and author of many books including *These Are the Words: A Vocabulary of Jewish Spiritual Life* (Jewish Lights).

Irving Greenberg: President of Jewish Life Network, a Judy and Michael Steinhardt Foundation. Rabbi Greenberg has published articles on Jewish thought and religion and in American Jewish history. His books include *The Jewish Way* and *Living in the Image of God: Jewish Teachings to Perfect the World.*

Tzipporah Heller: Contemporary writer and author of the book *More Precious Than Pearls: Selected Insights into the Qualities of the Ideal Woman: Based on Eshes Chayil.*

Theodor Herzl: (1860–1904) Founder of modern political Zionism. His solution to the problem of anti-Semitism was the creation of a Jewish State, which he describes in his book *The Jewish State.* He presided over five Zionist Congresses and is well known for his famous phrase of optimism, "If you will it, it is no dream."

Abraham Joshua Heschel: (1907–1972) A contemporary theologian whose knowledge encompassed the Bible, Talmud, Hasidism, and philosophy. A poet, mystic, and social reformer, he was an active participant in interreligious dialogue and marched with Martin Luther King, Jr. in Selma.

Abraham Kabak: (1880–1944) Hebrew author who finally settled in Palestine in 1921, where he played a central role in the literary, educational, and civic life of Jerusalem.

Mordecai Kaplan: (1881–1983) Philosopher; founder of Reconstructionism. He defined Judaism as an evolving religious civilization; his primary work articulating his beliefs is *Judaism as a Civilization.* He also founded Young Israel, an active young Orthodox community, and developed the idea of the bat mitzvah and the concept of a Synagogue Center.

Karyn D. Kedar: Contemporary rabbi who works as director of the Midwest Council of the Union of American Hebrew Congregations, with congregations in the Midwest, guiding people in their own spiritual and personal growth. Author of *God Whispers: Stories of the Soul, Lessons of the Heart* (Jewish Lights).

Rebekah Kohut: (1804–1951) Educator and community leader. President of the New York Council of Jewish Women from 1897–1901, after which she served in many governmental and Jewish communal positions of leadership.

Abraham Isaac Kook: (1865–1935) Religious thinker and first Ashkenazic chief rabbi of Palestine. He was an important bridge between the Orthodox and secular pioneers during the early years of building the State of Israel.

Harold Kushner: Conservative rabbi and popular theologian and writer who is best known for his book *When Bad Things Happen to Good People.*

Lawrence S. Kushner: Rabbi-in-residence at Hebrew Union College–Jewish Institute of Religion, New York, he served for more than twenty years as the spiritual leader of Congregation Beth El in Sudbury, Massachusetts. He is the author of many books, including *Invisible Lines of Connection: Sacred Stories of the Ordinary* (Jewish Lights).

Levi Yitzchak of Berditchev: (1740–1810) Hasidic rebbe who consolidated the Hasidic movement in Central Poland and Lithuania, he was one of the most famous rebbes in the third generation of the Hasidic leadership.

Yeshayahu Leibowitz: (1903–1994) An Orthodox, contemporary Israeli philosopher who critiqued Judaism in the light of the creation of the Jewish State.

Naomi Levy: A Conservative rabbi and writer. She is the author of *To Begin Again: The Journey Toward Comfort, Strength, and Faith in Difficult Times.*

Alan Lew: A Conservative rabbi and spiritual leader of Congregation Beth Shalom in San Francisco. He came to Judaism and the rabbinate after many years of Zen Buddhism and is the author of *One God Clapping: The Spiritual Path of a Zen Rabbi.*

Isaac Luria: (1534–1572) Also known as HaAri (the Lion), he was a kabbalistic master who lived in Safed and established his own philosophy of Kabbalah called Lurianic Kabbalah.

Moshe Hayyim Luzzatto: (1707–1747) Born in Padua, Italy, he became a controversial eighteenth-century Kabbalist whose saintly way of life gave rise to suspicion and opposition. His most important work is *The Path of the Just (Mesillat Yesharim).*

Moses Maimonides: (1135–1204) Moses ben Maimon, also called the Rambam, perhaps one of the greatest thinkers in all of Jewish history. Trained as a physician, Maimonides was also a commentator and philosopher. He is best known for his *Guide for the Perplexed* and his *Mishneh Torah,* an "easy-to-use" compilation of Jewish law.

Levi Meier: Rabbi, and chaplain of Cedars-Sinai Medical Center in Los Angeles. He is a licensed clinical psychotherapist and a marriage, family, and child therapist. He is the author of *Ancient Secrets: Using the Stories of the Bible to Improve Our Everyday Lives* and *Moses—The Prince, the Prophet: His Life, Legend & Message for Our Lives* (both Jewish Lights). He is special issues editor of the *Journal of Psychology and Judaism* and teacher of The Writer's Torah Study group of the Avi Chai Foundation.

Moses Mendelssohn: (1729–1786) Philosopher of the German Enlightenment and spiritual leader of German Jewry who worked tirelessly to improve the civic status of the Jews in Western Europe.

Yehiel Mihal of Zlotchov: (1731–1786) An early leader of Hasidim in Galicia, he preached in the town of Zlotchov from 1770 and was known for telling tales of miracles of piety and asceticism.

Barbara Myerhoff: (1935–1985) A social anthropologist who pioneered research with elderly Jews and the Hasidic community in Los Angeles. Author of *Number Our Days.*

Nachman of Breslov: (1772–1810) The great-grandson of the Baal Shem Tov and the founder of the Breslover Hasidim. Reb Nachman, as he is often called, is still considered to be the leader of the Breslover Hasidim. His followers believe that no other leader can follow as his successor.

Nachum of Rizhyn: Descendant of Israel Friedmann of Ruzhin (1797–1850). Hasidic leader who established a large center in Ruzhin, in Poland/Lithuania.

Jacob Neusner: Professor at the University of South Florida, Tampa, and the author of hundreds of books, many on the rabbinic period and the Talmud.

William Novak: Former editor of *Response, New Traditions,* and founder of *Moment* magazine. He is also the co-editor of *The Big Book of Jewish Humor.*

Debra Orenstein: Senior fellow of the Wilstein Institute of Jewish Policy Studies and author on Jewish spirituality and gender studies, she is the editor of *Lifecycles, Vol. 1: Jewish Women on Life Passages and Personal Milestones* and *Lifecycles, Vol. 2: Jewish Women on Biblical Themes in Contemporary Life* (both Jewish Lights).

Bachya ibn Pakuda: (mid–eleventh century) Moral philosopher who lived in Muslim Spain. His major work, *Duties of the Heart,* was written in the year 1000.

Shimon Peres: Israeli politician who has served in many governmental posts, including serving as prime minister from 1984 to 1986.

Letty Cottin Pogrebin: Founding editor of *Ms.* Magazine and renowned feminist and social activist. Author of many books, including *Deborah, Golda and Me.*

Justine Wise Polier: (1903–1987) First woman appointed as judge in the State of New York, she served as Justice of the Domestic Relations Court for thirty-eight years. Widely considered a voice of conscience of her era, she left a legacy of social activism. Daughter of Rabbi Stephen S. Wise, a renowned early American Reform rabbi and Zionist leader.

Rachel Naomi Remen: One of the earliest pioneers in the mind-body field and one of the first to develop a psychological approach to people with life-threatening illnesses. Cofounder and medical director of Commonweal Cancer Help Program and author of *Kitchen Table Wisdom* and *My Grandfather's Blessings.*

Arnold Resnicoff: The command chaplain for the U.S. European Common Command and advisor on religion, ethics, and morals for all U.S. forces in an area spanning 89 nations and 13 million square miles.

Steven Carr Reuben: Author, educator, and rabbi of Congregation Kehillat Israel in Pacific Palisades, California.

Julia Richmond: (1855–1912) A long-time educator in New York public schools who was also active in the improvement of Jewish education and was an early leader of the National Council of Jewish Women.

Ann Roiphe: Contemporary author and journalist.

Franz Rosenzweig: (1886–1929) Philosopher and theologian who is best known for his book, *Star of Redemption.* An exponent of existentialism, he rejected traditional philosophical methods and based his belief in God in personal, not objective, experience.

Zalman Schachter-Shalomi: Rabbi and founder of Pnai Or Religious Fellowship, and father of the Jewish Renewal movement. He is the author of many books and articles and has designed workshops on Spiritual Eldering and spirituality.

Solomon Schechter: (1848–1915) Scholar and theologian who emigrated to the United States to become the chancellor of The Jewish Theological Seminary of America, where he became the early architect of Conservative Judaism.

Menachem Mendel Schneerson: (1902–1994) Seventh successive leader of Lubavitch Hasidim. Under his leadership its institutions expanded beyond the Lubavitch community into the mainstream of Jewish life.

Arthur Schnitzler: (1862–1931) Austrian playwright and author.

Ismar Schorsch: The Chancellor of the Jewish Theological Seminary of America.

Harold M. Schulweis: The senior rabbi of Valley Beth Shalom in Encino, California. Founding chairman of the Jewish Foundation for the Righteous, and author of *For Those Who Can't Believe.*

Albert Schweitzer: (1875–1965) Nobel Peace Prize winner in 1952. Renowned for his work in science, theology, and music.

Moses Mendes Seixas: (1744–1809) One of the organizers of the Bank of Rhode Island and president of the Newport Synagogue in 1790.

Hannah Senesh: (1921–1944) A poet born in Budapest. In 1943 she joined parachutists from Palestine who jumped into Nazi-occupied Europe on rescue missions. She was the first to cross into Hungary from Yugoslavia, where she landed and fought with the partisans. At age twenty-three she was captured and executed.

Rami Shapiro: A rabbi of and director of the Simply Jewish Fellowship in Miami, Florida, and author of *Wisdom of the Jewish Sages, Minyan,* and *The Way of Splendor.*

Charles Sherman: The spiritual leader of Temple Israel in Tulsa, Oklahoma.

Isaac Bashevis Singer: (1904–1991) Beloved Yiddish American novelist whose stories were serialized in the Yiddish daily paper *Forward* and translated into many languages.

Henry Slominsky: (1884–1970) U.S. philosopher and professor.

Shalom Spiegel: (1899–1984) Scholar, writer and educator; professor of medieval Hebrew literature at The Jewish Theological Seminary of America.

Leo Stein: (1872–1947) American Jewish writer.

Milton Steinberg: (1903–1950) Conservative rabbi influenced by Reconstructionism who emerged as a leading writer of philosophical theology. Author of many books, including *Basic Judaism.*

Vilna Gaon: (1720–1797) Also known as Elijah ben Solomon Zalman. Great spiritual and intellectual leader of Jewry in modern times. He vociferously opposed both the *Haskalah* movement and Hasidism.

Sheila Peltz Weinberg: Contemporary Reconstructionist rabbi who heads the Jewish Community of Amherst congregation. She is well known for her work in leading discussions between Buddhists and Jews and teaches Jewish meditation.

Elie Wiesel: Author; the pivotal moral figure in intellectual culture related to the Holocaust.

Isaac Mayer Wise: (1819–1900) U.S. rabbi and architect of Reform Judaism who advocated the creation of a union of congregations, a common prayer book, and a college to train American rabbis. He served as the first president of Hebrew Union College upon its founding in 1875.

Elliot Yagod: Scholar and faculty member of the Shalom Hartman Institute in Jerusalem.

Yehiel ben Yekutiel ben Benyamin Harofe: Author of *Sefer Ma'alot HaMiddot,* which contains statements of moral living. He lived in Rome in the late thirteenth century.

Simcha Zissel Ziv: Nineteenth-century disciple of Israel Salanter, founder of the *Musar* movement from Lithuania.

Leopold Zunz: (1794–1886) A historian, and among the founders of the Science in Judaism movement. His chief interest was Hebrew literature.

SOURCES OF QUOTED TEXTS

While the texts we have shared in these pages provide the reader with a great deal of insight and inspiration, it is important to realize that most of them come from larger works. These are described below.

Avot de Rabbi Natan: Small tractate that provides an expansion to the trac-tate of the Mishnah called *Pirke Avot* (Ethics of the Fathers). Ascribed to Rabbi Nathan the Babylonian.

Babylonian Talmud: The rabbinic discussions called the Gemara, along with the Mishnah, is called the Talmud. The Babylonian Talmud was a product of 300 years of study and was compiled in about 500 C.E.

Derekh Eretz Zuta: The middle section of the talmudic section called Derekh Eretz, which talks about the need for self-examination and modesty.

Exodus Rabbah: Midrashim on Exodus. The first part was edited no earlier than the tenth century C.E. and the second half is thought to have been com-piled earlier.

Genesis Rabbah: Midrashim on Genesis, edited in Palestine in about 425 C.E.

The Guide for the Perplexed: Moses Maimonides' seminal philosophical work, completed ca. 1200.

Haggadah: Literally, "the telling (of the story)." A book, used during the Passover seder, that contains the story of the Exodus from Egypt in a ritual-ized form.

Jerusalem Talmud: Compilations of the laws and discussion of the early Rabbis in Israel, mainly in the Academy of Tiberias. Much smaller in length than the Babylonian Talmud and considered less authoritative; its final form was completed sometime at the beginning of the fifth century C.E.

Kohelet Rabbah: Also known as Ecclesiastes *Rabbah;* a midrash on the book of Ecclesiastes written in Palestine and redacted around the beginning of the seventh century.

Leviticus Rabbah: Palestinian *midrashim* composed around the fifth century C.E.

Mekhilta: Oldest rabbinic commentary on the Book of Exodus, dated no earlier than the fifth century C.E. in Palestine.

Midrash Tehillim: Midrashim on Psalms, containing material dated as early as the third century and as late as the thirteenth century.

Mishnah: Legal codification, expounding the Bible and constituting the core of Oral Law, compiled and edited by Rabbi Judah the Prince in the early part of the third century.

Numbers Rabbah: Midrashim on the books of Numbers based on the school of Moses ha-Darshan, the eleventh-century scholar of Narbonne.

Pirke Avot: The volume of the Mishnah that contains teachings on interpersonal, societal, and spiritual concerns. Also called *Ethics of the Fathers.*

Pesikta D'Rav Kahana: One of the oldest midrashic collections containing homilies on the portions of the Torah and *haftarah* thought to be a Palestinian text from the fifth century C.E.

Pesikta Zutarta: Also known as *Lekach Tov;* a medieval midrashic collection on the Torah composed in Germany at the end of the eleventh century.

Proverbs: A biblical book. The second in the Hagiographa, it is a collection of moral sayings.

Psalms: First book in the Hagiographa section of the Bible, it consists of 150 psalms traditionally ascribed to King David, who is often call the psalmist.

Ruth Rabbah: Midrashim on the book of Ruth, this is a Palestinian work compiled no earlier than the sixth century C.E.

Sefer Hasidim: An extensive work on Jewish ethics by Judah HeHasid (d. 1217), one of the great teachers of Hasidei Ashkenaz.

Siddur: The Jewish prayer book. From a Hebrew root meaning "to arrange in order," referring to the order of the prayers.

Sifre: Halakhic *midrashim* on the books of Numbers and Deuteronomy. Most probably a Palestinian work compiled no later than fourth century C.E.

Zohar: Mystical biblical commentary on sections of the Five Books of Moses and parts of the Hagiographa (Song of Songs, Ruth, Lamentations). The *Zohar* dwells on the mystery of creation and ascribes symbolic explanations to stories and events in the Bible.

CONTRIBUTORS

Yosef I. Abramowitz is the founder of *Jewish Family & Life!* and publisher of *Sh'ma*. Yossi and his wife, Rabbi Susan Silverman, are the co-authors of *Jewish Family & Life: Traditions, Holidays and Values for Today's Parents and Children*. He is the founder of JewishFamily.com, InterFaithFamily.com, GenerationJ.com, Jvibe.com, and JSkyway.com, the Jewish satellite network.

Bradley Shavit Artson is a Conservative rabbi serving as the dean of the Ziegler School of Rabbinic Studies at the University of Judaism in Los Angeles. He is the author of *It's a Mitzvah! Step-By-Step to Jewish Living* and *Dreams of Blessings: The Bedside Torah*.

Leila Gal Berner is a Reconstructionist rabbi and has a Ph.D. in medieval Jewish studies. A congregational rabbi, professor, musician, and liturgist, she is the first woman in history to edit a nationally distributed Shabbat prayer book, *Or Chadash*. Her liturgical commentaries appear in the *Kol Haneshamah* prayer book series published by the Reconstructionist Press.

Jonathan Jaffe Bernhard is a Conservative rabbi serving as the assistant rabbi at Adat Ari El at Los Angeles.

Tsvi Blanchard is a rabbi who serves as director of organizational development at CLAL, an organization devoted to empowering the many diverse views of the Jewish people. In addition to his work as a national Jewish teacher and lecturer, Tsvi is a university teacher, psychotherapist, and organizational consultant. His most recent publications relate to both health and healing and ecology and environmentalism.

Barry H. Block has served as the rabbi of Temple Beth-El in San Antonio, Texas, since 1992. A native of Houston, he was ordained at Hebrew Union College–Jewish Institute of Religion in New York in 1991.

Terry A. Bookman, known for his popular "Introduction to God" classes and "God: The Lab" workshops, as well as for his speaking, writing, and online spiritual forum, is senior rabbi at Temple Beth Am in Miami, Florida. He is also the author of *The Busy Soul* and *God 101*.

Herbert Bronstein is the senior scholar of North Shore Congregation Israel in Glencoe, Illinois, and faculty member in the Religion Department at Lake Forest College in Illinois. He has combined a successful vocation as a congregational rabbi and extensive community service with lifelong achievements in scholarship, academic teaching, lecturing, and writing.

Ayelet Cohen is a rabbinical student at The Jewish Theological Seminary of America. She has served as rabbi in Nice and Paris, France, and in Montreal, Canada, and is a Cooperberg-Rittmaster rabbinic intern at Congregation Beth Simchat Torah in New York City.

Jerome K. Davidson is senior rabbi at Temple Beth-El of Great Neck, New York. He serves on the faculty and Board of Governors of Hebrew Union College–Jewish Institute of Religion; he is the former president of the Synagogue Council of America, and the CCAR-elected representative to the UAHC Board of Trustees. He has been a leading voice in welcoming gays and lesbians into Reform congregational life. Rabbi Davidson has also created dialogue programs with Catholics, Muslims, and African-American congregations.

Avram Davis is the founder of Chochmat HaLev, a Jewish Meditation and Spirituality Center in Berkeley, California. He has a Ph.D. in comparative philosophy and religion from the University of California at Santa Cruz and has studied in numerous yeshivot in New York and Israel. He is the author of *The Way of Flame: A Guide to the Forgotten Mystical Tradition of Jewish Meditation,* and editor of *Meditation from the Heart of Judaism: Today's Teachers Share Their Practices, Techniques, and Faith* (both Jewish Lights).

Lavey Derby serves as the rabbi and spiritual leader of Congregation Kol Shofar in Tiburon, California, and is the founder of the Neshamah Minyan, dedicated to deepening a relationship to the Divine through meditation and prayer. He is on the faculty of the Wexner Heritage Foundation.

Malka Drucker is a rabbi and author of more than eighteen award-winning books for young people and adults. A spiritual leader in Santa Fe, New Mexico, she is currently working on a book about women as spiritual leaders of all faiths.

Amy Eilberg was the first woman ordained as a Conservative rabbi by The Jewish Theological Seminary. She currently serves as a pastoral counselor in private practice and teaches and writes on Jewish spirituality and healing.

Edward Feinstein is rabbi of Valley Beth Shalom in Encino, California, and an instructor at the Ziegler Rabbinical School of the University of Judaism.

Yehudah Fine is a rabbi, family therapist, and motivational speaker. An expert on teen issues, family problems, and recovery issues, he regularly appears on talk radio and television across the country. He is a member of the guidance staff at Yeshiva University and author of *Times Square Rabbi: Finding Hope in Lost Kids' Lives.*

Mordecai Finley serves as the rabbi of Ohr HaTorah Congregation and is co-rabbi of Makom Ohr Shalom, both in Los Angeles.

James A. Gibson serves as rabbi of Temple Sinai in Pittsburgh.

Melvin J. Glazer is the rabbi at Beth David Congregation in Miami, as well as a grief therapist. He has served various congregations in the United States, Canada, and South Africa.

James Scott Glazier serves as the rabbi of Temple Sinai in South Burlington, Vermont, and is Vermont's only Reform congregational rabbi.

Edwin C. Goldberg is the rabbi of Temple Judea in Coral Gables, Florida. He is the author of the book *Midrash for Beginners* and has published numerous articles and sermons. He also serves as an adjunct professor at the University of Miami in the Department of Religious Studies.

Elyse Goldstein is the director/rosh yeshiva of Kolel: The Adult Centre for Liberal Jewish Learning, a full-time progressive adult learning institute in Toronto. She is the author of *ReVisions: Seeing Torah through a Feminist Lens* and editor of *The Women's Torah Commentary: New Insights from Women Rabbis on the 54 Weekly Torah Portions* (both Jewish Lights).

James Stone Goodman is a rabbi, writer, and musician in St. Louis, Missouri. He serves Congregation Neve Shalom and the Central Reform Congregation.

Irving Greenberg is president of Jewish Life Network, a Judy and Michael Steinhardt Foundation. JLN's mission is to create new institutions and initiatives to enrich the inner life of American Jewry. Rabbi Greenberg has published articles on Jewish thought and religion and in American Jewish history. His books include *The Jewish Way* and *Living in the Image of God: Jewish Teachings to Perfect the World*.

Daniel Gropper is a rabbi at Temple Isaiah in Lexington, Massachusetts. He serves on the board of KAVOD: A Tzedakah Collective, and enjoys liturgy and modern midrash.

Judith HaLevy is the rabbi of Malibu Jewish Center and Synagogue, a Reconstructionist synagogue in Malibu, California. She is also the co-founder and rabbi of Sarah's Tent, a spiritual community in Los Angeles dedicated to a creative and innovative approach to Judaism. She has served as associate director of Metivta: A Center for Comtemplative Judaism.

Brad Hirschfield is the associate director for Professional Education at CLAL. He received his rabbinic ordination from the Institute of Traditional Judaism where he served as assistant dean. He received his M.A. and M. Phil. in ancient Jewish history from The Jewish Theological Seminary, where he taught in the department of Talmud and Rabbinics.

Elana Kanter served as associate rabbi at Temple Beth-El in Birmingham, Alabama.

Stuart Kelman is the rabbi of congregation Netivot Shalom in Berkeley, California.

Francine Klagsbrun is the author of more than a dozen books, including *Jewish Days: A Book of Jewish Life and Culture Around the Year* and *Voices of Wisdom: Jewish Ideals and Ethics for Everyday Living*. Her column "Thinking Aloud" appears monthly in the New York *Jewish Week*. She is also a regular columnist for *Moment* magazine.

Peter S. Knobel is senior rabbi of Beth Emet, the Free Synagogue, in Evanston, Illinois, and chairman of the Liturgy Committee of the Central Conference of American Rabbis.

Jeffrey Korbman is the assistant campaign director of the United Jewish Federation of MetroWest (New Jersey) where, along with fundraising, he writes a weekly Torah commentary.

Jonathan Kraus is the rabbi of Beth El Temple Center in Belmont, Massachusetts. He publishes *d'var Torah,* a free weekly available online.

Irwin Kula is the president of CLAL—National Jewish Center for Learning and Leadership. He previously served as CLAL's director of education. He received his M.A. in Rabbinics and his rabbinical ordination from The Jewish Theological Seminary of America. Rabbi Kula teaches and lectures throughout the United States and serves as a consultant on the issues of Jewish identity and institutional change to both corporate and family foundations, as well as to federations, synagogues, and agencies.

Neil Kurshan serves as the rabbi of the Huntington Jewish Center in Huntington, New York.

Mark H. Levin serves as the rabbi of Congregation Beth Torah in Overland Park, Kansas.

Levi Meier is a rabbi who serves as chaplain of Cedars-Sinai Medical Center in Los Angeles. He is a licensed clinical psychotherapist and a marriage, family, and child therapist. He is the author of *Ancient Secrets: Using the Stories of the Bible to Improve Our Everyday Lives* and *Moses—The Prince, the Prophet: His Life, Legend & Message for Our Lives* (both Jewish Lights). He is special issues editor of the *Journal of Psychology and Judaism* and teacher of the Writer's Torah Study group of the Avi Chai Foundation.

Steven Heneson Moskowitz serves as rabbi and spiritual leader of the Jewish Congregation of Brookville, on Long Island's North Shore. Prior to this he served as the assistant director of the 92nd St. Y's Bronfman Center for Jewish Life.

David Nelson is a senior teaching fellow at CLAL—National Jewish Center for Learning and Leadership, and a faculty member of the School of Sacred Music of Hebrew Union College–Jewish Institute of Religion, New York. He has been a contributing editor for *Sh'ma* and is currently working on a book on Judaism and modern physics.

Vanessa L. Ochs teaches in the Department of Religious Studies of the University of Virginia and is a CLAL senior associate. She is the author of *Words on Fire: One Woman's Journey into the Sacred*.

Nessa Rapoport is the author of a novel, *Preparing for Sabbath*, and of *A Woman's Book of Grieving*. With Ted Solotaroff, she edited *The Schocken Book of Contemporary Jewish Fiction*. Her short stories and essays have been widely published. Her column, "Inner Life," appears monthly in the New York *Jewish Week*.

Jack Riemer is the rabbi of Congregation Beth Tikvah in Boca Raton and the editor of *Jewish Reflections on Death; The World of the High Holy Days;* and co-editor of *So That Your Values Live On: Jewish Ethical Wills and How to Prepare Them* (Jewish Lights).

Jeffrey Salkin is the senior rabbi of The Community Synagogue in Port Washington, New York. A noted writer and teacher, he is the author of numerous articles and books, including *Putting God on the Guest List: How to Reclaim the Spiritual Meaning of Your Child's Bar or Bat Mitzvah* (Jewish Lights). His latest book is *Searching for My Brothers: Jewish Men in a Gentile World*.

Nigel Savage studied at the University of Sussex in the U.K., at Georgetown University in Washington, D.C., and at Machon Pardes and Yakar in Jerusalem. He is the director of Hazon (Hebrew for "vision"), a non-profit organization committed to fostering idealistic people and innovative projects in the Jewish community.

Ismar Schorsch is the chancellor of The Jewish Theological Seminary of America.

Harold M. Schulweis is the senior rabbi of Valley Beth Shalom in Encino, California, and founding chairman of the Jewish Foundation for the Righteous; he is the author of *For Those Who Can't Believe*.

Rami Shapiro is a rabbi of Temple Beth Or in Miami, Florida, and director of the Simply Jewish Fellowship. He is the author of *Wisdom of the Jewish Sages; Minyan;* and *The Way of Splendor*.

Rick Sherwin is the rabbi of Temple Israel in Orlando, Florida. His primary field of interest is creative liturgy.

Jeffrey Sirkman is the rabbi of Larchmont Temple, a past president of the Westchester Board of Rabbis, and a member of the Board of Governors of the New York Board of Rabbis.

Marcia Cohn Spiegel is co-author of *The Jewish Woman's Awareness Guide* and *Women Speak to God: The Poems and Prayers of Jewish Women.* She is the founder of the Alcohol Drug/Action Program and L'Chaim: 12 Steps to Recovery.

Elisabeth "Liza" Stern is the interim rabbi at Temple Beth El in Sudbury, Massachusetts.

Michael Strassfeld is co-author of *Night of Questions: A Passover Haggadah,* author of *The Jewish Holidays,* and co-editor of the *Jewish Catalogs.* He is working on a *New Jewish Catalog: A Guide to Jewish Spiritual Practice.*

Michael White is the senior rabbi of Temple Sinai of Roslyn and a Ph.D. candidate in religion at the University of Southern California.

Arnold Jacob Wolf is rabbi emeritus of the Midwest's oldest congregation, KAM Isaiah Israel in Chicago. He is the author of five books and numerous articles. Rabbi Wolf serves as the theology editor of *Judaism* and has also published articles in *Commentary,* the *CCAR Journal, Tradition, The Christian Century,* and the *New York Times.*

Joel H. Zaiman is the senior rabbi at Chizuk Amuno Congregation in Baltimore, Maryland.

Josh Zweiback serves as a rabbi at Congregation Beth Am in Palo Alto, California, where he directs its program in adult education.

Raymond A. Zwerin is the rabbi of Temple Sinai in Denver, Colorado. In 1973, he co-founded A.R.E. Publishing, Inc., with Audrey Friedman Marcus. He is the author of a textbook on the Jewish community and a booklet on the Jewish attitude toward abortion, as well as children's books and minicourses. Many of his sermons have been published in *The American Rabbi.*

CONTRIBUTOR INDEX

Each contributor is identified at the end of the essay that he or she has written, while the authors are identified only by their initials.

THEME INDEX

Permissions

We gratefully acknowledge permission from the following sources to reprint material or adapt from the original:

Yosef I. Abramowitz for adaptations from *Learn Torah with... Parshat Ki Tissa* © 1999 by Yosef I. Abramowitz; CLAL—The National Jewish Center for Learning and Leadership to reprint selections from CLAL Spotlight online © 2000, *In the Name of Heaven* © 1997, and *These Are the Words* © 1995 (Tsvi Blanchard, Irving Greenberg, Irwin Kula, David Nelson, Vanessa Ochs); Rabbi Edward Feinstein for materials from the Valley Beth Shalom congregational website, © by Rabbi Edward Feinstein; Rabbi James A. Gibson for selections from Temple Sinai congregational website; Rabbi Daniel Gropper for adaptations from December 1999 *Temple Isaiah Bulletin*; Jewish Lights Publishing for selections from *Ancient Secrets: Using the Stories of the Bible to Improve Our Everyday Lives* © 1996 by Levi Meier, *The Earth Is the Lord's: The Inner World of the Jew in Eastern Europe* © 1995 by Sylvia Heschel, Executrix of the Estate of Abraham Joshua Heschel, *The Empty Chair: Finding Hope & Joy—Timeless Wisdom from a Hasidic Master, Rebbe Nachman of Breslov* © 1994 by The Breslov Research Institute, *The Gentle Weapon: Prayers for Everyday and Not So-Everyday Moments* © 1999 by The Breslov Research Institute, *God Whispers: Stories of the Soul, Lessons of*

About JEWISH LIGHTS Publishing

People of all faiths and backgrounds yearn for books that attract, engage, educate and spiritually inspire.

Our principal goal is to stimulate thought and help all people learn about who the Jewish People are, where they come from, and what the future can be made to hold. While people of our diverse Jewish heritage are the primary audience, our books speak to people in the Christian world as well and will broaden their understanding of Judaism and the roots of their own faith.

We bring to you authors who are at the forefront of spiritual thought and experience. While each has something different to say, they all say it in a voice that you can hear.

Our books are designed to welcome you and then to engage, stimulate and inspire. We judge our success not only by whether or not our books are beautiful and commercially successful, but by whether or not they make a difference in your life.

We at Jewish Lights take great care to produce beautiful books that present meaningful spiritual content in a form that reflects the art of making high quality books. Therefore, we want to acknowledge those who contributed to the production of this book.

Stuart M. Matlins, Publisher

PRODUCTION
Bridgett Taylor & Marian B. Wallace

EDITORIAL
Martha McKinney & Sandra Korinchak

TEXT DESIGN
Susan Ramundo, SR Desktop Services

COVER DESIGN
Stacey Hood, Big Eyedea Design

COVER / TEXT PRINTING AND BINDING
Versa Press, East Peoria, Illinois

Spirituality

THE GENTLE WEAPON
Prayers for Everyday and Not-So-Everyday Moments
Adapted by *Moshe Mykoff* and *S.C. Mizrahi*,
together with the *Breslov Research Institute*

4 x 6, 144 pp., 2-color text, Deluxe PB, ISBN 1-58023-022-9 **$9.95**

THE EMPTY CHAIR: FINDING HOPE & JOY
Timeless Wisdom from a Hasidic Master,
Rebbe Nachman of Breslov
Adapted by *Moshe Mykoff* and the *Breslov Research Institute*

4 x 6, 128 pp., 2-color text, Deluxe PB, ISBN 1-879045-67-2 **$9.95**

FINDING JOY
A Practical Spiritual Guide to Happiness
by *Dannel I. Schwartz* with *Mark Hass*

6 x 9, 192 pp. Quality PB, ISBN 1-58023-009-1 **$14.95**
HC, ISBN 1-879045-53-2 **$19.95**

MY PEOPLE'S PRAYER BOOK
Traditional Prayers, Modern Commentaries
Vol. 1—The *Sh'ma* and Its Blessings
Vol. 2—The *Amidah*
Vol. 3—*P'sukei D'zimrah* (Morning Psalms)
Vol. 4—*Seder K'riat Hatorah* (The Torah Service)
Edited by *Rabbi Lawrence A. Hoffman*

Vol. 1: 7 x 10, 168 pp. HC, ISBN 1-879045-79-6 **$23.95**
Vol. 2: 7 x 10, 240 pp. HC, ISBN 1-879045-80-X **$23.95**
Vol. 3: 7 x 10, 240 pp. HC, ISBN 1-879045-81-8 **$23.95**
Vol. 4: 7 x 10, 264 pp. HC, ISBN 1-879045-82-6 **$23.95**

Spirituality

THE HANDBOOK OF
JEWISH MEDITATION PRACTICES
A Guide for Enriching the Sabbath
and Other Days of Your Life
by *Rabbi David A. Cooper*

6 x 9, 208 pp. Quality PB, ISBN 1-58023-102-0 **$16.95**

DISCOVERING JEWISH MEDITATION
Instruction & Guidance for Learning
an Ancient Spiritual Practice
by *Nan Fink Gefen*

6 x 9, 208 pp. Quality PB Original, ISBN 1-58023-067-9 **$16.95**

THE WAY OF FLAME
A Guide to the Forgotten Mystical Tradition
of Jewish Meditation
by *Avram Davis*

4½ x 8, 176 pp. Quality PB, ISBN 1-58023-060-1 **$15.95**

THE DEATH OF DEATH
Resurrection and Immortality in Jewish Thought
by *Neil Gillman*

6 x 9, 336 pp. Quality PB, ISBN 1-58023-081-4 **$18.95**
HC, ISBN 1-879045-61-3 **$23.95**

Mystery & Science Fiction

MYSTERY MIDRASH
An Anthology of Jewish Mystery & Detective Fiction
Edited by *Lawrence W. Raphael*
Preface by *Joel Siegel*, ABC's Good Morning America
6 x 9, 304 pp. Quality PB Original, ISBN 1-58023-055-5 **$16.95**

CRIMINAL KABBALAH
An Intriguing Anthology of
Jewish Mystery and Detective Fiction
Edited by *Lawrence W. Raphael*
Foreword by *Laurie R. King*
6 x 9, 288 pp. (est.) Quality PB Original, ISBN 1-58023-109-8 **$16.95**
(Avail. April 2001)

WANDERING STARS
An Anthology of Jewish Fantasy & Science Fiction
Edited by *Jack Dann*
Introduction by *Isaac Asimov*
6 x 9, 272 pp. Quality PB, ISBN 1-58023-005-9 **$16.95**

MORE WANDERING STARS
An Anthology of Outstanding Stories of
Jewish Fantasy & Science Fiction
Edited by *Jack Dann*
Introduction by *Isaac Asimov*
6 x 9, 192 pp. Quality PB, ISBN 1-58023-063-6 **$16.95**

Life Cycle

The Art of Jewish Living Series
for Holiday Observance

HANUKKAH
by *Dr. Ron Wolfson*
Edited by *Joel Lurie Grishaver*
7 x 9, 192 pp. Quality PB, Illus., ISBN 1-879045-97-4 **$16.95**

THE SHABBAT SEDER
by *Dr. Ron Wolfson*
7 x 9, 272 pp. Quality PB, Illus., ISBN 1-879045-90-7 **$16.95**
Booklet of Blessings and Songs **$5.00**
Audiocassette of Blessings **$6.00**
Teacher's Guide **$4.95**

THE PASSOVER SEDER
by *Dr. Ron Wolfson*
7 x 9, 352 pp. Quality PB, Illus., ISBN 1-879045-93-1 **$16.95**

Passover Workbook **$6.95**
Audiocassette of Blessings **$6.00**
Teacher's Guide **$6.95**

A HEART OF WISDOM
Making the Jewish Journey from
Midlife through the Elder Years
Edited by *Susan Berrin*
6 x 9, 384 pp. Quality PB, ISBN 1-58023-051-2 **$18.95**
HC, ISBN 1-879045-73-7 **$24.95**

Life Cycle

LIFECYCLES

Volume 1: Jewish Women on Life Passages & Personal Milestones

Edited and with Introductions by *Rabbi Debra Orenstein*

6 x 9, 480 pp. Quality PB, ISBN 1-58023-018-0 **$19.95**
HC, ISBN 1-879045-14-1 **$24.95**

Volume 2: Jewish Women on Biblical Themes in Contemporary Life

Edited and with Introductions by
Rabbi Debra Orenstein and *Rabbi Jane Rachel Litman*

6 x 9, 464 pp. Quality PB, ISBN 1-58023-019-9 **$19.95**
HC, ISBN 1-879045-15-X **$24.95**

GRIEF IN OUR SEASONS
A Mourner's Kaddish Companion
by *Rabbi Kerry M. Olitzky*

4½ x 6½, 448 pp. Quality PB Original, ISBN 1-879045-55-9 **$15.95**

PARENTING AS A SPIRITUAL JOURNEY
Deepening Ordinary & Extraordinary Events into Sacred Occasions
by *Rabbi Nancy Fuchs-Kreimer*

6 x 9, 224 pp. Quality PB, ISBN 1-58023-016-4 **$16.95**

SO THAT YOUR VALUES LIVE ON
Ethical Wills & How to Prepare Them
Ed. by *Rabbi Jack Riemer* & *Professor Nathaniel Stampfer*

6 x 9, 272 pp. Quality PB, ISBN 1-879045-34-6 **$17.95**

Healing/Recovery/Wellness

TWELVE JEWISH STEPS TO RECOVERY
A Personal Guide to Turning from
Alcoholism & Other Addictions …
Drugs, Food, Gambling, Sex …
by *Rabbi Kerry M. Olitzky & Stuart A. Copans, M.D.*
Preface by *Abraham J. Twerski, M.D.*
Intro. by *Rabbi Sheldon Zimmerman*
"Getting Help" by *JACS Foundation*

6 x 9, 144 pp. Quality PB, ISBN 1-879045-09-5 **$13.95**

HEALING OF SOUL, HEALING OF BODY
Spiritual Leaders Unfold the Strength and
Solace in Psalms
Edited by *Rabbi Simkha Y. Weintraub, CSW,*
for The Jewish Healing Center

6 x 9, 128 pp. Quality PB Original, illus., 2-color text
ISBN 1-879045-31-1 **$14.95**

ENTERING THE TEMPLE OF DREAMS
Jewish Prayers, Movements, and Meditations
for the End of the Day
by *Tamar Frankiel* and *Judy Greenfeld*

7 x 10, 192 pp. Illus., Quality PB Original, ISBN 1-58023-079-2 **$16.95**

Spirituality

BROKEN TABLETS
Restoring the Ten Commandments and Ourselves
Edited by *Rabbi Rachel S. Mikva*
Introduction by *Lawrence Kushner*
Afterword by *Arnold Jacob Wolf*
6 x 9, 192 pp. HC, ISBN 1-58023-066-0 **$21.95**

A HEART OF MANY ROOMS
Celebrating the Many Voices within Judaism
by *David Hartman*
6 x 9, 352 pp. HC, ISBN 1-58023-048-2 **$24.95**

The Way Into... Series

THE WAY INTO TORAH
by *Norman J. Cohen*
6 x 9, 176 pp. HC, ISBN 1-58023-028-8 **$21.95**

THE WAY INTO JEWISH PRAYER
by *Lawrence A. Hoffman*
6 x 9, 224 pp. HC, ISBN 1-58023-027-X **$21.95**

THE WAY INTO
ENCOUNTERING GOD IN JUDAISM
by *Neil Gillman*
6 x 9, 240 pp. HC, ISBN 1-58023-025-3 **$21.95**

THE WAY INTO JEWISH MYSTICAL TRADITION
by *Lawrence Kushner*
6 x 9, 176 pp. HC, ISBN 1-58023-029-6 **$21.95**

Children's Spirituality

A PRAYER FOR THE EARTH
The Story of Naamah, Noah's Wife
by *Sandy Eisenberg Sasso*
Full-color illustrations by *Bethanne Andersen*
For ages 4 and up NONDENOMINATIONAL, NONSECTARIAN

9 x 12, 32 pp. HC, Full-color illus., ISBN 1-879045-60-5 **$16.95**

SHARING BLESSINGS
Children's Stories for Exploring the Spirit of the Jewish Holidays
by *Rahel Musleah* and *Rabbi Michael Klayman*
Full-color illustrations by *Mary O'Keefe Young*
For ages 6 and up

8½ x 11, 64 pp. HC, Full-color illus., ISBN 1-879045-71-0 **$18.95**

THE BOOK OF MIRACLES
A Young Person's Guide to Jewish Spiritual Awareness
by *Lawrence Kushner*
For ages 9–13

With a Special 10th Anniversary Introduction and all new illustrations by the author.

6 x 9, 96 pp. HC, 2-color illus., ISBN 1-879045-78-8 **$16.95**

GOD'S PAINTBRUSH
by *Sandy Eisenberg Sasso*
Full-color illustrations by *Annette Compton*
For ages 4 and up
MULTICULTURAL, NONDENOMINATIONAL, NONSECTARIAN

11 x 8½, 32 pp. HC, Full-color illus., ISBN 1-879045-22-2 **$16.95**
Teacher's Guide: A Guide for Jewish & Christian Educators and Parents
8½ x 11, 32 pp. PB, ISBN 1-879045-57-5 **$6.95**

Spirituality

ANCIENT SECRETS
Using the Stories of the Bible to Improve
Our Everyday Lives
by *Rabbi Levi Meier, Ph.D.*

5½ x 8½, 288 pp. Quality PB, ISBN 1-58023-064-4 **$16.95**

SELF, STRUGGLE & CHANGE
Family Conflict Stories in Genesis
and Their Healing Insights for Our Lives
by *Norman J. Cohen*

6 x 9, 224 pp. Quality PB, ISBN 1-879045-66-4 **$16.95**
HC, ISBN 1-879045-19-2 **$21.95**

MEDITATION FROM THE HEART OF JUDAISM
Today's Teachers Share Their Practices,
Techniques, and Faith
Edited by *Avram Davis*

6 x 9, 256 pp. Quality PB, ISBN 1-58023-049-0 **$16.95**
HC, ISBN 1-879045-77-X **$21.95**

VOICES FROM GENESIS
Guiding Us through the Stages of Life
by *Norman J. Cohen*

6 x 9, 192 pp. Quality PB, ISBN 1-58023-118-7 **$16.9**
HC, ISBN 1-879045-75-3 **$21**

Spirituality

EYES REMADE FOR WONDER
A Lawrence Kushner Reader

Introduction by *Thomas Moore*

6 x 9, 240 pp. Quality PB, ISBN 1-58023-042-3 **$16.95**
HC, ISBN 1-58023-014-8 **$23.95**

INVISIBLE LINES OF CONNECTION
Sacred Stories of the Ordinary

by *Lawrence Kushner*

6 x 9, 160 pp. Quality PB, ISBN 1-879045-98-2 **$15.95**
HC, ISBN 1-879045-52-4 **$21.95**

THE BUSINESS BIBLE
10 New Commandments for Bringing Spirituality & Ethical Values into the Workplace

by *Rabbi Wayne Dosick*

5½ x 8½, 208 pp. Quality PB, ISBN 1-58023-101-2 **$14.95**

THE JEWISH GARDENING COOKBOOK
Growing Plants & Cooking for Holidays & Festivals

by *Michael Brown*

6 x 9, 224 pp. Quality PB, Illus., ISBN 1-58023-116-0 **$16.95**
HC, ISBN 1-58023-004-0 **$21.95**

GOD & THE BIG BANG
Discovering Harmony Between Science & Spirituality

y *Daniel C. Matt*

9, 216 pp. Quality PB, ISBN 1-879045-89-3 **$16.95**

Spirituality

DOES THE SOUL SURVIVE?
A Jewish Journey to Belief in Afterlife, Past Lives & Living with Purpose
by *Rabbi Elie Kaplan Spitz*

6 x 9, 288 pp. HC, ISBN 1-58023-094-6 **$21.95**

SIX JEWISH SPIRITUAL PATHS
A Rationalist Looks at Spirituality
by *Rabbi Rifat Sonsino*

6 x 9, 208 pp. HC, ISBN 1-58023-095-4 **$21.95**

MOONBEAMS
A Hadassah Rosh Hodesh Guide
Edited by *Carol Diament, Ph.D.*

8½ x 11, 240 pp. Quality PB Original, ISBN 1-58023-099-7 **$20.00**

THE WOMEN'S TORAH COMMENTARY
New Insights from Women Rabbis on the 54 Weekly Torah Portions
Edited by *Rabbi Elyse Goldstein*

6 x 9, 496 pp. HC, ISBN 1-58023-076-8 **$34.95**

ReVISIONS
Seeing Torah through a Feminist Lens
by *Rabbi Elyse Goldstein*

5½ x 8½, 224 pp. Quality PB, ISBN 1-58023-117-9 **$16.95**
208 pp. HC, ISBN 1-58023-047-4 **$19.95**